Computational Enginee
Historical Memories

Nanetti outlines a methodology for deploying artificial intelligence and machine learning to enhance historical research.

Historical events are the treasure of human experiences, the heritage that societies have used to remain resilient and express their identities. Nanetti has created and developed an interdisciplinary methodology supported by practice-based research that serves as a pathway between historical and computer sciences to design and build computational structures that analyse how societies create narratives about historical events. This consilience pathway aims to make historical memory machine-understandable. It turns history into a computational discipline through an interdisciplinary blend of philological accuracy, historical scholarship, history-based media projects, and computational tools. Nanetti presents the theory behind this methodology from a humanities perspective and discusses its practical application in user interface and experience.

An essential read for historians and scholars working in the digital humanities.

Dr. Andrea Nanetti is an award-winning and internationally recognised expert in Digital Humanities. He has carried out trailblazing research in Europe, the United States, China, Africa, and South-East Asia for over 30 years. Since 2013, he has been a Professor at Nanyang Technological University, Singapore. Using the history of Venice as contextualised within late medieval Afro-Eurasian trade systems, he achieved international standing within a broad research spectrum that spans from critical editions of primary historical sources to computational applications and web-based media. As a result, several world's top-level institutions, including Harvard University, Princeton University, Shanghai Jiao Tong University, Brown University, Johns Hopkins University, and Ca' Foscari University of Venice, invited him to be a visiting fellow.

"Dr. Nanetti's research reimagines history in the golden age of AI. Computational history is not simply a stagnant past or the point of departure for an impending future but the anywhere door for other realities."

Dr. Chin-Yew Lin, *Senior Principal Research Manager of the Knowledge Computing Group at Microsoft Research, Beijing, PRC.*

"Sitting at the intersection of history, computer science, media studies, and philosophy, Nanetti's work justifies and maps a way forward for historians grappling with the implications of the digital turn. Computational methods offer solutions to obstacles of language and culture, not just those that separate regional scholarly traditions, but also those that separate academic scholarship from the public sphere. Put into practice in the Engineering Historical Memory platform, his ideas show the promise of digital approaches for expanding, rather than just streamlining, the production of historical knowledge."

Dr. Adam Kosto, *Professor, Department of History, Columbia University, New York, USA.*

"Professor Nanetti has compiled a beautiful book demonstrating a vital step towards bringing traditional expert-intensive inquiries in historical materials and engineering tools and practices together into an integral system. This must-read book lays the groundwork for enabling machines to work with historical materials, leveraging extensive digital resources, including datasets and models in engineering and humanities. The book and its realization as interactive applications, the Engineering Historical Memory, will be the essential resource for anyone interested in designing and building engineering systems that can empower researchers in humanities and engage a broad audience in the general public. In a world with countless AI applications powering our daily life, this book showcases how we could work together to integrate new engineering technologies and historical materials and create powerful interactive systems encoding human experiences in the long term."

Dr. Yao-Yi Chiang, *Professor of Computer Science and Engineering, University of Minnesota.*

"'Computational Engineering of Historical Memories' is a particularly timely book – digital humanities is currently in danger of dissipating into a number of digital sub-disciplines. Andrea Nanetti introduces a suite of techniques to help understand global human history and then demonstrates how his approaches can be applied through some practice-based research. Professor Nanetti's vision is to make historical memory machine-understandable and, ultimately, to turn history into a computational discipline. This is nothing if not revisionist and I commend this book for its ambition."

Roger Kain FBA, *Professor of Humanities, School of Advanced Study, University of London, UK.*

Computational Engineering of Historical Memories

With a Showcase on Afro-Eurasia
(ca 1100-1500 CE)

Andrea Nanetti

Routledge
Taylor & Francis Group

LONDON AND NEW YORK

First published 2023
by Routledge
4 Park Square, Milton Park, Abingdon, Oxon OX14 4RN

and by Routledge
605 Third Avenue, New York, NY 10158

Routledge is an imprint of the Taylor & Francis Group, an Informa business

British Library Cataloguing-in-Publication Data
A catalogue record for this book is available from the British Library

ISBN: 9781032316802 (hbk)
ISBN: 9781032316819 (pbk)
ISBN: 9781003310860 (ebk)

DOI: 10.4324/9781003310860

Typeset in Times New Roman
by KnowledgeWorks Global Ltd.

To those scholars, media artists, software engineers, web developers, UX/UI practitioners, publishers, cultural institutions, and others who, through their collaboration with the international web-based initiative for the engineering of historical memories (EHM), contribute to the open and free access to primary historical sources and recognise it as a fundamental human right for the advancement of knowledge and peacebuilding in our glocal societies.

Facesti come quei che va di notte,
che porta il lume dietro e sé non giova,
ma doppo sé fa le persone dotte
Dantis ALAGHERII *Comedia*, Purgatorio XXII, vv. 67–69

Contents

Figures

Abbreviations

ABMS	agent-based modelling and simulation
AI	artificial intelligence
AIIB	Asian Infrastructure Investment Bank
API	application programming interface
AVOD	advertising-based video on demand
BRI	Belt and Road Initiative
CRUD	create, read, update, delete [operations]
DAO	data access objects
EHM	[The] Engineering [of] Historical Memory
FAIR	findability, accessibility, interoperability, and reusability
HTTP	Hypertext Transfer Protocol
ICT	information and communications technology
ML	machine learning
NTU	Nanyang Technological University, Singapore
OBOR	One Belt One Road/一带一路
OTT	over-the-top
PRC	People's Republic of China
SRB	Silk Road Fund
SVOD	subscription video on demand
UGC	user-generated content

Foreword

I often used to see, and occasionally talked to, Stephen Hawking, as he was a fellow of the same college at Cambridge University as myself. He would often raise the question of time travel, with all its philosophical problems and paradoxes (for instance, could one travel back in time and kill one's grandmother, thereby extinguishing her descendants including oneself?). But in one sense, time travel is not so difficult after all. Historians have the capacity to take us on journeys through time. The images of people that we see may be indistinct and the background may be fuzzy, and as with a guided tour around a historic city, different guides will tell different stories—how true that is I often witness when passing tour guides in Cambridge, although I resist breaking in and telling them that they are talking nonsense. Just as we rely on roads, rivers, and railways to take us from place to place and miss out many beautiful or ugly vistas that lie off our path, in studying the past, we are guided by the great stream of documents that figuratively cascades down upon us from the shelves and storerooms of archives and libraries. We try often unsuccessfully to see beyond them, and the further we go back in time, the more difficult this becomes, even with the help of objects found in the soil, including the mortal remains of distant ancestors—we can end up feeling that we know a great deal more about the ancient dead than the ancient living, whether among the ancient Egyptians or the Etruscans.

As Andrea Nanetti points out in this intriguing and path-breaking book, there are many ways of presenting the past to a modern audience. I am always struck on visits to bookshops in Spain by the fact that the section on historical fiction is often larger than the section on what I would call real history. People want to come close to the experience of those who lived before our time, and so many aspects of life are very difficult to reconstruct, including emotions (unless a record has been preserved in someone's writings) that it is easy to prefer the imaginative reconstructions we are offered on paper and in film. Frequently this moulds the way most people think about past events. In Britain, the unstoppable fascination with the Tudor period in the sixteenth century has generated a number of television series; even the presence of academic advisors does little to restrain the enthusiasm of directors and producers who, as Nanetti observes, want to tell the liveliest story and are not as fixated with the need to be accurate with the evidence as professional historians should be. So we settle into the view that this is how a famous person looked, dressed and spoke, and confuse modern confabulation with real evidence.

This is not to say that imagination is unimportant for a historian. Far from it! Anyone who has ploughed through a massive *Habilitationsschrift*, the additional thesis required in Germany from candidates for professorships, will know how deadly some advanced research can be—as readable as an old-fashioned telephone directory. But history should not be presented as a scientific report. As historians write, they will be generating in their mind images of the people they are mentioning and the setting in which they moved, and they will be hoping to communicate some of that to their readers, whether they are writing for fellow-historians or for a wider public—but always in the knowledge that while they arbitrarily have King Roger dressed in red in their own imagination, maybe their readers have him dressed in blue.

In an age of globalisation, it has become increasingly important to understand not just the history of one's own country and its immediate neighbours, but the global context in which local histories sit—as Nanetti points out, this is sometimes described as 'glocal' history. In doing so, we must hold back from simplistic generalisations, while respecting the pioneering work of figures such as Fernand Braudel and Immanuel Wallerstein, who attempted to map out ways of doing this. We must also be wary of brilliant but biased historians, such as Eric Hobsbawm, who were wedded to particular political viewpoints and in some case wrote about the past with the intention of validating those viewpoints. Marxist theory is based on the mountain of research conducted by Marx, Engels, and their successors and was an enormous scholarly achievement, whatever one thinks of its political assumptions. But it also placed the past within a straitjacket of inevitable processes, and awareness that the world beyond Europe did not fit these theories has grown over the last few decades. The attempts by Edward Said, Eric Williams, and others to extend the argument beyond Europe in books now rated as 'modern classics' have failed because of their political obsessions and their simplistic generalisations based on misread facts, and Nanetti's methods should help us understand these issues more sensibly. His attention to the relationship between Europe and Africa as far back as the Middle Ages is therefore very welcome.

This politicisation of the past is still a problem, now that the 'culture wars' in the United States and Great Britain have pitched a new wave of historians with a radical political agenda against what they term 'old-fashioned' historians. As the great playwright Tom Stoppard has acutely observed, we now live in the age of 'personal truth' and 'truth truth' and it is imperative that we pursue the latter, rather than trying to bend our narrative of the past to match beliefs about race, gender, and identity that have merged in the late twentieth century and—even when they mark an improvement on past values—were not the values of our ancestors and cannot be used to pass judgement on our ancestors. To get things right, we have to move beyond spontaneous instinct and personal feelings and instead need to accumulate all the evidence we can, and Nanetti's project opens up ways in which we can hope to do this.

All this makes the harnessing of advanced technologies, including digital humanities, ever more important. Our understanding of the past must be guided not by political and social concerns of our own day but by an honest and passionate commitment to accurate representation of people, places, and events. We strive to be objective, even though we know that on this score we are fallible, as in so many areas of life. With the help of the methodologies outlined in this book, we can hope to achieve a fuller and more nuanced understanding of the past. For the time travel offered by historians to their readers is often jerky, poorly illuminated, and mysterious. With the help of Andrea Nanetti, we can make it less so.

David Abulafia
Cambridge University, June 2022

Preface

This book follows up on a recurrent desideratum when I present the virtual system of interactive applications called Engineering Historical Memory (EHM, https://engineeringhistoricalmemory. com/) at international conferences and other invited talks. Students and colleagues ask for a reference work about EHM. Indeed, EHM has been mentioned in or the subject of several publications of mine, between 2007 and 2022. With this monographic publication, I share topics already investigated and discussed on various occasions and under different circumstances (e.g., traditional and online publications, public lectures, conference papers) in a new unitary form with a coherent narrative. In essence, this book results from a long process of summarising, expanding, reworking, and updating research materials conceived and only partially published in English, Italian, Chinese, and Korean between 2007 and 2022. In this book, I acknowledged these previous publications and public presentations in the references.

Thus, this book provides a robust theoretical discussion on the opportunities and limits of the use of computers in the historian's craft. Specifically, it focuses on (1) the explanation of methods that historians can apply to overcome the challenges of the digital time machine and (2) the exemplification of computational tools relevant to historians. Finally, the book elucidates the overall EHM's design process as (1) selecting critical primary sources, (2) decoding the information that philology has presented in traditional publications, (3) curating the encoding of this information into machine-readable systems, (4) parsing and analysing of historical information to make it machine-understandable, (5) information visualisation, (6) mashup of secondary literature available online which is related and relevant to the information searched by the user, (7) creation of new insights in an open and collaborative digital space, and (8) engagement of video makers and other creators of history-based media products.

Furthermore, this book provides the theoretical background that underlines EHM's practice-based research in archives and libraries and practice-led research in computational history. Thus, it is expected to be of interest to historians and computer scientists at the research, teaching, and student levels. In addition, it presents and discusses core concepts that digital historians, computer scientists, and digital-born students must understand to make independent contributions. Finally, it aims to bring the reader beyond the frontiers of existing knowledge to educate responsible citizens for peacebuilding through computational history, historical memory, tradition, legacy, and, ultimately, a new science of heritage to empower the study and design of a better present and sustainable futures of life on planet Earth.

Acknowledgements

Under its Academic Research Fund Tier 1 (2020–2023, RG45/20), the Singapore Ministry of Education supported this open-access book project. Furthermore, as this book is a theoretical counterpart to the virtual system of interactive applications called *Engineering Historical Memory* (EHM, https://engineeringhistoricalmemory. com/), the author also wants to acknowledge the other research institutions and funding agencies that supported his research on this topic as follows.

- Università degli Studi di Bologna (1999–2011)
- Associazione per Imola Storico-Artistica (1999–2000, 2007–2008)
- Università di Venezia Ca' Foscari (2010–2012, and 2019–ongoing)
- Meduproject Srl (spin-off company, Università degli Studi di Bologna, 2013)
- Microsoft Research (2014–2015, 2016–2017)
- Microsoft Azure for Research (2015–2016, 2016)
- NTU Singapore (StartUp Grant, 2014–2016, M4081357)
- Guangzhou Ruifeng Culture & Communication Co., Ltd (2017–2018)
- Ministry of Education, Singapore, under its Academic Research Fund Tier 1 (2017–2020, RG55/17NS)
- Digimagic Communications Pte Ltd, Singapore (2019)
- Ministry of Education, Singapore, under its Academic Research Fund Tier 1 (2019–2021, RG45/19NS)
- Techno India NJR Institute of Technology (2020–2021)
- Ministry of Education, Singapore, under its Academic Research Fund Tier 1 (2022–2025, RT20/21)
- Università degli Studi di Firenze (2020–2022)
- Singapore United Traineeship Programme released by Singapore Business Foundation and Workforce Singapore (2021–2022)

- Taylor & Francis Group (2020–ongoing)
- Scopus Elsevier (2020–ongoing)

This book results from a long process of summarising, expanding, reworking, and updating research materials conceived and only partially published by the author in English, Italian, Chinese, and Korean between 2007 and 2022. During the drafting of the work, additions were made to complete gaps and better coordinate the overall narrative of the discourse on the engineering of historical memories into one single and coherent piece of scholarship. In particular, the author sought and obtained clearance for the use of contents extracted from the following publications: Nanetti and Cheong (2018), Nanetti (2021, 2022).

Last but not least, the author expresses his warmest thanks to all colleagues and students who contributed to EHM and discussed its theoretical foundations with him between 2007 and 2022. A complete list of over 130 research collaborators and about 100 students is available on the EHM credits page.

References

Nanetti, Andrea (2021). "Defining Heritage Science. A Consilience Pathway to Treasuring the Complexity of Inheritable Human Experience through Historical Method, AI and ML". *Complexity*, 2021, special issue on *Tales of Two Societies: On the Complexity of the Coevolution between the Physical Space and the Cyber Space*, edited by Shu-Heng Chen (Lead Editor), Simone Alfarano and Dehua Shen (Guest Editors), Article ID 4703820. https://www.hindawi.com/journals/complexity/2021/4703820/

Nanetti, Andrea (2022). "Waterways Connecting the Peoples of the World. A presentation of the EHM application for Fra Mauro's *mappa mundi* as a virtual laboratory for investigating the Maritime Silk Road discourse in the digital time machine". In *Venezia e il senso del mare. Percezioni e rappresentazioni [Venice and the sense of the sea. Perceptions portrayals]*. Venice: Istituto Veneto di Scienze, Lettere ed Arti.

Nanetti, Andrea, & Siew Ann Cheong (2018). "Computational History: From Big Data to Big Simulations". In *Big Data in Computational Social Science and Humanities*, edited by Shu-Heng Chen, 337–363. Cham: Springer International Publishing AG. https://link.springer.com/chapter/10.1007/978-3-319-95465-3_18

1   Computational Engineering of Historical Memories

1.1 Vision, Mission, and Motivation from a Human Sciences Perspective

The vision behind the engineering of historical memories is inspired by the Greek/Roman stoic concept of φιλαντρωπία/humanitas (Zetzel 1972, 173, Grafton & Jardine 1986, Higgins 2014, 429–430, Bettini 2019, 50–62, 92–100) as it is witnessed in the statement by Publius Terentius Afer (ca 190–185–159 BCE), *Homo sum, humani nihil a me alienum puto* ('I am human, I consider nothing human to be alien to me'), in his comedy *Heautontimorumenos* (Act I, Scene 1, 25, 77) that is based on Menander's Ἑαυτὸν τιμωρούμενος, *The Self-Tormentor*, and in the concept of *studia humanitatis ac litterarum* expressed by Marcus Tullius Cicero (106–43 BCE) in his oration in defence of the poet Aulus Licinius Archias, *Etenim omnes artes, quae ad humanitatem pertinent, habent quoddam commune vinclum et quasi cognatione quadam inter se continentur* ('In truth, all the arts which concern the civilising and humanising of men [better read: all the sciences which concern the human nature], have some link which binds them together, and are, as it were, connected by some relationship to one another'; refer to Yonge 1856, 2 and II.3).

However, Cicero's *De officiis* had already warned that 'taking care of other people's things is difficult …. Although Cremete, the famous character of Terentius, claims that nothing human is foreign to him (*humani nihil a se alienum putat*), however, since we perceive and feel with greater intensity the fortunes or adversities that touch us than those that affect others, as if we were separated from them by a long interval, we express different judgments about them from those that concern us' (Picone & Marchese 2012, I, 30, cited by Bettini 2019, 87). Moreover, Cicero expresses the different proximity between the larger human society and the 'domus' (home). In between, there are the 'gens'

DOI: 10.4324/9781003310860-1

(those who speak our same language and have common origins with us), our own 'civitas' (hometown), our 'propinqui' (relatives), and our spouse and children (Bettini 2019, 84–85). As Martha Nussbaum stated, Cicero's *De officiis* 'has been a kind of Bible' for thinkers and statesmen worldwide. In other words, to achieve justice among humans, it is necessary to overcome the Ciceronian principle, according to which 'common generosity' must stop when the care we must take for 'our people' is undermined (Nussbaum 2004).

Today, the closest English word to φιλαντρωπία/*humanitas* seems to be empathy, viz. the ability to understand and share the feelings of another human being, to serve the needs of our contemporary globalised youth as human beings. In Europe, Giacomo Leopardi (1798–1837) epitomised an example of the philosophical understanding of empathy as the ultimate human quality and hope. Leopardi called it *social catena* ('social chain') in his poem *Broom* (*La Ginestra*, v. 149), composed in 1836 at Villa Ferrighi in Torre del Greco (refer to Ranieri 1845, I, 119–127, for the text; and Galassi 2010, 286–309, for the English translation). This Leopardi's thought results from his vast philosophical erudition that ranged between eras and disciplines through ancient and modern languages, encompassing the heritage available in Europe at his time. After taking stock of what science had discovered on the materialist structure of reality, he asserted the groundlessness of human values and the total indifference of nature towards the destiny of humankind. Leopardi anticipated Nietzsche in overturning the religious and humanistic values of the Christian order of the world and setting the human condition in a new framework (Pogue Harrison 2014).

The Roman author and grammarian Aulus Gellius (ca 125–post 180 CE) 'links the Roman notion of *humanitas* not so much to the Greek word *philantropía* but *paidéia*, that is to education and culture' (Marche 1967, Marshall 1990, Bettini 2019, 95: *Noctes Atticae*, 13, 17). Gellius refers to the Roman polymath Marcus Terentius Varro (116–27 BC), who uses the term *humanus* for those who know because of having studied a subject in books (Bettini 2019, 95, referring to Leonardis 2018). Thus, in the Roman world and subsequently during the Renaissance, the Latin word *humanitas* embeds the semantics of two Greek words, *philantropía* and *paideia* (Bettini 2019, 97).

The vision is that, on planet Earth, *l'aiuola che ci fa tanto feroci* ('the little threshing-floor which makes us so fierce'), as iconically defined by Dante Alighieri (*Paradiso*, xxii, 151), the human ability to plan the future (Preston 2018) requires the ban on violence and the capability of fostering out ethics of freedom as a generator of responsibility.

Against violence in the resolution of all human disputes and conflicts, humanity can leverage the legacy of Mahatma Gandhi to use peaceful means to bring about political or social change and solve incompatibility between two or more opinions, principles, or interests (Pontara 2019, 135–161). Individuals, institutions, and societies can agree on common goals that they want to achieve for the good of everybody (Ignatieff 2017). For this huge but inevitable task, humans have developed education and laws to mitigate the exploitation of humans perpetrated by humans against other humans. Scholarship can set a new science of heritage to decode-encode the treasure of human experiences and transmit it to the next generation of world citizens, raising awareness of the importance of immunisation against blind faith in technology and progress (Nanetti 2021a).

Hannah Arendt (1906–1975), in her widely celebrated book, *The Human Condition*, published in 1958 (Arendt 1998), discussed the evolution of the relationship between freedom and responsibility. Arendt's analysis was made in the aftermath of World War II and is still sharply relevant in the human search for ways of living together without violence. The need for a metamorphosis, a gesture of civilisation, which—as the poet Giuseppe Ungaretti said to Pier Paolo Pasolini in an interview in 1965—'is an act of human bullying against Nature', requires responsibility. Cultures (i.e., ideas, customs, and social behaviour of the world's peoples) nurture this responsibility. In the tradition of Alfred Weber (1868–1958) and Robert King Merton (1910–2003), civilisation denotes the human control of nature and is used in the singular, while culture indicates the social construction of meaning and is used in the plural (Schäfer 2001, 302). Michelangelo Pistoletto, with the symbol of the Third Paradise, enhanced this relationship between freedom and responsibility within the framework of the 17 Sustainable Development Goals that the United Nations is targeting to achieve by 2030 (Pistoletto 2010, 64–73).

The mission to foster this vision has three critical steps. First, it aims to develop a transcultural advancement in understanding the human condition with a 'glocal' approach (i.e., designing global futures with local heritage). 'The neologism *glocal* was coined by Manfred Lange who, in his work for the May 1990 Global Change Exhibition, sought to capture the complex interplay between the local, the regional, and the world-wide' as reported by Jeffrey Schnapp (2013, 80). From the historian's perspective, in the preface to his book about the perception of the past in our globalised world, the French historian Serge Gruzinski has discussed the relationship between 'local' historiographies and the different histories produced by the globalisation of the cultural industry (Gruzinski 2015, Preface).

Second, it wants to nurture human citizenship as κοσμοπολιτεία/ cosmopolitanism. This concept follows the pre-Socratic philosopher Diogenes of Sinope, also known as Diogenes the Cynic (ca 412–323 BCE). According to the account given by Diogenes Laërtius (180–240 CE) in his *Vitae Philosophorum* (*Βίοι καὶ γνῶμαι τῶν ἐν φιλοσοφίᾳ εὐδοκιμησάντων/Lives and Opinions of Eminent Philosophers*; Yonge 1853, VI, 63), when Diogenes of Sinope was asked where he came from, he answered: 'I am a citizen of the cosmos [κοσμοπολίτης/ kosmopolitês (cosmopolite or cosmopolitan)]'. Third and eventually, there is the ambition to educate the next generation of human scientists and decision-makers who are called upon to take up humanity's grand challenges in the twenty-first century (Vasbinder et al. 2018).

The human condition is the most vital and burning issue (Langlois 1977, Arendt 1998). The focus is on the life of individual human beings in space-time and their experiences embedded in artefacts. Humanity (i.e., human beings collectively) embraces notions and conceptions related to humankind, the totality of the individual human beings living on the Earth at present, and human kindness. Humankind identifies a living species that benefits from the privileges of Darwinian evolution. Instead, individual human beings are subject to all the laws of physicochemical transformations that affect both living and non-living beings. Individual human beings are all different. As they look different outside, they are different inside. Their minds and consciousnesses are other. There is no normality. Instead, it is the variegated treasure of human experience on planet Earth. The knowledge of religious and secular humanities (i.e., learning concerned with human culture, especially literature, history, art, music, and philosophy) is grounded on the treasure of the experiences that individuals, institutions, and societies accumulated across space and time. These experiences are embodied in artefacts (human-made things such as books, paintings, music, sculptures). Unity of intent can only be reached in shared projects for the future. Individuals, institutions, and societies can agree on common goals (*ut unum sint*; New Testament, John, 17, 21). Trust is our most valuable commodity. The wisdom of knowing under which situation to act as individuals, institutions, and societies is a choice that must be (re)discussed in every present with *virtus/* virtue (Gardini 2019, 191).

In the second century CE, a wealthy Greek called Diogenes, who lived in the city of Oenoanda of Lycia (in today's southwest Turkey), commissioned a large public inscription displaying Epicurus' teachings, of which archaeologists excavated several fragments (Casanova 1984, Ferguson Smith 1993, 2003). This inscription was not only for the inhabitants of his city, as stated in the fragment that illustrates its purpose. Indeed, it was 'even for those called foreigners, but who are not in reality. In fact, according to the various divisions of the earth, who has one country, who has another; but if we look at the whole complex of this world, there is only one homeland for all, the whole earth, and the world is the only home' (Casanova 1984, fr. 30 I–II). Thus, it makes no sense to speak of foreigners because no man can be called such on the Earth (Bettini 2019, 91).

In terms of motivation, the overall research process for the engineering of historical memories, both society-driven and scholarly, is focused on historical sciences and rooted in the academic domain of the assembled human sciences (i.e., it deals with people and their actions, encompassing all social sciences, humanities, and arts). The French historian Fernand Braudel (1902–1985), in his 1960 essay, *Unité et diversité des sciences de l'homme* (Braudel 1960; English translation, *Unity and Diversity in the Human Sciences*, Braudel 1980, 55–63), shaped the concept of the forthcoming *Maison des Sciences de l'Homme* ('House of Human Sciences', enacted on 4 January 1963), when he epitomised 'gathering the human sciences together' as follows:

> It must be *all* the human sciences which are examined ..., the most classic, the oldest, and the newest. These last would rather call themselves social sciences and would like to form the four of five "major" sciences in our world. Now I would maintain that in order to build up a unity, all research has a contribution to make .... Can sociologists, economists (in the wider sense), psychologists, linguists really, by themselves, mobilize the entire forces of the human sciences? I think not .... Soon the *Maison des Sciences de l'Homme* will bring together in Paris all the centers of research and all the laboratories that are valuable in this huge field. All this fresh vigor, all the new methods are within arm's reach, while at the same time we have the indispensable framework of all classic human "sciences", which is more precious than anything and doubtless unique in the world, and without which no decisive action can be possible.
>
> (Braudel 1980, 61–62)

Michel Foucault (1926–1984), in his seminal book on the history of the human sciences (Foucault 1966 in French, and 1970 in English), made this discourse famous worldwide. As showcased by Rens Bod (2013), this discussion regathered momentum during the first four international conferences on the History of the Humanities organised by Rens Bod, Jaap Maat, and Thijs Weststeijn at the University of Amsterdam on 'The Making of the Humanities', in 2008 (Bod et al. 2010, 7–14) and 2010 (Bod et al. 2012, 9–20), and at the Royal Netherlands Institute in Rome in 2012 (Bod et al. 2014) and 2014. These events were very successful and had significant institutional and academic outcomes. They nurtured, among others, the establishment of the Society for the History of the Humanities in 2016. Furthermore, the society started the scientific journal 'History of Humanities' (2016 onwards) with the proceedings of the fourth conference and institutionalised the international conferences series on the History of the Humanities as its annual conference (Bod et al. 2016, 1–2).

Accordingly, the motivation by which the above vision and mission plan to be achieved focuses on enhancing the 'study of humans in their social context' and, thus, 'belongs to the social sciences' (Bod et al. 2010, 8). Finally, the day-to-day research activity in historical sciences explores engineering solutions (i.e., computer science and technology concerned with the design, building, and use of engines, machines, and structures) and experiments with computational technologies (i.e., the use of computers) to expand the human capacity of processing data and information, in terms of quantity and speed (Galleron & Idmhand 2020, Golub & Liu 2021). Ultimately, it focuses on one of the computation's key technologies, machine learning algorithms, to open new horizons of discovery to the human sciences (Domingos 2015, 299; referring to Bradshaw et al. 1987, for example on how to approach the automation of the discovery of scientific laws).

1.2   Reloading the Treasure of Human Experiences into the Digital Time Machine

The philosopher and poet Giacomo Leopardi (1798–1837) inspired Andrea Nanetti's vision that neglecting heritage, the treasure of human experience, would leave humanity impoverished and less prepared for the uncertainties and increasing complexities of living together on planet Earth (Nanetti 2021a). According to Leopardi, there is stagnation if society is incapable of redesigning its heritage for the future. Leopardi expresses a deep aversion to the present when it loses its connections with the past. He was horrified by the present when it was stripped of its ties with the past (Pogue Harrison 2014). This vision images that with a clearer understanding of where we came from, we can better understand who we are, where we are now, and what we want to become (Nanetti & Simpson 2015, 82–90, 83–84, 89). Human societies have always used their heritage, viz. the inheritable treasure of human experiences (i.e., knowledge and values) accumulated across space and over time, to remain resilient, express cultural identities in their national narratives, and imagine desirable futures by integrating the new with the old (Kahane 2020).

Nowadays, the rapid development of life in the digital time machine (Nowotny 2020) is endangering the traditionally spontaneous adaptation process to change (Moreau 2020). Although 'the research paths of cultural heritage and AI have increasingly found shared interests, leading to a successful merge of these two disciplines' (Bordoni et al. 2016, vii–viii), the risk of an endangered cultural-heritage transmission is a call to action for the humanities (Borgman 2009). Given the increasing pace of technological innovation, many traditional modes of knowledge and value transmission have become obsolete or are at the risk of vanishing. As a result, societies might lose their usual means before they could master new methods to keep available their so-far treasured human experiences in the present and for the future. This loss of cultural heritage would, thus, compromise societal resilience and adaptability to change when they are needed more than ever. Public and private synergies in higher education, science, and research (humanities complemented by other natural science disciplines) could play a significant role in dealing with this challenge. They should provide the vision to prototype, and engineer solutions, with imagination (i.e., the faculty of conceiving new ideas and seeing external entities not present to the senses), empathy (i.e., a strong feeling of relationships with others), and curiosity (i.e., a strong desire to know and acquire knowledge by study, experience, or being taught).

The second Singapore Heritage Conference, 'Heritage and the Creative Industries', held at Nanyang Technological University in Singapore on 15–16 January 2015, emphasised that the multidisciplinary domain of heritage science focuses on recording, accessing, interpreting, conserving, and managing cultural heritage seen as the treasure of human experiences. Today, heritage science considers the knowledge and values acquired in all relevant disciplines, from arts and humanities (e.g., philosophy, ethics, art and art history, economics, sociology, and anthropology) to fundamental sciences (e.g., chemistry, physics, mathematics, and biology), as well as to computer science and engineering, communication and media studies. In particular, the conference speakers and audience wrestled with the tensions between age-old practices and our modern digital lifestyles. New media and non-conventional communications have risen as a challenge, creating new possibilities for cultural expressions and the advancement of learning. However, during the conference, there was a sense that we might be losing our humanity as lives become more and more digital, and the criteria of digital-data preservation are left to the neoliberal rules of the free market. Nevertheless, in his keynote address at the conference mentioned above, an expert like Harold Thwaites talks about past experiences and draws from them creative inspirations for the future. In hearing him, one can realise that human qualities like ethics, empathy, identity, and spirituality are bonding resources serving to bind people together. In short, to be human is to be connected to other humans, to our environments and, for some, to a cosmic significance (refer to Nanetti 2015).

Information communication technology (ICT) has indeed opened a new frontier for the advancement of data sharing. One can agree with Sandra Rendgen that 'professional data and information management will be a central cultural tool in the decades to come' (Rendgen & Wiedemann 2013, 9). However, ICT alone cannot support substantial advancement of learning because the exponentially growing volume of digital data is a solution and a problem at the same time. Technology allows us to access more and more information faster and faster from almost everywhere. However, current ICT cannot retain, structure, and process the amount of digital data produced by society. Moreover, unstructured data per se is of minor or negligible value. To become an asset, data needs to be filtered, organised, and become machine-readable. This data processing requires considerable natural and human resources that our society may be unable or unwilling to allocate. Thus, many traditional modes of knowledge and value transmission might become obsolete or risk vanishing soon. Due to this risk, our society needs to decide the selection criteria of what human knowledge and values to preserve and keep available for the next generation in a digital form.

In human history, when communication media underwent major technological innovations (e.g., writing, electromagnetic signals), society experienced the new with sceptical doubt, because of the potential impoverishment of communication (Ong 1982, IV). For example, according to the Greek philosopher Plato, writing is dead when compared to orality in sharing human thought (*Phaedrus*, 274–277). Today, traditional information processing (e.g., human mind, social interactions), knowledge aggregation (e.g., mental memories, epics, myth, social imaginary, culture), and storage systems (e.g., human brain, rituals, paintings, books, maps, archives, libraries) seem to be sentenced to death by the new solutions empowered by the advent of the electronic computer, which offers to human communication all the opportunities of orality and writing at the same time. On the contrary, new media and technologies give more freedom to the previous ones, which continue not only to survive, but also to flourish in new and unexpected forms (e.g., painting after the advent of photography).

In nature, genes have physiological criteria to preserve or discard the information. Heredity—viz. the passing on of physical or mental characteristics genetically from one generation to another to ensure the existence of intelligent life itself—obeys the laws of function and convenience in relation to the environment where life spreads and evolves. Human genes are the naturally curated repository of all the experiences accumulated by humanity on planet Earth. Human societies added cultural criteria as a complementary trove of valuable knowledge. Cultural heritage—viz. the experiences accrued by human communities and transmitted by artificial (i.e., human-made) means such as orality, artefacts, and rituals—needs to be curated by humans. As mentioned above, traditional selection criteria are put at risk by today's rapid development of society, globalisation, and digital revolutions. Our society is, thus, urged to decide what to store and what to discard in the digital trove of human experiences.

Today, there is a clear need of taking over the responsibility of discussing the best desirable principles for this new digital trove because society needs to reinforce, with more human selection criteria, the algorithms that are already dealing with the selection of valuable data. Machines increasingly write these algorithms and work mainly on pattern recognition to collect the data that is considered worthy of being stored because of free-market rules. However, our society has not yet developed a conscious selection and discards systems (Eco 2014, 87–89, 94). Therefore, in the elaboration of the selection criteria for heritage science, it is essential to add ethics to pattern recognition if we want to avoid the risk of relying only on the authority of the free market whilst deciding on the usefulness of the treasure of human experiences. For example, a report published by the Capgemini Research Institute in September 2020 demonstrated that one-third of the leaders in charge of artificial intelligence (AI) systems are not competent in understanding the potential biases of their products (Capgemini Research Institute 2020). Considering that we can only assume what the next generation will need or appreciate in the future, transcultural and intergenerational empathy becomes an essential human value along with the functional and necessary preservation of the environmental characteristics compatible with human life on Earth (UNEP 1972–2022). For the recent debate on the early-twentieth-century cultural approach known as 'transculturalism', refer to Madeleine Herren et al. (2012, 1–3, and 45–46). In 2013, Massimo Recalcati explained the debate on the intergenerational discussion based on Lacan's psychoanalytic perspective (Recalcati 2013).

Heritage science can step up new gear and provide a crucial contribution to implementing this plan and empower human imagination and wisdom. This unique heritage science should first decode the knowledge and values humanity embedded in tangible and intangible heritage. Then, it should encode them in a digital knowledge aggregator (i.e., a 'knowledge engineering tool that allows its user to assemble information of different kinds from different sources, guided by what the user *wants to do* with the synthesized whole'; Nanetti et al. 2015, 159). Finally, it could make relevant information available to decision-making (where, when, and how it is needed) algorithmically (i.e., using computational procedures). In general, to improve this kind of advancement of learning, historians need to develop specific ontologies to parse data and recognise entities from historical sources. These data can then be mapped into an electronic database and used in analytical environments to build linkages between parsed texts and recognised entities from other heterogeneous sources (e.g., Wikipedia, OpenStreetMap) and search engines (e.g., Google Scholar, Microsoft Academic). For this to happen, historical data must be published online, and open-access databases must be appropriately shared. As a collective whole, historians have big digital data organised in databases. Still, these databases are not very useful because most of them sit within organisations on the hard disk of individual researchers.

Scholars partially share their data via published books and journal papers. Data is manipulated in descriptive narratives and needs a reverse-engineering process to be used again for a different kind of thinking. Citations and notes are the 'procedures intended to communicate an effect of authenticity' (Ginzburg 2012). Since Modern times, historians typically use the footnote as 'the one form of proof supplied in support of their assertions' (Grafton 1994, 1995, 1997). However, these footnotes can become an unwieldy web that takes considerable effort to navigate. Superhuman efforts are thus required to take all the pieces and put them together into a recognisable whole.

Therefore, first, the database interface must be adequately designed so that it is user-friendly and does not require computer-engineering skills. Second, and perhaps most importantly, data must be curated and tagged by scholars using the same identified ontologies and vocabularies used to aggregate the data into the database. Finally, data can be publicly accessible to the international scholarly community. Any researcher who needs a particular piece of data can find it easily and quickly (e.g., on MSRA Graph Engine, Linx Analytics). The same identified ontologies and vocabularies can be used to model historical data from historical sources as Linked Data (i.e., best practices to export, share, and connect pieces of data on the Semantic Web) and generate, for example, graph representations of the data (e.g., RDF using JSON-LD-JavaScript Object Notation for Linked Data), among other solutions (Grinin & Korotayev 2014, Flanders & Jannidis 2015, Graham et al. 2016).

Unfortunately, nearly all historical databases were designed to be the end products of research projects or programs. To further proceed, databases need to be constantly expanded with new data sets. Among others, examples of such excellent historical databases include the *Digital Atlas of Roman and Medieval Civilizations* directed by Michael McCormick, the biology-informed *Seshat: Global History Databank* initiated by Peter Turchin, the *Big History Project* conceived by David Christian, *Trismegistos* founded by Mark Depauw, and, to link different databases, *Pelagios* coordinated by Leif Isaksen, and the *Collaborative for Historical Information and Analysis* (CHIA) for creating a world-historical data set initiated by Patrick Manning with support from the US National Science Foundation (Manning 2013, 2015). These databases and others can become portals of historical knowledge if they also offer functionalities to combine data with metadata, show visualisations of this combination, and run simulations based on insights gained from such visualisations.

Beyond the mandatory identifying metadata associated with each piece of historical data, databases should also record the interactions between researchers from different disciplines. These interactions between experts could not happen quickly without the computer database because most expert assessments are pre-publication level and theoretical, so we will not see them in journal publications or books, however long we wait. In this sense, having very diverse data made available on a database and having metadata to augment the data sets themselves is one way the digital computer revolutionises the study of history. It allows historians more intimate interactions with the data and, consequently, closer interactions with each other.

However, if we stop at this stage, data sets and metadata will quickly accumulate. The volume of data and metadata available will be so large that no one expert can comprehend them anymore. Therefore, to take advantage of the third wave of 'really' computational history's opportunities, historians can be helped by the computer to comprehend the collection of data and metadata better. This process means going from simple data management aided by the computer (Graham et al. 2016, 73–111) to more sophisticated topic modelling and data visualisations. This process involves 'deforming, compressing, or otherwise manipulating data to see them in new and enlightening ways' (Graham et al. 2016, 113–158 and 159–194) and network analysis (Hitzbleck & Hübner 2014, 7–15, Graham et al. 2016, 195–264).

In this data visualisation stage, the historian will borrow various machine learning strategies from the computer scientist to discover patterns in the data. Because historians traditionally spend long hours working directly with data, they become very good at formulating hypotheses and, after that, finding from memory other pieces of data that would support such hypotheses. However, they likely miss many different patterns in the data that do not fit into their modes of theorising. The suite of data visualisation and machine learning methods developed by computer scientists can help discover most of these patterns. Unfortunately, such methods have been underutilised because (1) the historical databases are fragmented and, therefore, patterns across different data sets cannot be detected, and (2) the methods are not traditionally included in the training of historians. More importantly, the historical databases are designed for human queries and not necessarily structured for machine queries and thus machine learning.

The final stage that history must reach to become a full-fledged computational discipline is modelling and simulation to explore big historical data in extensive simulations, algorithmically—as John Holland would say (Holland 1975, Mitchell 1996, 2–3). Models can be top-down (equation-based) or bottom-up (rule-based). They can be analysed (by following the chain of logic in the equations or rules until we arrive at conclusions) or simulated (by letting the computer follow the chain of logic so that we can interpret the conclusions). Models help us understand the big picture by functioning (in conjunction with analysis, or more likely, simulation, when the model becomes too complex) as a *macroscope* synthesising our incomplete knowledge and insights into a complete whole.

As summarised by Shawn Graham, Ian Milligan, and Scott Weingart, it was Joël de Rosnay who first used the term *macroscope* to discuss complex societies (de Rosnay 1979). In literary criticism, a similar concept was called 'distant reading' by Franco Moretti (2005) and 'macroanalysis' by Matthew L. Jockers (2013). As for cultural history, an exemplar demonstration of the 'data-driven macroscopic' approach is given by Maximilian Schich and his research team (2014, 562). Murray Gell-Mann (2013), in his keynote lecture, *A Crude Look at the Whole,* given at the international conference *A Crude Look at the Whole: A Reflection on Complexity* hosted by Nanyang Technological University, Singapore, from 4 to 6 March 2013, pointed out the fact that to increase the understanding of historical processes, we should improve the approach pioneered by the British historian Toynbee, rather than simply criticising and marginalising. In his 12-volume magnum opus, *A Study of History,* Arnold Joseph Toynbee presented the development of major world civilisations starting from the history of the Byzantine Empire (Toynbee 1934–1961, Gell-Mann 1997, 9, Schäfer 2001, 301). Others, like Erez Aiden and Jean-Baptiste Michel (2013), also wrote about 'a [macro] scope to study human history' (Graham et al. 2016, 2).

Ultimately, the purpose of having models is to make predictions, which can be qualitative or quantitative. If we resimulate the past, we can end up with a simulated world (Gavin 2014, 24), interwoven by counterfactual histories. If we simulate the future, we will be exploring different scenarios. The debate over contingency versus inevitability explicitly discusses counterfactuals in modern evolutionary biology. This focus has happened at least since Stephen Jay Gould's book about evolution and how to interpret evidence from the actual past was published in 1989. The discussion became relevant for the history of science in general (Radick 2005), and Osvaldo Pessoa Jr has been exploring the role of computer models in assessing the history of science counterfactuals (Pessoa 2001). This discussion fits in the discourse of 'the social logic of the text', as discussed in 1997 by Gabrielle Spiegel. She argued that 'while cultural anthropology and cultural history (together with the New Historicism) have successfully reintroduced a (new) historicist consideration of discourse as the product of identifiable cultural and historical formations, they have not been equally successful in restoring history as an active agent in the social construction of meaning' (Spiegel 1997, 9).

1.3 The Online System Engineering Historical Memory (EHM): Methods and Tools

In recent years, the influence of visual imagery has advanced, and new tools and techniques have been increasingly exploited to the benefit of interdisciplinary research (Strandgaard Jensen 2021).

Information visualisation has become an essential and meaningful approach for digital history to explore complex data sets (Bertin 2010, Schnapp 2014, 8–15, Cheng et al. 2020). It can be construed as a powerful guide for exploring primary historical information and generating new research opportunities in online secondary literature repositories (Cohen 2008). Nowadays, several visualisation solutions can be tested and successfully used by historians in their perennial chase for the truth (Nanetti & Cheong 2018, 341–343). Therefore, good information visualisation can aid in discovering relationships in different historical information and promoting the sharing and participatory interpretation of historical memory (Fan et al. 2020). Designing, developing, and sharing such visualisation tools for digital history implies multiple collaborations between the curators of the actual artefacts. These curators are occupied in institutions such as museums, archives, libraries, sites, and galleries. They collaborate with a plurality of different professions spanning the humanities to computer science, from conservation to communication sciences, and from copyright law to free access to knowledge (Proctor 2010, Macchia & Salgado 2015, Olafson 2015) to create trustworthy systems (Duranti 2016).

These new and complex professional interactions need innovative and flexible methods to avoid or solve potential conflicts and create effective working teams and environments. Ultimately, they can provide the users with web services and digital experiences of artefacts that satisfy the requirements of scholars, conservation institutions, and the public. Following the century-old tradition of learning at a high level, the shift into the digital must safeguard scholarly accuracy in the delivery of information. At the same time, web technologies can provide the user with sophisticated tools to confront authorities with facts, viz. to confirm the provenance of data and validate the reliability of the information, discover new insights, and search for newly published relevant evidence and interpretation (Nanetti et al. 2016a, b). Since 2007, Engineering Historical Memory (EHM) has been working in this direction. Umberto Eco inspired the inception of this research in theory (Eco 2007, 2014) and Antonio Carile in practice. The theoretical starting point of this research is Umberto Eco's essay *Dall'albero al labirinto*, which gives the title to his collected studies on the history of semiotics published by Bompiani in Milan in 2007, and later translated into English as *From the Tree to the Labyrinth* (Eco 2014). In practice, Antonio Carile's studies on the *Partitio TImperii Romanie* (i.e., 'Partition of the Byzantine Empire' made by the Latin powers of the Fourth Crusade in the aftermath of the second conquest of Constantinople in 1204) were the example (Carile 1965).

In the absence of the original document, Carile worked on its critical edition, searching for copies in the manuscripts of about 2,000 Venetian chronicles. During this research, he discovered several different versions of the *Partitio* and classified the codices of the Venetian chronicles into families accordingly (Carile 1969). However, this classification does not necessarily apply to the entire manuscript codex, where a version of the *Partitio* is recorded. It is confirmed only for the specific text of the *Partitio* itself. In 2007, based on this factual consideration, Andrea Nanetti conceived a new method for 'the engineering of historical memories' (EHM). Firstly, he applied it to the critical analysis of the early modern chronicles of the Italian municipality of Imola that record the story of the city from its legendary Trojan origins until the annexation by the State of the Roman Church (Nanetti 2008). The EHM method worked on the historical identification of individual stories (i.e., accounts of past events that can be philologically construed as modular components with a probable independent textual tradition) across all available manuscript codices. Furthermore, their content was matched with the secondary literature that had used them to close the historiography loop.

EHM is an ongoing research project that welcomes international and multidisciplinary collaboration to design and test interactive applications for the virtual (re)organisation and delivery of historical knowledge in the digital age. EHM engages and connects cultural and educational institutions, scholars, software engineers, user interface, and user-experience designers. The EHM research team studies and practices 'by what means' traditional historical scholarship can supply machine-readable information. The aim is to empower historical sciences with AI and machine learning. This process can enable all users to read primary historical sources interactively. The user's different knowledge and expertise levels are taken into consideration by a series of on-demand steps in the information retrieval process. In the history domain, EHM makes a cross-disciplinary use of established research processes. These research processes aim to facilitate the exploration of primary historical sources (Nanetti et al. 2016a, b). They include mapping as understood in mathematics and linguistics (i.e., an operation that associates each element of a given set, the domain, with one or more items of a second set, the range) and parsing as understood in computing (i.e., analyse narratives into logical syntactic components). EHM uses these operations of mapping and parsing for individual primary historical sources to associate semantic elements. Given sets of information provided by the domain of the traditional disciplines (e.g., history, art history, philology, palaeography, diplomatics, codicology, archaeology, epigraphy, sigillography) are associated with one or more elements of the range of machine-readable content management systems (e.g., spreadsheets, computational notebooks).

The level of accuracy of this preliminary human activity is directly proportional to that of the aggregations generated and visualised by the EHM algorithms from different sets of similar written or depicted elements in the EHM database (e.g., geographical names, people's names, goods, ships, governments, events, architectures, drawings) and potentially relevant publications, images, and videos retrieved in online repositories. To understand and emphasise the unity of EHM as an interactive system in the approach to historical information, the rhetorical and conceptual linking of 'ping and visualisation' and 'search and visualisation' should be hendiadys. Thus, in its primary meaning, the term 'mapping' is understood as the localisation and description of elements, facts, or phenomena that relate to a circumscribed area, historically understood at the intersection of precise space and time coordinates. The aim is to provide and test an example of an innovative epistemological process to distil historical data visually. On EHM, the 'visualisation' process is seen not as a reductive representation to epitomise and illustrate written narratives but as an investigative tool for the historian intending to enter fully into the digital era. Historians can use EHM for discovering and organising new relationships between objects in a new historical landscape where past, present, and future can merge into a democratised whole (Bolick 2006, Altman 2008).

This EHM application shows how making information machine-understandable allows digital systems to satisfy different audiences simultaneously and the various queries that come from individual audiences under other circumstances. The EHM process starts with aggregating traditionally acquired scholarship (e.g., books and papers) into two main streams: texts and images. Then, information is parsed and transferred into machine-understandable formats using Google Spreadsheet as a content management system and data storage solution. This system has several concurrent advantages: powerful, popular, secure, robust, customisable, easy backup, and, finally, the similarity with MySQL database in table-like construction. The structure is ready to engage an automatic approach for generating rich, linked geo-metadata from historical map images (Li et al. 2020).

Each item is identified using a relevant Wikipedia page whenever available. Based on this identification, EHM picks keywords and filters to aggregate knowledge from leading online repositories about any item selected by the user in the online application in real time. Some resources are searched through their API (application programming interface). APIs are either public (e.g., Europeana, Gallica, YouTube, Vimeo, Google Images, Bing Images) or shared upon research collaboration agreements (e.g., Taylor & Francis, Scopus-Elsevier). Other online repositories do not have the policy to publicly share their APIs for federated searches. In these cases, the user is prompted to link to the official websites in separate tabs; an automated query consistent with the selected item is automatically filled to facilitate the search. Online repositories without API are not included in the EHM search (e.g., SmartHistory).

With most resources, search APIs work by looking for input keywords in the digital documents accessible online (title, author, abstract, full text). Notably, Taylor & Francis also provides a cutting-edge service, which allows searching by 'concepts' related to the set keywords. On EHM, the search results are visualised under four categories as follows:

- Scholarly publications from Europeana, Gallica, Taylor & Francis, Scopus-Elsevier, via API.
- Images from Google Images, Bing Images, via API.
- Videos from YouTube, Vimeo, I-Media-Cities, via API.
- Guided search in other relevant resources that do not publicly share their API (e.g., Old Maps Online, Getty Images, Google Scholar, JSTOR, China National Knowledge Infrastructure, Wanfang Data, Pelagios, Blackwell).

Additionally, other EHM tools are in the pipeline to empower the user experience in discovering new knowledge across the primary historical sources published on EHM. In early 2021, Justin Dauwels and Andrea Nanetti, assisted by a team of undergraduate and graduate students from Delft University of Technology (the Netherlands), started to work on a new algorithm for image search to allow users to find images without the need for keywords (van Mastrigt et al. 2021). Keywords place severe limitations on image search. First, words belong to one specific language: all images with metadata in another language are left behind. Also, the choice of keywords is arbitrary and generates ambiguity. To address these challenges, EHM searches for images visually using a set of different methods (e.g., template matching, feature matching, nearest neighbour search, transfer learning, second-order loss and attention for image retrieval, deep learning) (Nanetti 2021b, Yao et al. 2022).

In mid-2021, Erik Cambria, Andrea Nanetti, and Siew Ann Cheong, in collaboration with John Pavlopoulos and assisted by Ng Yue Jie Alphaeus (NTU Singapore, URECA project), began to experiment with the SenticNet API for sentiment analysis (SenticNet n.d.) to the primary historical sources published on EHM (Ng et al. 2022). Sentiment analysis is one of the fastest growing research areas in computer science (Mäntylä et al. 2018). However, applying sentiment analysis methods to historical texts is still in its infancy and faces several challenges (Sprugnoli et al. 2016, Koncar et al. 2020, Schmidt et al. 2021, Vázquez-González et al. 2022). Most challenges are because available algorithms are trained on today's social media. So, EHM explores different methods (e.g., concept parsing, intensity ranking, personality recognition, aspect extraction, polarity classification, emotion categorisation, and subjectivity detection) and tests them on each paragraph/story of the chronicles and travel accounts (Nanetti & Vu 2019).

All these EHM tools can be linked to the original artefact or its replicas (e.g., physical copies, cloud-based reproductions, projections, large interactive screens) and used as gateways to access the knowledge embedded in the artefact in any exhibition setting via intelligent devices. For example, in the BYOD (Bring Your Own Device) era, via a quick-response (QR) code displayed in the exhibition caption, the camera of the visitor's smart device can read the uniform resource locator (URL) and access the relevant EHM application. The user can also continue the experience on mobile and desktop devices after and outside the exhibition. This continuity of engagement allows EHM to involve the user online in co-designing the experience as experimented by the EU Research Project MeLa— European museums in an age of migrations (Lanz & Montanari 2015, Capurro & Lupo 2016, 89–93). This model goes towards a laboratory for continuous innovation in designing digital history to structure the advancement of learning in cloud-based systems (Celaschi & Lupo 2016, Formia 2016). The EHM learning tools are cloud-based and, thus, accessible anywhere by anyone with an internet connection. Working on real-time knowledge aggregation, the EHM information is constantly updated and possibly targeted on the visitor's profile when logged into the system. A diagram in Figure 1.1 illustrates the EHM workflow.

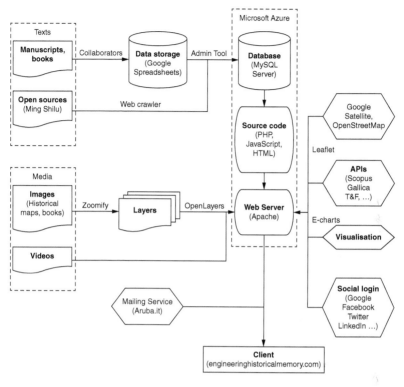

Figure 1.1 Workflow of the EHM search.

Source: Diagram created by Khoi Vu and Andrea Nanetti.

The historical accounts work on 'what happened' (i.e., the factual), while computer simulations tell us 'what could have happened' (i.e., the counterfactual). Only by combining both the most accurate assessment of what actually happened and what could have happened, we can address the question if in history there are such things as universal laws, from which we cannot deviate in a cause-and-effect 'mechanism-based understanding' (Paolucci & Picascia 2011, 135) of historical phenomena. The power of computer simulations can support historical sciences to develop a shared prescriptive mode of inquiry in assessing primary and secondary sources. It will also provide new freedom in the historian's subjective and descriptive identification and assessment of problems to be investigated. Figure 1.2 illustrates the stages through which history can improve as a computational discipline.

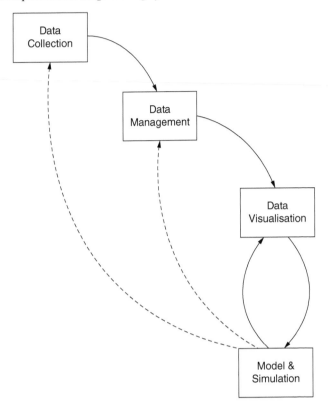

Figure 1.2 The stages a discipline must progress through to become computational.

Source: Nanetti & Cheong 2018, 338.

References

Aiden, Erez, & Jean-Baptiste Michel (2013). *Uncharted: Big Data as a Lens on Human Culture*. New York: Riverhead. https://archive.org/details/uncharted bigdata0000aide

Altman, Rick (2008). *A Theory of Narrative*. New York: Columbia University Press.

Arendt, Hannah (1998). *The Human Condition*, Second edition, with an *Introduction* by Margaret Canovan. Chicago, IL and London: The University of Chicago Press (first edition, Chicago and London: The University of Chicago Press, 1958). https://monoskop.org/images/e/e2/Arendt_Hannah_ The_Human_Condition_2nd_1998.pdf

Bertin, Jacques (2010). *Semiology of Graphics: Diagrams, Networks, Maps*, translated [from French to English] by William J. Berg. Redland, CA: Esri Press.

Bettini, Maurizio (2019). *Homo sum. Essere "umani" nel mondo antico*. Turin: Einaudi.

Bod, Rens, Jaap Maat, & Thijs Weststeijn (Eds.) (2010). *The Making of the Humanities*, Volume 1. *Early Modern Europe*. Amsterdam: Amsterdam University Press. http://www.jstor.org/stable/j.ctt46n1vz

Bod, Rens, Jaap Maat, & Thijs Weststeijn (Eds.) (2012). *The Making of the Humanities*, Volume 2. *From Early Modern to Modern Disciplines*. Amsterdam: Amsterdam University Press. http://www.jstor.org/stable/j.ctt45kdfw

Bod, Rens, Jaap Maat, & Thijs Weststeijn (Eds.) (2014). *The Making of the Humanities*, Volume 3. *The Modern Humanities*. Amsterdam: Amsterdam University Press. http://www.jstor.org/stable/j.ctt45kdfw

Bod, Rens (2013). *A New History of the Humanities: The Search for Principles and Patterns from Antiquity to the Present*. Oxford: Oxford University Press. DOI: 10.1093/acprof:oso/9780199665211.001.0001

Bod, Rens, Julia Kursell, Jaap Maat, & Thijs Weststeijn (2016). "A New Field: History of Humanities". *History of Humanities*, *1*(1), 1–8. https://doi.org/10.1086/685056

Bolick, Cheryl Mason (2006) "Digital Archives: Democratizing the Doing of History". *International Journal of Social Education*, *21*(1), 122–134. https://files.eric.ed.gov/fulltext/EJ782136.pdf

Bordoni, Luciana, Francesco Mele, & Antonio Sorgente (2016). *Artificial Intelligence for Cultural Heritage*. Newcastle upon Tyne: Cambridge Scholars Publishing

Borgman, Christine L. (2009). "The Digital Future Is Now: A Call to Action for the Humanities". *Digital Humanities Quarterly*, *3*(4). http://www.digitalhumanities.org/dhq/vol/3/4/000077/000077.html

Bradshaw, Gary L., Pat Langley, Herbert A. Simon, & Jan M. Zytkow (1987). *Scientific Discovery: Computational Explorations of the Creative Processes*. Cambridge, MA: MIT Press. https://doi.org/10.1177/027046768800800417

Braudel, Fernand (1960). "Unité et diversité des sciences de l'homme". *Revue de l'enseignement supérieur*, *1*, 17–22.

Braudel, Fernand (1980). *On History*, translated by Sarah Matthews. Chicago, IL: The University of Chicago Press [originally, *Écrits sur l'histoire*. Paris: Flammarion, 1969]. https://archive.org/details/onhistory00brau

Capgemini Research Institute (2020). *AI and the Ethical Conundrum. How Organizations Can Build Ethically Robust AI System and Gain Trust*. https://www.capgemini.com/wp-content/uploads/2020/09/AI-and-the-Ethical-Conundrum-Infographic.pdf

Capurro, Rita, & Eleonora Lupo (Eds.) (2016). *Designing Multivocal Museums. Intercultural Practices at 'Museo Diocesano, Milano'*. Research Project MeLa – European museums in an age of migrations, funded within the European Union's Seventh Framework Programme (SSH-2010-5.2.2, project officer Mr Zoltán Krasznal – work package of the *Politecnico di Milano*, Department of Design). Milan: Politecnico di Milano, Department of Design. http://www.mela-project.polimi.it/upl/statics/Designing_Multivocal_Museums.pdf

Carile, Antonio (1965). *"Partitio Terrarum Imperii Romanie.* Edizione e commento". *Studi Veneziani, 7,* 125–305.

Carile, Antonio (1969). *La cronachistica veneziana (secoli XIII-XVI) di fronte alla spartizione della Romania nel 1204.* Florence: Leo S. Olschki.

Casanova, Angelo (Ed.) (1984). *I frammenti di Diogene di Enoanda.* Firenze: Università degli Studi di Firenze, Dipartimento di Scienze dell'Antichità «Giorgio Pasquali».

Celaschi, Flaviano, & Eleonora Lupo (2016). *Verso un modello di laboratorio per l'innovazione continua,* in Celi, & Formia 2016, 234–242.

Celi, Manuela, & Elena Formia (Eds.) (2016). *Humanities Design Lab. Le culture del progetto e le scienze umane e sociali.* Santalcargelo di Romagna: Maggioli Editore.

Cheng, Xiandong, Hao He, Yan Ren, & Shengqi Ba (2020). "Teaching Discussion on Information Visualisation Design". In *Design, User Experience, and Usability. Case Studies in Public and Personal Interactive Systems (HCII 2020),* edited by Aaron Marcus, & Elisabeth Rosenzweig, 393–404. Cham: Springer. https://doi.org/10.1007/978-3-030-49757-6_28

Cohen, Daniel J. (2008). "Interchange: The Promise of Digital History". *Journal of American History, 95,* 452–491. https://doi.org/10.2307/25095630

de Rosnay, Joël (1979). *The Macroscope: A New World Scientific System.* New York: Harper & Row.

Domingos, Pedro (2015). *The Master Algorithm: How the Quest for the Ultimate Learning Machine Will Remake Our World.* New York: Basic Books. https://archive.org/details/masteralgorithmh0000domi_q9v1

Duranti, Luciana (2016). "What Will Trustworthy Systems Look Like in the Future?" In *Building Trustworthy Digital Repositories. Theory and Implementation,* edited by Philip C. Bantin, 336–346. Lanham, MD: Rowman & Littlefield Publishing Group.

Eco, Umberto (2007). *Dall'albero al labirinto.* Milan: Bompiani.

Eco, Umberto (2014). *From the Tree to the Labyrinth.* Cambridge, MA and London: Harvard University Press. https://doi.org/10.4159/9780674728165

Fan, Luwei, Bo Hu, Fuqiang Li, & Jixiang Sui [范陆薇, 胡波, 李富强, 隋吉祥] (2020). "博物馆解说牌的信息可视化设计 [Information Visualisation Design for Museum Exhibition Panels]". 东南文化 *[Journal of Dongnan Culture], 4,* 163–169, 191–192. http://dnwh.njmuseum.com/pdf/2020/202004/20200419.pdf

Ferguson Smith, Martin (Ed.) (1993). "Diogenes of Oinoanda". In *The Epicurean Inscription,* edition, with introduction, translation, and notes. Naples: Bibliopolis.

Ferguson Smith, Martin (Ed.) (2003). "Supplement to Diogenes of Oinoanda". In *The Epicurean Inscription.* Naples: Bibliopolis.

Flanders, Julia, & Fotis Jannidis (2015). *Knowledge Organization and Data Modeling in the Humanities.* http://www.wwp.northeastern.edu/outreach/conference/kodm2012/flanders_jannidis_datamodeling.pdf

Formia, Elena (2016). *Design/Humanities. Una mappatura critica come apertura per la ricerca,* in Celi, & Formia 2016, 213–232.

Foucault, Michel (1966). *Les mots et les choses. Une archéologie des sciences humaines*. Paris: Éditions Gallimard. https://monoskop.org/images/4/40/Foucault_Michel_Les_mots_et_les_choses.pdf

Foucault, Michel (1970). *The Order of Things: An Archaeology of the Human Sciences*, translated from French into English by Alan Sheridan. London and New York: Tavistock Publications and Pantheon Books. https://archive.org/details/orderofthingsarc00fouc/mode/2up

Galassi, Jonathan (2010). *Giacomo Leopardi, Canti*, poems bilingual edition translated and annotated by J. Galassi. New York: Farrar, Straus, and Giroux.

Galleron, Ioana, & Fatiha Idmhand (2020). "Why Go from Texts to Data, or The Digital Humanities as A Critique of the Humanities". *Word & Text: A Journal of Literary Studies & Linguistics 10*(1), 53–69.

Gardini, Nicola (2019). *Rinascere. Storie e maestri di un'idea italiana*. Milan: Garzanti.

Gavin, Michael (2014). "Agent-Based Modeling and Historical Simulation". *Digital Humanities Quarterly*, *8*(4). http://www.digitalhumanities.org/dhq/vol/8/4/000195/000195.html

Gell-Mann, Murray (1997). "The Simple and the Complex". In *Complexity, Global Politics, and National Security*, edited by David S. Alberts, & Thomas J. Czerwinski, 2–12. Washington, DC: National Defense University. http://www.dodccrp.org/files/Alberts_Complexity_Global.pdf

Gell-Mann, Murray (2013). *A Crude Look at the Whole*, transcript by Jonathan Sim (18 July 2018). Para Limes. https://www.paralimes.org/2018/07/transcript-of-a-crude-look-at-the-whole-by-murray-gell-mann

Ginzburg, Carlo (2012). "Microhistory, Two or Three Things that I Know About It". In *Threads and Traces. True False Fictive*, edited by Idem, translated from Italian to English by Anne C. Tedeschi, & John Tedeschi, 193–214. Berkeley, Los Angeles, London: University of California Press (Original work: *Il filo e le tracce. Vero falso finto*. Bologna: Feltrinelli, 1986). https://doi.org/10.1086/448699

Golub, Koraljka, & Ying-Hsang Liu (2021). *Information and Knowledge Organization in Digital Humanities: Global Perspectives*. London: Routledge. https://doi.org/10.4324/9781003131816

Gottlieb, Halina, & Marcin Szeląg (2015). "Engaging Spaces. Interpretation, Design and Digital Strategies." In *Proceeding of the NODEM 2014 Conference* (Poland, Warsaw, 1–3 December 2014). Warsaw: Museum of King Jan III's Palace at Wilanów. http://nodem.org/wp-content/uploads/2015/08/NODEM-2014-Proceedings.pdf

Gould, Stephen Jay (1989). *Wonderful Life: The Burgess Shale and the Nature of History*. London: Hutchinson Radius. https://archive.org/details/wonderfullifebur0000goul

Grafton, Anthony (1994). "The Footnote from de Thou to Ranke". In Idem & Suzanne L. Marchand (Eds.), Proof and persuasion in history. *History & Theory*, *33*, 53–76. https://doi.org/10.2307/2505502

Grafton, Anthony (1995). *Die tragischen Ursprünge der deutschen Fußnote*. Berlin: Wagenbach.

Grafton, Anthony (1997). *The Footnote: A Curious History*. Cambridge, MA: Harvard University Press. https://archive.org/details/footnotecurioush 0000graf/mode/2up

Grafton, Anthony, & Lisa Jardine (1986). *From Humanism to the Humanities. Education and the Liberal Arts in 15th and 16th Century Europe*. London: Duckworth. https://archive.org/details/fromhumanismtohu0000graf/mode/2up

Graham, Shawn, Ian Milligan, & Scott Weingart (Eds.) (2016). *Exploring Big Historical Data. The Historian's Macroscope*. London: Imperial College Press. https://doi.org/10.1142/p981

Grinin, Leonid, & Andrey Korotayev (Eds.) (2014). *History & Mathematics. Trends and Cycles*. Volgograd: 'Uchitel' Publishing House. https://philpapers. org/archive/GRIHM-4.pdf

Gruzinski, Serge (2015). *L'histoire, pour quoi faire?* Paris: Librairie Arthème Fayard.

Herren, Madeleine, Martin Rüesch, & Christiane Sibille (2012). *Transcultural History: Theories, Methods, Sources*. Heidelberg: Springer Verlag. https://doi. org/10.1007/978-3-642-19196-1

Higgins, Chris (2014). "Humanism, Cosmopolitanism, and the Ethics of Translation". *Educational Theory*, *64*(5), 429–437. https://doi.org/10.1111/ edth.12073

Hitzbleck, Kerstin, & Klara Hübner (Eds.) (2014). *Die Grenzen des Netzwerks 1200–1600*. Ostfildern: Jan Thorbecke Verlag der Schwabenverlag AG.

Holland, John (1975). *Adaptation in Natural and Artificial Systems. An Introductory Analysis with Applications to Biology, Control, and Artificial Intelligence*. Ann Arbor, MI: University of Michigan Press. https://archive. org/details/adaptationinnatu0000holl/mode/2up

Ignatieff, Michael (2017). *The Ordinary Virtues: Moral Order in a Divided World*. Cambridge, MA: Harvard University Press.

Jockers, Matthew L. (2013). *Macroanalysis: Digital Methods & Literary History*. Champaign, IL: University of Illinois Press. http://dx.doi.org/10.5406/ illinois/9780252037528.001.0001

Kahane, Bernard (2020). "La dimension identitaire de l'information à l'ère des algorithmes et de l'intelligence artificielle". In *La transmission en question(s)*, edited by Michel Gad Wolkowicz, 633–656. Paris: éditions IN PRESS.

Koncar, Philipp, Alexandra Fuchs, Elisabeth Hobisch, Bernhard C. Geiger, Martina Scholger, & Denis Helic (2020). "Text Sentiment in the Age of Enlightenment: An Analysis of Spectator Periodicals". *Applied Network Science*, *5*(1), 1–32. https://doi.org/10.1007/s41109-020-00269-z

Langlois, Walter (1977). "André Malraux (1901-1976)". *The Future Review*, *50*(5), 683–687. https://www.jstor.org/stable/390398

Lanz, Francesca, & Elena Montanari (2015). *Proactive Spaces. An Insight on the Statial and Museographical Features of 21st Century 'Post-museum'*, in Gottlieb, & Szeląg 2015, 43–50. http://nodem.org/wp-content/uploads/2015/ 08/NODEM-2014-Proceedings.pdf

Leonardis, Irene (2018). "L'humanitas, secondo Varrone. La memoria della stirpe umana". *Athenaeum*, *106*(2), 487–503.

Li, Zekun, Yao-Yi Chiang, Sasan Tavakkol, Basel Shbita, Johannes H. Uhl, Stefan Leyk, & Craig A. Knoblock (2020). "An Automatic Approach for Generating Rich, Linked Geo-Metadata from Historical Map Images". In *Proceedings of the 26th ACM SIGKDD International Conference on Knowledge Discovery & Data Mining*, 3290–3298. New York: Association for Computing Machinery. https://doi.org/10.1145/3453172

Macchia, Teresa, & Mariana Salgado (2015). *You Could Have Told Me!" Collaboration on the Design of Interactive Pieces for Museums. A Case Study*, in Gottlieb, & Szeląg 2015, 91–97. http://nodem.org/wp-content/uploads/2015/08/NODEM-2014-Proceedings.pdf

Manning, Patrick (2013). *Big Data in History*. Basingstoke: Palgrave Macmillan. https://doi.org/10.1057/9781137378972

Manning, Patrick (2015). "A World-Historical Data Resource: The Need is Now". *Journal of World-Historical Information, 2–3*(2), 1–6.

Mäntylä, Mika V., Daniel Graziotin, & Miikka Kuutila (2018). "The Evolution of Sentiment Analysis—A Review of Research Topics, Venues, and Top Cited Papers". *Computer Science Review, 27*, 16–32. https://doi.org/10.1016/j.cosrev.2017.10.002

Marche, René (Ed.) (1967). *Aulu-Gelle, Les nuits attiques. Livres I–IV*. Paris: Les Belles Lettres.

Marshall, Peter K. (Ed.) (1990). *A. Gellii Noctes Atticae*. [Reissue with corrections.] Oxford: Oxford University Press.

Mitchell, Melanie (1996). *An Introduction to Genetic Algorithms*. Cambridge, MA: MIT Press. https://www.boente.eti.br/fuzzy/ebook-fuzzy-mitchell.pdf

Moreau, Thibault (2020). "Héritage, transfert, mémoire. Ce qui se reçoit, s'élabore, se transmet – avec qui?" In *La transmission en question(s)*, edited by Michel Gad Wolkowicz, 361–370. Paris: éditions IN PRESS.

Moretti, Franco (2005). *Graphs, Maps, Trees: Abstract Models for a Literary History*. London and New York: Verso. https://docdrop.org/static/drop-pdf/Pages-from-Moretti-2007—Graphs-Maps-bkBff.pdf

Nanetti, Andrea (2008). *Imola antica e medievale nella cronachistica cittadina di età moderna: indagine esemplare per una ingegnerizzazione della memoria storica [Ancient and medieval Imola in the city chronicles of the modern age: exemplary investigation for an engineering of the historical memory]*. Imola: Editrice La Mandragora.

Nanetti, Andrea (2015). "Heritage and the Creative Industries". In *Videorecording of the 2nd Singapore Heritage Science Conference* (Nanyang Technological University, Singapore, 15–16 January 2015). http://www.paralimes.ntu.edu.sg/NewsnEvents/HeritageandtheCreativeIndustry/Pages/Video%20Gallery.aspx

Nanetti, Andrea (2021a). "Defining Heritage Science. A Consilience Pathway to Treasuring the Complexity of Inheritable Human Experience through Historical Method, AI and ML". *Complexity*, 2021, special issue on *Tales of Two Societies: On the Complexity of the Coevolution between the Physical Space and the Cyber Space*, edited by Shu-Heng Chen (Lead Editor), Simone Alfarano and Dehua Shen (Guest Editors), Article ID 4703820. https://www.hindawi.com/journals/complexity/2021/4703820/

Nanetti, Andrea (Director) (2021b). Image Search for Digital History. September 8, 2021. Engineering Historical Memory, 2:09. https://ehm-video. s3.ap-southeast-1.amazonaws.com/ImageSearch.mp4

Nanetti, Andrea, & Anna Simpson (2015). "Sharing our Heritage to Shape our Future. How Effective Are Multi-User Sharing Platforms in Supporting Collaborative Visioning for the Future, and why is Heritage Centre-Stage?" In *SOTICS 2015. The Fifth International Conference on Social Media Technologies, Communication, and Informatics* (Barcelona, Spain, 15–20 November 2015), 82–90. Wilmington, DE: IARIA XPS Press. http://www. thinkmind.org/index.php?view=article&articleid=sotics_2015_4_20_60070

Nanetti, Andrea, & Siew Ann Cheong (2018). "Computational History: From Big Data to Big Simulations". In *Big Data in Computational Social Science and Humanities*, edited by Shu-Heng Chen, 337–363. Cham: Springer International Publishing AG. https://link.springer.com/ chapter/10.1007/978-3-319-95465-3_18

Nanetti, Andrea, & Nguyen Khoi Vu (Eds.) (2019). *EHM – Chronicles and Travel Accounts of Afro-Eurasia (1205-1533 CE)*. https://engineeringhistori calmemory.com/AfroEurasia.php

Nanetti, Andrea, Angelo Cattaneo, Siew Ann Cheong, & Chin-Yew Lin (2015). "Maps as Knowledge Aggregators: From Renaissance Italy Fra Mauro to Web Search Engines". *The Cartographic Journal*, *52*(2), 159–167. https://doi. org/10.1080/00087041.2015.1119472

Nanetti, Andrea, Siew Ann Cheong, & Mikhail Filippov (2016a). "Digital Maps and Automatic Narratives for Interactive Global Histories". *The Asian Review of World Histories*, *4*(1), 83–123. https://doi.org/10.12773/arwh.2016.4.1.083

Nanetti, Andrea, Chin-Yew Lin, & Siew Ann Cheong (2016b). "Provenance and Validation from the Humanities to Automatic Acquisition of Semantic Knowledge and Machine Reading for News and Historical Sources Indexing/ Summary". *The Asian Review of World Histories*, *4*(1), 125–132. https://doi. org/10.12773/arwh.2016.4.1.125

Ng, Yue Jie Alphaeus, Erik Cambria, Andrea Nanetti, Siew Ann Cheong, & Nguyen Khoi Vu (Eds.) (2022). "EHM – Sentiment Analysis for Digital History". Last modified May 2022. DOI https://engineeringhistoricalmemory. com/Sentiment.php

Nowotny, Helga (2020). *Life in the Digital Time Machine*. The Second Wittrock Lecture held in Uppsala on 25 February 2020. Uppsala: Swedish Collegium for Advanced Study.

Nussbaum, Martha C. (2004). "Duties of Justice, Duties of Material Aid. Cicero's Problematic Legacy". In *Stoicism. Tradition & Transformations*, edited by Steven K. Strange, & Jack Zupko, 214–249. Cambridge: Cambridge University Press.

Olafson, Rikke (2015). Wonderful Stories on Digital Devices – How Museums Have the Power to Ignite Feelings of Resonance and Wonder, in Gottlieb, & Szeląg 2015, 158–164. http://nodem.org/wp-content/uploads/2015/08/ NODEM-2014-Proceedings.pdf

Ong, Walter G. (1982). *Orality and Literacy. The Technologizing of the Word.* London and New York: Routledge. https://monoskop.org/images/d/db/ Ong_Walter_J_Orality_and_Literacy_2nd_ed.pdf

Paolucci, Mario, & Stefano Picascia (2011). "Enhancing Collective Filtering with Causal Representation". In *2011 Culture and Computing*, 135–136. Los Alamitos, CA: IEEE Computer Society. https://doi.org/10.1109/Culture-Computing.2011.37

Pasolini, Pier Paolo (Director) (1965). *Comizi d'amore [Love Meetings].* Documentary film. Rome: Arco Film.

Pessoa, Osvaldo Jr. (2001). "Counterfactual Histories: The Beginning of Quantum Physics". *Philosophy of Science*, *68*, 519–530. https://doi.org/ 10.1086/392933

Picone, Giusto, & Rosa Rita Marchese (Eds.) (2012). Marco Tullio Cicerone, *De officiis. Quel che è giusto fare.* [Latin text and translation into Italian.] Turin: Einaudi.

Pistoletto, Michelangelo (2010). *The Third Paradise.* Venice: Marsilio Editori.

Pogue Harrison, Robert (2014). "La magia di Leopardi". *451 Via della Letteratura della Scienza e dell'Arte.* URL: https://www.451online.it/la-magia-di-leopardi/ and https://www.youtube.com/watch?v=XBN715JD-OY

Pontara, Giuliano (2019). *L'antibarbarie. La concezione etico-politica di Gandhi e il XXI secolo*, [second revised, updated, and augmented edition]. Turin: Edizioni Gruppo Abele [first edition, 2006]: 135-161 (*Contro la violenza nei conflitti umani [Against violence in human conflicts]*. This relevant book has not been translated into English yet.

Preston, Christopher J. (2018). *The Synthetic Age. Outstanding Evolution, Resurrecting Species, and Reengineering Our World.* Cambridge, MA and London: The MIT Press. https://ieeexplore.ieee.org.remotexs.ntu.edu.sg/ servlet/opac?bknumber=8564055

Proctor, Nancy (2010). "Digital: Museum as Platform, Curator as Champion, in the Age of Social Media". *Curator: The Museum Journal*, *53*(1), 35–43. https://doi.org/10.1111/j.2151-6952.2009.00006.x

Radick, Gregory (2005). "Other Histories, Other Biologies". In *Philosophy, Biology, and Life*, edited by Anthony O'Hear, 21–47. Cambridge, MA: Cambridge University Press. https://doi.org/10.1017/CBO9780511599729.003

Ranieri, Antonio (1845). *Opere di Giacomo Leopardi*, edited by A. Ranieri. Florence: Felice Le Monnier. https://books.google.com.sg/books?id= NPwrott0O-0C&pg=PR5&source=gbs_toc_r&cad=4#v=onepage&q&f=false

Recalcati, Massimo (2013). *Il complesso di Telemaco. Genitori e figli dopo il tramonto del padre [The Telemachus complex. Parents and children after the father's sunset].* Milan: Feltrinelli.

Rendgen, Sandra, & Julius Wiedemann (2013). *Information Graphics.* Köln: Taschen. https://archive.org/details/informationgraph0000rend/mode/2up

Schäfer, Wolf (2001). "Global Civilisation and Local Cultures: A Crude Look at the Whole". *International Sociology*, *16*(3), 301–319. https://doi.org/10.117 7%2F026858001016003004

Schich, Maximilian, Chaoming Song, Yong-Yeol Ahn, Alexander Mirsky, Mauro Martino, Albert-László Barabási, & Dirk Helbing (2014). "A Network Framework of Cultural History". *Science, 345*, 558–562. https://doi.org/10.1126/science.1240064

Schmidt, Thomas, Katrin Dennerlein, & Christian Wolff (2021). "Towards a Corpus of Historical German Plays with Emotion Annotations". In *3rd Conference on Language, Data and Knowledge (LDK 2021, September 1-3, 2021, Zaragoza, Spain)*, edited by Dagmar Gromann, Gilles Sérasset, Thierry Declerck, John P. McCrae, Jorge Gracia, Julia Bosque-Gil, Fernando Bobillo, & Barbara Heinisch, Article No. 9, 9:11-9:11. Saarbrücken/Wadern Schloss Dagstuhl – Leibniz-Zentrum für Informatik GmbH, Dagstuhl Publishing. https://doi.org/10.4230/OASIcs.LDK.2021.9

Schnapp, Jeffrey T. (2013). "Animating the Archive". In *Animated Archive*, edited by Fulvio Irace, & Graziella Leyla Ciagà, 72–80. Milan: Electa, 2013. https://doi.org/10.5210/fm.v13i8.2218

Schnapp, Jeffrey T. (2014). *Knowledge Design. Incubating New Knowledge forms/Genres/Spaces/in the Laboratory of the Digital Humanities*, keynote delivered at the Herrenhausen Conference '(Digital) Humanities Revisited – Challenges and Opportunities in the Digital Age' (Germany, Hanover, 5–7 December 2013). Bramsche: Rasch Druckerei und Verlag. https://jeffreyschnapp.com/wp-content/uploads/2011/06/HH_lectures_Schnapp_01.pdf

SenticNet (n.d.). *Sentic APIs*. Accessed May 22, 2022. https://sentic.net/api/

Spiegel, Gabrielle M. (1997). *The Past as Text*. Baltimore and London: The Johns Hopkins University Press.

Sprugnoli, Rachele, Sara Tonelli, Alessandro Marchetti, & Giovanni Moretti (2016). "Towards Sentiment Analysis for Historical Texts". *Digital Scholarship in the Humanities, 31*(4), 762–772. https://doi.org/10.1093/llc/fqv027

Strandgaard Jensen, Helle (2021). "Digital Archival Literacy for (All) Historians". *Media History, 27*(2), 251–265. https://doi.org/10.1080/13688804.2020.1779047

Toynbee, Arnold Joseph (1934–1961). *A Study of History*, 12 Vols. London: Oxford University Press. https://archive.org/search.php?query=A+study+of+history

UNEP (1972–2022). *Environment Programme*, incepted by the United Nations in 1972. https://www.unenvironment.org.

van Mastrigt, Philippe, Justin Dawels, Andrea Nanetti, & Nguyen Khoi Vu (Eds.) (2021). "EHM – Image Search for Digital History". Last modified May 2022. DOI https://engineeringhistoricalmemory.com/ImageSearch.php

Vasbinder, Jan Wouter, Balázs Gulyás, & Jonathan Y. H. Sim (Eds.) (2018). *Grand Challenges for Science in the 21st Century*. Singapore: World Scientific. https://doi.org/10.1142/11161

Vázquez-González, Stephanie, María Somodevilla-García, Rosalva Loreto López, Helena Gómez-Adorno, David Pinto, Beatriz Beltrán, & Vivek Singh (2022). "Creating a Corpus of Historical Documents for Emotions Identification". *Journal of Intelligent & Fuzzy Systems, 42*(5), 4779–4787. https://doi.org/10.3233/JIFS-219265

Yao, Yuanyuan, Qi Zhang, Yanan Hu, Cristian Meo, Yanbo Wang, Andrea Nanetti, & Justin H. G. Dauwels (2022). "Image Search Engine by Deep Neural Networks". In *Proceedings of the 42nd WIC Symposium on Information Theory and Signal Processing in the Benelux (SITB 2022; Louvain-la-Neuve, Belgium, 1–2 June 2022)*. Delft, The Netherlands: Delft University of Technology, 134.

Yonge, Charles Duke (1853). "Diogenes Laertius". In *Βίοι καὶ γνῶμαι τῶν ἐν φιλοσοφίᾳ εὐδοκιμησάντων/Lives and opinions of eminent philosophers*, translated from Greek to English by Charles D. Yonge. London: Henry G. Bohn. https://standardebooks.org/ebooks/diogenes-laertius/the-lives-and-opinions-of-eminent-philosophers/c-d-yonge/text

Yonge, Charles Duke (1856). "Marci Tullii Ciceronis". In *Pro Archia peoeta*, translated from Latin to English by Charles D. Yonge. London: Henry G. Bohn.

Zetzel, James Eric Guttman (1972). "Cicero and the Scipionic Circle". *Harvard Studies in Classical Philology*, 76, 173–179.

2 Historians and Computers

2.1 Computers in the Historian's Craft. Opportunities and Limits

The electronic computer radically changed at all levels the ways our globalised societies and economies work (Cortada 1993). The changes that the advent of the electronic computer brought to the twentieth-century society have been critically discussed, among others, by Douglas S. Robertson (1998, 2003) and Helga Nowotny, who focused on artificial intelligence (AI) and life in the digital time machine (2020, 2021). Science methods are in the process of being transformed by the scientific infrastructure of data-intensive computing (Hey et al. 2009, 109–172, Edmond et al. 2020, 207–209) and machine learning (ML) engineering into eScience as, for example, Jim Gray discussed in a talk that he gave for the Computer Science and Telecommunications Board of the US National Research Council in Mountain View on 11 January 2007 (Gray 2009). In 2001, from a computer science and engineering perspective, Eric Mjolsness and Dennis DeCoste had already pointed out how disruptive is ML to science while highlighting 'some useful characteristics of modern machine learning methods and their relevance to scientific applications' (Mjolsness & DeCoste 2001, 2051). Referring to Tom M. Mitchell's book on ML (Mitchell 1997), they opened their article with the following definition of ML, which can be considered a working definition for the purposes of the present essay.

> Machine Learning (ML) is the study of computer algorithms capable of learning to improve their performance of a task on the basis of their own previous experience. The field is closely related to pattern recognition and statistical inference. As an engineering field, ML has become steadily more mathematical and more successful in applications over the past 20 years … it will lead

DOI: 10.4324/9781003310860-2

to appropriate, partial automation of every element of scientific method, from hypothesis generation to model construction to decisive experimentation. Thus, ML has the potential to amplify every aspect of a working scientist's progress to understanding. It will also, for better or worse, endow intelligent computer systems with some of the general analytic power of scientific thinking.

(Mjolsness & DeCoste 2001, 2051)

Since the introduction of punched cards to enter data into computers, historians have started to create large data sets that may be analysed computationally and they are fully aware of the importance of this technological turn for the advancement of historical research: all historians went digital, in one way or another (Le Roy Ladurie 1973, 1978, 2–5, Galasso 2000, 311–315, Ginzburg 2001, Cohen & Rosenzweig 2006, Nanetti & Cheong 2018, 343–344). The French historian Emmanuel Le Roy Ladurie (1973, 1978) was one of the first, if not the very first, to clearly foresee and phrase the implications of the use of the computer in historical studies:

History based on computers/information technology is not limited to a very specific category of research, but also leads to the establishment of an 'archive'. Once transferred to tape or punched cards, and after having been used by a first historian, the data can in fact be stored for future researchers, who want to find non-experimented correlations.

(Le Roy Ladurie 1973, 1978, 3)

The reflections on computation made by the French historian Fernand Braudel (1902–1985), as discussed in Chapter 1, involve some scepticism and link the early 1960s' electronic archival forms to present debates on AI and ML algorithms. Both periods are characterised by the exponential growth of interdependencies between artificial actions (i.e., human-made) and computational operations (i.e., completed by electronic devices able to store and process data, typically in binary form, according to instructions given to them in a variable program or machine learning, which allows algorithms to learn through experience, and do things that humans are not able to programme). This process has been showcased by Nils Nilsson in a critical history of AI from its early stages to the early 2000s (Nilsson 2010), as outlined by Pedro Domingos in his work on the search for a master algorithm (Domingos 2015, 298). More recently, Helga Nowotny made a comprehensive and deep reflection on the power and illusions accompanying the unstoppable advance of predictive algorithms in our society (Nowotny 2021).

Shawn Graham, Ian Milligan, and Scott Weingart called the 'Digital Humanities Moment', the time when historians started delving into data management and experimenting with various software to generate new insights from their data sets (Graham et al. 2016, 37–72). Since then, historians seem to find it more difficult to move forward to take full advantage of the fact that computation itself is again 'morphing', as William Brian Arthur would say (Brian Arthur 2009, 150–151). Indeed, ML algorithms, one of computation's disruptive technologies, underwent radical change and have now opened new horizons to the automation and speed of discovery during what Pedro Domingos called the ML revolution (Domingos 2015, 1–22). Christine L. Borgman outlined the role of data scholarship in the humanities (Borgman 2015, 161–204), and Graham, Milligan, and Weingart recognised this as the opportunity for a third wave of computational history, because entry barriers to powerful computing and big data have never been lower for the historian (Graham et al. 2016, 58).

The same Pedro Domingos stated that 'the engine that turns data into knowledge is no longer a black box: you know how the magic happens and what it can and can't do' (Domingos 2015, 291). In this ambition, there are opportunities and limits. The debate is open and can be represented by a discussion published in the journal of the American Association for the Advancement of Science in 2010. From a sociological viewpoint, James Evans and Andrey Rzhetsky stated that 'soon, computers could generate many useful hypotheses with little help from humans' (Evans & Rzhetsky 2010a, 399). Soon after this publication, three letters of disagreement were sent to the journal *Science* by Sabina Leonelli (2010), from a genomics perspective, Francesco Gianfelici (2010), from an engineering perspective, and a team of researchers comprising Chris Haufe, Kevin C. Elliott, Richard M. Burian, Maureen A. O'Malley (2010), from a philosophy perspective. From their different disciplinary viewpoints, they all heavily criticised Evans and Rzhetsky with a common argument base on the role of the scientist in research processes.

According to the criticisers mentioned above, Evans and Rzhetsky 'misrepresent the crucial role played by humans in using computational tools for automated hypothesis generation' (Leonelli 2010); 'despite the effectiveness of computer tools, the centrality of the researchers has not changed in science. Scientists define the computation of models, the analysis of data, and the validation of scientific hypotheses, as well as the guidelines for ad hoc software and large-scale computations. Technology is a useful tool for the scientists, but it cannot solve open problems such as the Riemann Conjecture' (Gianfelici 2010); and that the topic 'needs to be placed within a broader understanding of scientific practice … by focusing on computational generation and selection of simplified lego-like hypothesis, Evans and Rzhetsky rip scientific practice out of this context. Even the simplest hypotheses are generated within a complex system of not only discovery-oriented activities, but also human actors with intuition and expertise, disciplinary traditions, social norms, funding structures, and anticipation of future research directions' (Haufe et al. 2010).

Following up on the three above-mentioned letters, the editors of the journal 'Science' published the weak response given them by James Evans and Andrey Rzhetsky.

> Leonelli and Gianfelici misinterpret our perspective as a call for 'full automation' of science. The approach we describe advocates a symbiotic partnership between scientists and machines to make scientists and science much more productive. Our title 'Machine science' emphasizes that computation is expanding beyond data analysis and entering hypothesis generation, becoming part of the scientific creative process, not unlike computer-aided design (CAD) tools used in present-day engineering.
>
> (Evans & Rzhetsky 2010b, 318)

In the response to the research team led by Chris Haufe, Evans, and Rzhetsky make a general reference to the book *The Fourth Paradigm* edited by Tony Hey, Stewart Tansley, and Kristin Tolle in 2009, with the following statement.

> Perhaps the strongest disagreement with this community is not whether hypotheses are useful, but whether they should be invoked before or after the data are collected (or both).
>
> (Evans & Rzhetsky 2010b, 318–319)

Therefore, it should be more attractive and easier for historians to step into algorithmic thinking, now that computer programs can make scientific discoveries in different ways (Mjolsness & DeCoste 2001, 2051). As showcased for Afro-Eurasian pre-modern history in Chapter 5, the present generation of historians, in passing the baton to the next one, can nurture the ambition to overcome cultural barriers and linguistic obstacles (refer to Chapter 4) that each previous generation of scholars encountered in the recurrent exercise of (re)reading primary sources from the perspective of its own present—that is, the epitome of the historian's craft. The reason being that, for the first time ever, all pre-modern historiographical works could be parsed by ML tools (probabilistic graphical models, deep learning, reinforcement learning, representation learning) and scholars can encode their information into machine-readable databases, which could enable natural language processing tools (discourse processing, question answering, machine translation, text summarisation, sentiment analysis) to ultimately include big historical data as explored by Shawn Graham, Ian Milligan, and Scott Weingart (2016) and agent-based modelling and simulations as proposed by John H. Holland and John H. Miller (1991) and discussed by Andrea Nanetti and Siew Ann Cheong (2018, 353–357) into the historian's toolkit and pioneer the beginnings of a distinctive epoch in the history's perennial search for truth.

In practice, it is more complicated than that because the accurate philological study and deep critical interpretation of each piece of evidence are fundamental to the historian's craft. The question of the sources keeps on being of the essence to the historian's craft at each dramatic technological turn (oral-to-written, handwritten-to-printed, analogue-to-electronic, and now from mathematical to algorithmic computation). It is acting as a bottleneck as demonstrated by Andrea Nanetti and Siew Ann Cheong (2018, 346) as follows:

> Firstly, historical data are seen by computer science people as unstructured, that is, historical records cannot be easily decomposed into unambiguous fields, except for the population and taxation ones, which are rare and scattered throughout space and time till the nineteenth century. This fact, in a computational perspective, prevent taxation and population databases to be scalable and aggregated with other datasets. An evident demonstration for taxation records is the *Online Catasto of Florence*. It is a searchable database of tax information for the city of Florence in 1427-1429 (c. 10,000 records uploaded till 1969) based on the work by David Herlihy and Christiane Klapisch-Zuber (1981).
>
> Secondly, machine-learning tools developed for structured data cannot be applied as they are for historical research. Both the exegesis of primary historical sources, and the analysis of how those same primary sources have been selected and interpreted in various historiographical narratives are of the essence in this issue. The historians are required to shift from generalisation to conceptualisation, because univocal distinctions among theoretical units (e.g., evidence, fact, event) and historical phenomena (e.g., trade, conflict, diplomacy) become necessary conditions to

generate new computational ontologies for databases (Gruber 1993; 1995, Guarino et al. 2009) and their application in agent-based modelling for historical simulations.

(Gavin 2014)

Quantitative historical analyses seem not to be immune when they nurture the belief that human societies evolve in predictable ways and build up top-down models, aggregate data, and promote possible futures because the way in which time is organised has deep roots in disciplinary assumptions with cascades of consequences. The organisation of time is based on substantial prejudice, biological and geographical determinism, and anthropology-driven periodisation (Nanetti & Cheong 2016, 12–14). Also, Peter Turchin's research team stressed on the high need of a new grammar for eScience to overcome the biases of disciplinary assumptions in interdisciplinary investigations. (Turchin et al. 2018). A team of 40 researchers at Google identified 'underspecification as a key reason' for the fact that 'ML models often exhibit unexpectedly poor behavior when they are deployed in real-world domains' (D'Amour et al. 2020, 2). The phenomenon of underspecification was already known as an issue in statistics. Alexander D'Amour, who has been trained in causal reasoning, verified that this failure was common to a variety of distinct AI applications from image recognition and natural language processing (NLP) to medical predictions (D'Amour et al. 2020).

Human sciences can leverage this research even if Alexander D'Amour and his research team (2020) did not mention any example in this field. Indeed, the training of ML models (i.e., the creation of ML algorithms) requires many examples and finally a test on a set of similar but new and challenging examples. However, the training process uses too many random values in lab simulations and this factor becomes a critical weakness when it comes to performing in the real world. The advantage of having history as a lab is that we can operate in the real world since the very beginning. To do so, the work of the historian needs to be observed, described, analysed, and engineered to build a highly performative AI application.

2.2 Reflections on the Training of Machine Learning Algorithms for the Next Generation of Historians

The dreaming about a Robot Scientist for the human sciences like Adam, the one created in the United Kingdom for genomics by an interdisciplinary research team of computer scientists and biologists to identify 'genes encoding orphan enzymes in *Saccharomyces cerevisiae*' (King et al. 2009), dissolves and changes gradually into a series of reflections. Indeed, automation for human sciences has its own peculiarities. However, the discourse on formalisation through ontology and language can be instructive, because 'the development of Robot Scientist "Adam" advances the automation' of two scientific fundamental methods: 'the hypothetico-deductive method and the recording of experiments in sufficient detail to enable reproducibility. Adam has autonomously generated functional genomics hypotheses about the yeast *Saccharomyces cerevisiae* and experimentally tested these hypotheses by using laboratory automation' (King et al. 2009, 85). The UK researchers 'have confirmed Adam's conclusions through manual experiments' and 'developed an ontology and logical language' to describe Adam's research and formalise 'how a machine contributed to scientific knowledge' (King et al. 2009, 85).

The creation of learning algorithms needs conceptual solutions. In 2015, computer scientist Pedro Domingos justified his use, with poetic license, of the term *master algorithm* in the *Prologue* to the homonymous book and explains it in the context of the advancement of learning.

> If it exists, the Master Algorithm can drive all knowledge in the world-past, present, and future-from data. Inventing it would be one of the greatest advances in the history of science .... The Master Algorithm is to machine learning what Standard Model is to particle physics or the Central Dogma to molecular biology: a unified theory that makes sense of everything we know to date, and lays the foundation for ... future progress .... What it requires is stepping back from the mathematical arcana to see the overarching pattern of learning phenomena .... Once we have the conceptual solution, we can fill in the mathematical details ... convinced that learning is the key to solving AI ... nothing could have more impact that teaching computers to learn.
>
> (Domingos 2015, xviii–xix)

To approach this huge task, a robust method—for the identification of key academic disciplines and the definition of their major contributions to a new interdisciplinary theory or science—is provided by the work published in September 1959 by John H. Holland as *Willow Run Laboratories Technical Memorandum 2900-52-R*. The work surveys how four academic disciplines contribute to the foundation of 'Automata theory (presently more formally named, at the Massachusetts Institute of Technology and The University of

Michigan, *The Communication Sciences*)': logic and metamathematics provide the axiomatic method and decision procedures (formal system), effective definition, and computability (Turing machines); the studies on electronic computers contribute programming and simulations; information theory (Shannon's mathematical theory of communication) is used for the measure of information and channel capacity; neurophysiology offers theories on the formation of concepts in the nervous system, and in particular on the recognition of macroscopic patterns by a sequential process (Holland 2018).

On the basis of the above reflections, to access 'automatic programming and artificial intelligence' (Holland 2018, 21) human sciences need a formal system (which in logic and metamathematics 'consists of four parts: a set of primitives, a definition of what constitutes a term or well-formed formula, a set of rules, and a set of axioms') to be able to run simulations: 'In automata theory, one always has some set of complex systems in mind, and the axioms are chosen so that upon interpretation they become true statements about important or characteristic properties of the system' (Holland 2018, 8).

From a human sciences perspective, there is 'an inventory of human knowledge which might provide the material for the art of combination' and assist AI specialists in the exploration of the origins of their own field and open new horizons to ML algorithms. This brings us back to the very beginning of modern science, where AI can find the origins of its field of studies as well; it is the Catalan philosopher, TOSF, Ramon Llull's *Ars Magna Combinatoria* manuscript work dated 1305. Llull elaborated his *ars*, a universal logic, able to discover and demonstrate the truth starting from simple terms and combining them in a mathematical way (Bonner 1985). Llull's combinatorial logic and memory techniques had wide influence until the early eighteenth century on authors such as Giovanni Battista aka Giambattista Della Porta (1535–1615), Bernardino Telesio (1509–1588), Filippo aka Giordano Bruno OP (1548–1600), Tommaso Domenico Campanella OP (1568–1639), Francis Bacon (1561–1626), and Gottfried Wilhelm Leibniz (1646–1716). The latter, in his *Dissertatio de Arte Combinatoria* (1666, Dissertation on the Art of Combinations) 'had long wondered what would be the best way of providing a list of primitives and, consequently, of an alphabet of thoughts or of an encyclopedia'; in his *Initia et Specimina Scientiae Generalis de nova ratione instaurationis et augmento scientiarum, ita ut exiguo tempore et negotio si modo velint homines, magna praestari possint ad felicitatis humanae incrementum* (1679, Beginnings and Specimens of General Science, a new concept of establishment and increasing of sciences, so that within a little time and

effort, who is willing to do it, with high hopes can perform the increasing of human happiness) 'described an encyclopedia as an inventory
of human knowledge which might provide the material for the art of
combination' (Eco 1995, 275, referring to Gerhardt 1875, Band I, VII,
57–60); and in his *Historia et Commendatio Linguae Characteristicae
Universalis quae simul sit ars inveniendi et iudicandi* (first published
posthumously in Raspe 1765, History and Commending of the
Universal Characteristic Language which is at the same time an art
for finding and evaluating) recalled:

> a time when he had aspired after 'an alphabet of human thoughts'
> such that 'from the combination of the letters of this alphabet,
> and from the analysis of the vocables formed by these letters,
> things might be discovered and judged'. It had been his hope,
> he added, that in this way humanity might acquire a tool which
> would augment the power of the mind more than telescopes and
> microscopes had enlarged the power of sight. This was not only
> a matter of convention. The identification of primitives cannot
> precede the formulation of the *lingua characteristica* because such
> a language would not be a docile instrument for the expression
> of thought; it is rather the *calculating apparatus through which
> those thoughts must be found* (on Leibniz and *The Foundation of
> Modern Historical Linguistics (1697-1716;* Eco 1995, 277, quoting
> Gerhardt 1875, Band I, VII, 184)*, see the chapter with this same
> title in Carhart 2019, 240-ff.).

From a computer science and engineering perspective, we are at a very
early stage in the construction of robust and sustainable automation
tools and processes for the human sciences.

> The main problem, to put it roughly, is representing words in a for-
> mal framework, similar to what Gottfried Wilhelm Leibniz had
> proposed more than 340 years ago. With his famous *Calculemus!*
> he intended to resolve any differences of opinion: 'The only way
> to rectify our reasoning is to make them as tangible as those of
> the Mathematicians, so that we can find our error at a glance, and
> when there are disputes persons, we can simply say: Let us calcu-
> late [*calculemus*], without further ado, to see who is right.
>
> (Seising 2002, 51)

We can find this idea of reducing reasoning to calculation already
in the late 13th century in the work of the Catalonian, Ramon

Llull. In his *Art Abreujada d'Atrobar Veritat* ('The Abbreviated Art of Finding Truth'), later published under the title of *Ars generalis ultima* or *Ars magna* ('The Ultimate General Art' [Llull]). Leibniz had written his dissertation about Llull's *Ars magna* and named it 'ars conbinatoria'.

(Lee & Zadeh 1969, 430)

Llull and Leibniz's arts have been steps on the plan for computing with concepts. All this deserves to be explained step-by-step; and in the first place, particularly the determination of words admitting of such a representation and where and by means of what is actually possible.

(Trillas & Seising 2018, 2)

The structure of graph databases can facilitate or prevent access to information across languages, because using English as an inter- and cross-cultural lingua franca, NLP algorithms cope with a serial multilingual translation process via all sorts of interpretations expressed in different languages, which constantly modify, subtract, and add meaning to words and objects across time and space (Young et al. 2018).

Discussing on this topic with one of the authors of the article mentioned above, Erik Cambria, he added that 'NLP has become increasingly powerful due to data availability and various techniques developed in the past decade. This increasing capability makes it possible to capture semantics in a more nuanced way. Naturally, many applications are starting to seek improvements by adopting cutting-edge NLP techniques. Machine translation is no exception. However, there are so many things that we unconsciously do when we read a piece of text. Reading comprehension requires multiple inter-related tasks, which have not been accounted for in past attempts to automate translation. The biggest issue with machine translation today is that we tend to go from the syntactic form of a sentence in the input language to the syntactic form of that sentence in the target language. That's not what we humans do: we first decode the meaning of the sentence in the input language and then we encode that meaning into the target language' (2021).

It seems that the revolution has not happened yet, as Michael I. Jordan stated that 'for the foreseeable future, computers will not be able to match humans in their ability to reason abstractly about real-world situations' (Pretz 2021). According to Erik Cambria and Bebo White (2014), NLP needs yet to evolve from its current 'Syntactics Curve' (i.e., a stage that provides a 'Bag-of-Words') to a new 'Pragmatics Curve' (providing a 'Bag-of-Narratives'), through an intermediate 'Semantics Curve' ('Bag-of-Concepts') (Cambria & White 2014, 51, Figure 1). In this path, the main risks—as highlighted by the philologist Lorenzo Tomasin in 2017—are (1) techno-science as the new Gramscian hegemonic and anti-humanistic culture, (2) technological banalisation of the humanistic discourse, (3) hybrid scholarship with low intellectual impact, and last, but not least (4) the loss of accuracy which since ever has been one of the characterising traits of qualitative disciplines (e.g., history and textual criticism) (Tomasin 2017, 42–46). Effective actions to mitigate these risks would need to be considered in research integrity policies for the human sciences in addition to the ones derived from the key risks in the natural science. This is the proposed pathway to steer a new consilient science capable of propelling a more mature field of both NLP and Digital Humanities into a new science of heritage via computational history (Nanetti & Cheong 2018).

2.3   Towards a Computational Approach to History. The Principle of Computational Equivalence and the Phenomenon of Computational Irreducibility in Historical Sciences

As a continuation of what has been discussed in Sections 2.1 and 2.3, this section reviews what a computational approach to history means by considering Stephen Wolfram's statement that the computational approach is different because of 'the principle of computational equivalence', which implies the phenomenon of 'computational irreducibility'. The question is whether historians need a computational approach to understand better the treasure of human experiences accumulated in the traces they left in historical sources. As described in Section 5.1, an EHM research team (Siew Ann Cheong, Nguyen Khoi Vu, and Andrea Nanetti) started to work on ABMS for historical sciences in 2019. In theory, computer simulations can support historical sciences to develop a shared prescriptive mode of inquiry in assessing primary and secondary sources. It can also provide new freedom in the historian's subjective and descriptive identification and assessment of problems to be investigated. In practice, the historical accounts work on 'what happened' (i.e., the factual), while computer simulations tell us 'what could have happened' (i.e., the counterfactual). Only by combining both, the most accurate assessment of what happened and what could have happened, we can address the question if, in history, we have laws that can be used as the universal laws in natural sciences. In historical phenomena, we cannot deviate from these rules in a cause-and-effect 'mechanism-based understanding' (Nanetti & Cheong 2018, 338, Paolucci & Picascia 2011).

According to Stephen Wolfram, computation and information are the central ingredients for building any scientific theory. Thanks to computation, he developed a different perspective on the whole enterprise of science, starting from mathematics (e.g., calculus, geometry, and algebra) construed as the proper fundamental language of science and nature. He discovered that beginning with elementary programmes and rules, and wheeling them for some time, then searches result in extreme complexity, and this output is not immediately understandable by usual mathematical techniques. In synthesis, this is the methodological process that Stephen Wolfram explained in detail in his famous book *A New Kind of Science*, a project to find the fundamental theory of physics (Wolfram 2002). This book tells the story of the success of the computational paradigm, and Andrea Nanetti studied this lesson and compared it to René Descartes' *Discourse on the Method* (Descartes 1637) in shaping the idea of EHM to apply AI for modelling complex systems (Gil et al. 2021).

Section 1.3 describes how Andrea Nanetti's exploration of interdisciplinary approaches to the historian's craft started. Between 1991 and 2021, his research showcased how digital humanities can empower philological accuracy and historical method with computational processes. To achieve this synergistic approach, he started with the edition and commentary of a broad spectrum of primary historical sources for the history of the Venetian State of the Sea (archival documents, chronicles, maps, archaeological findings, paintings, epigraphs). Attention can be drawn to the four-volume critical edition, *The Morosini Codex: The World as Seen from Venice* (Nanetti 2010). Based on this research on primary sources, his *Atlas of Venetian Messenia* (Nanetti 2011) and the recent books *At the Origins of the Venetian Sea State* (Nanetti 2018) and *Venice and the Peloponnese, 992–1718* (Nanetti 2021b) can be considered traditional scholarly outputs. In parallel, the award-winning paper *Interactive Global Histories: For a New Information Environment to increase the Understanding of Historical Processes* (*Culture and Computing*, Kyoto; Nanetti et al. 2013) and the special issue on *Revisiting the World of Fra Mauro's Map and the Morosini Codex from an AI Perspective*, invited by the editor-in-chief of the journal *The Asian Review of World Histories* (Nanetti & Cheong 2016), introduce new approaches to digital history. The paper *Defining Heritage Science: A Consilience Pathway to Treasuring the Complexity of Inheritable Human Experiences Through Historical Method, AI and*

ML (Nanetti 2021a) and this book on *Computational Engineering of Historical Memories* share a new original and interdisciplinary path to Digital Humanities.

Concurrently, EHM began pioneering digital humanities projects and building visualisation and other computational tools. For scholars, these tools offer what is needed for reading and discussing a primary source in one single interactive environment. On the other hand, they provide the user of the historian's work with all that is required to trace provenance and validate the historian's explicit and silent narratives, as discussed in Section 1.3. This path motivated Andrea Nanetti to learn about the foundations of computational methods, practices, and theories available to the historian's craft. In 2007–2008, when he was at Princeton University, he had on his desk not only Umberto Eco's *Dall'Albero al Labirinto* (Eco 2007, 2014) but also Stephen Wolfram's *A New Kind of Science* (Wolfram 2002). Thus, he developed the idea of EHM to accomplish tasks such as visualising digitalised artefacts on the web (2D and 3D), information management and visualisation, and text and image searches on the internet. However, all this was not enough to take full advantage of both historical and computational methods. The EHM research path led Andrea Nanetti to understand the foundations of computation applied and applicable to historical sciences. The need was to investigate the fundamental primitives of computational processes that need to be understood and addressed to accomplish what he wanted to achieve for the advancement of learning in history.

As discussed in Section 5.1, Andrea Nanetti, Siew Ann Cheong, and Nguyen Khoi Vu started to model agents in the historical landscape. The question was 'Can we use the methods that we know from physics, or will they get stuck?' What they found was that when they wanted to study systems where the behaviour was quite complex (e.g., the system of the Venetian state convoys in the fifteenth century), the methods that they knew from physics (e.g., solving differential equations) did not seem to go the distance in being able to understand what was happening in historical systems that show complex behaviour. Then, at the beginning of the 1980s, Stephen Wolfram started to study complex systems. He thought about taking the idea—which was so successful in natural sciences over the last 300 years—of using mathematical equations to make formal models of systems in nature. Nanetti, Cheong, and Vu took the same idea and used mathematical equations to make the underlying models to engineer historical memory. The critical questions were 'Can we generalise beyond that? And what does it look like when we generalise beyond that?'.

If we want to explore this question and define models of historical things, we need to have a certain kind of belief that there are certain kinds of definite rules that say how the system to be modelled behaves. From a historical perspective, we are talking about the laws that underlie human actions and their interactions with the natural and social environments. The aim is to use computation and model how these systems behave. Sir Arthur Stanley Eddington (1882–1944), in his 1927 *Gifford Lectures,* said that 'the contemplation in natural science of a wider domain than the actual leads to a far better understanding of the actual' (Eddington 1929, 266–277, Nanetti & Cheong 2018, 337). Before the advent of computational technologies, the value of thought experiments, which Albert Einstein was very fond of, was to present scenarios different from those humans observe. The physical scientist would then follow the systems through their logical ends. They identify what they might have missed and realise what else could be possible if we had lived in a different universe, ultimately understanding the physical laws we have at a much deeper level (Callaway 2014).

Notoriously, historicism (in German, *Historizismus*, i.e., the belief that natural laws govern historical events) was heavily criticised by the Austrian-British philosopher Karl Raimund Popper (1902–1994) in his 1936 paper on *The Poverty of Historicism* (Popper 1957, iii). Popper reviews historicism as 'an approach to the social sciences which assumes that *historical prediction* is their primary aim, and which assumes that this aim is attainable by discovering the "rhythms" or the "patterns", the "laws" or the "trends" that underlie the evolution of history'. Popper wrote concerning the teleological theory of history by the German philosopher Georg Wilhelm Friedrich Hegel (1770–1831) and criticised the consequential idealist idea of history but not 'historism' (in German, *Historismus*) traditionally linked to the German historian Leopold von Ranke (1795–1886) as emphasised by Stefan Berger (2001, 28–29).

Stephen Wolfram argues that the computational approach is different because of 'the principle of computational equivalence', which implies the phenomenon of 'computational Irreducibility'. To know what the system is going to do, we have to simulate what the system will do (Wolfram 2002, 6). From this computational perspective, it is remarkable the criticism made of the idealist historicism by the Italian art historian Cesare Brandi (1906–1988) in the aftermath of World War II (Brandi 1950; reprinted in Brandi 1979, 57–125). Brandi discusses and criticises the determination, rooted in Romanticism and Idealism, to resolve history, all history, into a contemporary account.

According to Brandi, this vision—which, in his cultural environment, was embraced by the Italian idealist philosopher Benedetto Croce (1866–1952)—cannot but lead to renouncing the past and losing the sense of historical depth that is offered by the sedimentation and mutual tension of the different human experiences over time. Thus, he highlighted how, with this idealist approach, contemporary art was stuck in the present and lost the diversity of temporal and cultural perspectives. Brandi hopes that historical perspective can rebuild the dialectics between past, present, and future and reactivate the demiurgic power of tradition (Marchesini 2004, 321–322).

Furthermore, Stephen Wolfram's inquiry about the most general kind of rules in physics realised that at the foundations of computation, there are more general sources of possible rules for systems than the kind of things that he happened to have studied in mathematics, calculus, etc. (Wolfram 2002, 7–8).

> In the history of science, it is fairly common that new technologies are ultimately what make new areas of basic science develop. And thus, for example, telescope technology was what led to modern astronomy, and microscope technology to modern biology.
>
> (Wolfram 2002, 42)

The Italian rhetorician and historian Emanuele Tesauro (1592–1675) operated similarly when Galileo's telescope model was established to develop the natural sciences. Tesauro's *Cannocchiale aristotelico* (1654, first edition, and 1670, fifth and final edition) proposed to use a telescope named after the Greek philosopher Aristotle (384–322 BCE) as an instrument for a renewal of what we would now call human sciences, given that he proposed to use metaphor to generate new ontologies in rhetoric (Hatzfeld 1961, 4–8). Possibly inspired by Giordano Bruno's concept of metaphor (Gatti 2010, 165), Tesauro suggests utilising the model of metaphor to discover relationships that are still hidden between the folds of knowledge, as outlined by Umberto Eco (in Italian, 2007, 44, 67–72; English, 2014, 38, 62–67).

> To construct a repertoire of known things along which the metaphorical imagination can discover unknown relationships, Tesauro elaborates on the idea of a Categorical Index. He presents his Index (with baroque complacency for the marvellous gimmick) as a *secreto veramente secreto* ['truly secret secret'], an inexhaustible mine of infinite metaphors and ingenious concepts. Since genius is nothing more or less than the ability of *penetrar gli obietti*

altamente appiattiti sotto diverse categorie e di riscontrarli tra loro
['penetrate the objects that are highly flattened under different
categories and compare them with each other']—or the ability to
find analogies and similarities that would have passed unnoticed
if everything had remained classified under its category.

(Eco 2007, 45, translated from Italian into English by
Andrea Nanetti; 2014, 38)

Tesauro follows the trend of its time. But what seems to us a lack
of systematic spirit is, on the contrary, evidence of the encyclopae-
dist's effort to escape the arid classification by genus and species. It
is the still disordered accumulation (or barely ordered, as Tesauro
does, under the rubrics of the ten categories and their members)
which will then allow the invention (in the Baconian sense, not
as a finding but as a discovery) of unexpected and unprecedented
relationships between the objects of knowledge. The 'cumber-
someness' is the price you pay not to achieve completeness but to
avoid the poverty of any arborescent classification.

(Eco 2007, 47, translated from Italian into English by
Andrea Nanetti; 2014, 41)

The Index, and precisely because of its labyrinthine nature, allows
for connections to be made between everything and anything
else—such that it seems that Tesauro's metaphorist does nothing
else (and is pleased with it) other than to draw new knowledge
from the deconstruction of a Porphyrian tree. If, for the sake of
the master of those who know ['*l maestro di color che sanno*, Dante
Alighieri, *Comedia, Inferno*, IV, 131], Tesauro wanted to call his
index categorical. He provides us with a sort of procedure to follow the infinite paths of a labyrinth, where the subdivisions into
categories are nothing but temporary and entirely artificial con-
structions to somehow contain material in full boiling.

(Eco 2007, 48, translated from Italian into English by
Andrea Nanetti; 2014, 41–42)

The application of Tesauro's procedure, as explained by Umberto
Eco, and the use of Wolfram's foundations for a new kind of science
in historical memories have been at the theoretical and practical
groundworks of EHM since 2007. As envisioned by Andrea Nanetti,
historical memories can be engineered using computation models
and representations for a new kind of history. As Wolfram tested
what the computational telescope can see using a universal cellular

automaton (Wolfram 2002, 638–641), EHM chose to use ABMS (refer to Section 5.2) to test 'what-if' scenarios in the historical landscape. Umberto Eco traces a similar research trajectory in *Dall'albero al Labirinto*, the first chapter of his homonymous book (Eco 2007, 13–96) translated from Italian into English by Anthony Oldcorn as *From the Tree to the Labyrinth* (Eco 2014, 3–94). Thus, the EHM programmes are written and trained to follow the curatorial path that leads the treasure of historical information on human experiences, from traditional critical editions to dynamic encyclopaedic dictionaries and atlases. The user can experience the vertigo of the labyrinth guided by a Virgil-like computational machine, which does not need to put any still-available knowledge in latency.

The most overarching principle that Wolfram derived from extensive studies of the computational universe is what he called 'the principle of computational equivalence'. This principle says that as soon as we see a system whose behaviour is not simple, it will correspond to a computation that is of maximal sophistication (Wolfram 2002, 716–718). This principle implies a magic leap. We start from the statement made by the Catalan philosopher Ramon Llull TOSF (ca 1232–1316) that to do different computations, you need different devices (Bonner 1985). And, we reach the machine invented by the British mathematician Alan Mathison Turing (1912–1954), who demonstrated that with different programmes, we could have the same machine doing different computations (Dyson 2012). The question is how sophisticated needs the system to be to compute the treasure of human experiences. Then, it goes to Wolfram's curiosity about the kind of programmes. Do historical sciences need million-line extended new programmes or elementary programmes already available? For Wolfram, it was easy enough to demonstrate that simple programmes do not only do simple things. In the computational universe, he experienced that when simple rules are run randomly and relatively quickly, they can produce advanced complexity of behaviour (Wolfram 2002, 23–39).

This fact leads to another implication of the principle of computational equivalence, the phenomenon of 'computational irreducibility' (Wolfram 2002, 739). If we look at the history of exact sciences, for about 300 years, mathematical equations were the foundational raw materials for all accurate models of things in nature. In the first two decades of the twenty-first century, there has been this transition that almost all new models that have been made are program-based models and not mathematics-based models. It is a fascinating shift to see after such a long period. Once we deal with computationally based models, there are very different kinds of phenomena, such as the computational irreducibility that we have to deal with (Wolfram 2002, 737–740).

Traditional exact science believed that mathematical functions could predict what would happen. Science believes that there is a formula to predict Earth's location a million years from now instead of following its orbitals. This computational reducibility is a core value in traditional exact science. It implies that we can jump ahead and computationally reduce what's going on by being sort of smarter than the system and figure out what the system is going to do much more efficiently than the system itself. However, according to Wolfram, to outsmart a system, we need to do more sophisticated computation than what the system is doing. But this action is against the principle of computational equivalence, which says that we are all equivalent in the level of sophistication we can do. That's why the behaviour of some systems seems computationally irreducible because we are not capable of any more sophisticated computation than it is. Thus, to know what these systems are going to do, we have essentially to simulate what the systems are going to do, step by step (Wolfram 2002, 741–750).

The phenomenon of computational irreducibility will have many consequences for the digital-born historian. These consequences range from AI ethics (Nowotny 2021) to how free will arises from deterministic systems (Wolfram 2002, 750–753). There is a lot of rich and complex behaviour in the historical landscape. Mathematically, we cannot determine whether a specific feature of human experience is going on forever or dying out. The only way we must answer an infinite time question is to run the system for an endless time. We can't tell what a system is going to do. We can only mine systems and make models of existing systems in the real world. The issue is to bridge the gap between what is possible in the computational universe and what historians want to achieve. History, as other disciplines did before, must produce a way of taking out thoughts and making them computational. Stephen Wolfram spent a significant fraction of his life building a computational language. This language allows us to express what we want to think about in computationally enough terms that we can use what is possible in the computational universe to work out what we want. This is the story of Wolfram Language & System. Wolfram Research, Inc. was founded in 1987; Mathematica 1.0 was released on 23 June 1988; the company and successive versions of Mathematica continue to be significant parts of his life (Wolfram 2022).

Another thing that Stephen Wolfram realised increasingly as important is that this computational language is a way for us to start thinking computationally about things. Historically, the analogue is when people began to use fewer and fewer words in mathematics, started to use algebra and calculus, and ultimately started to think mathematically about 400 years ago. For example, the Italian philosopher and natural scientist Bernardino Telesio (1509–1588) was labelled as 'the first of the moderns' (*novorum hominum primum*) by the English philosopher Francis Bacon (1561–1639) (Spedding et al. 1887, V, 339, van Deusen 1932). Because Telesio was the first to challenge the authority of the Greek philosopher Aristotle (384–322 BCE), the master of those who know ('*l maestro di color che sanno*, Dante Alighieri, *Comedia, Inferno*, IV, 131). He also discussed the medical rules of the Greek physician and surgeon Galen of Pergamon (129–ca 216 CE), the most credited ancient expert of materia medica. Telesio's seminal work 'On the nature of things according to their principles' (*De rerum natura iuxta propria principia*) argued that, instead of abstract reason, science should rely on the data provided by the human senses (Ottaviani 2006). His work inspired the blossoming of the scientific method in the Italian philosophers Filippo aka Giordano Bruno OP (1548–1600) and Tommaso Domenico Campanella OP (1568–1639), Francis Bacon, and the French philosopher René Descartes (1596–1650), notwithstanding their widely different outcomes (Principe 2011).

In historical studies, this cultural and scientific revolution was prepared by some ground-breaking achievements. In 1440, the humanist Lorenzo Valla (1407–1457) pioneered the critical study of historical documents (Latin text, Setz 1976; English translation, Bowersock 2007). Later, the Renaissance statesmen and historians Niccolò di Bernardo dei Machiavelli (1469–1527) and Francesco Guicciardini (1483–1540) turned the writing of history into an object of study 'focusing on their views of human agency and individuality' (Bos 2010, 352). Then, in sixteenth-century England appeared the history play (Goy-Blanquet 2014, 195–201). The seventeenth century produced most famous and long-lasting, *De re diplomatica* ('On Diplomatics', 1681) by the French scholar Jean Mabillon OSB (1632–1707), who formalised a discipline to determine the authenticity of a document investigating its writing style, extrinsic and intrinsic features, and the *tenor formularis*. Mabillon's work also included *ante litteram* palaeography, even if the term was formally coined and used for the first time by Bernard de Montfaucon OSB (1655–1741) in his *Palaeographia Graeca* (1708). Later, on these strong foundations, the French historian, abbé Nicolas Lenglet du Fresnoy (1674–1755), worked on a method to study history (Lenglet du Fresnoy 1713, Eriksen 2015), and the German historian Leopold von Ranke (1795–1886) founded modern source-based history (Gilbert 1990, 11–45).

Today, we have a new opportunity. We can establish an empirical methodology to systematically train ML algorithms to assist historians in the (re)reading of primary sources and secondary literature in different languages. The training consists of programming instructions. The goal is the automatic performance of ontologies ascertained and processes refined by the centuries-old cumulative scholarship of diplomatics, palaeography, codicology, ecdotics, philology, and history. And thus, we can teach the next generation of digital-born historians to think algorithmically (Nanetti 2020). As defined by Donald Knuth in 1977, 'an algorithm is a set of rules for getting specific outputs from specific inputs. Each step must be so precisely defined that it can be translated into computer language and executed by machine' (Denning & Tedre 2019, 1). On a small scale, individuals can code and design algorithms. At large, teams and communities of people write multi-version programs consisting of millions of lines of code ported to numerous platforms and compatible with a range of different system set-ups. Computationally, ML algorithms write and execute code that humans cannot programme (Denning & Tedre 2019).

The import of ideas from physics into distributive computing made very effective models of biology evolution (Barton et al. 2007, Chapter 28). However, there is an additional computational language design problem in the historical landscape, which drives by questions such as the following. Can we invent a language to describe the human condition as Wolfram did to explain what's going on in the universe? Does the principle of computational equivalence tell us that we can model the human condition according to human and non-human rules? When we get into a causal graph, we generate transformations between elements in the original graph. We can get to infinite categories represented in the Eulerian graph. And, again, we get a further question. How do deterministic and non-deterministic Turing machines work in a multi-way Eulerian path? Mathematics has about 3 million theorems. How many rules would a machine need to model and simulate human history? Agent-based modelling and simulations are the EHM way to address these challenging questions and walk the computational path to advance learning in historical sciences.

In practice, EHM is working on a new interdisciplinary research methodology to prepare traditional historical data sets for the semantic web. Digitalised historical maps are used as knowledge aggregators (Nanetti et al. 2015). Digital mapping is the epistemological tool to pioneer experimental narrative and non-narrative operations in scientific studies (Chiang et al. 2020). The result associates each element of a given set of data coming from traditional disciplines (history, archaeology, art history, etc.) with one or more elements of a range of automatically generated sets of different things of the same general type (places, people, buildings, events, dates, ideas, and so on). Andrea Nanetti theorised this methodology (Nanetti 2014, 256–258). He then exemplified it in collaboration with Mario Giberti to support the re-discovery, re-reading, and reviewing of the different sources (archival, archaeological, cartographic, chronicle, art historical) and historiographical narratives related to the medieval history of the Italian town of Imola (Nanetti & Giberti 2014).

From 2011 to 2014, Nanetti and Giberti decided to explore a two-folded approach to the organisation and presentation of historical data sets; analytic (the mapping of the sources by Andrea Nanetti) and synthetic (the visualisation of the results by Mario Giberti) at the same time. The name of this method, 'mapping and visualisation', must be seen as a hendiadys to emphasise its conceptual and practical unity. The term mapping is taken in its primary meaning of localisation and description of elements, facts, or phenomena that relate to a circumscribed area, historically understood at the intersection of precise space and time coordinates. The aim was to provide and test a specimen of an innovative epistemological process to distil historical data visually. The visualisation process is not seen as a reductive representation to epitomise and/or illustrate written narratives but as an investigative tool for digitally born historians to organise and discover relationships between objects in a new historical landscape where past, present, and future can merge in a democratised whole (Bolick 2006).

This 'mapping and visualisation' method wants to be a first step towards the experimentation with automatic narratives (Nanetti et al. 2013, 107–109). From a knowledge-production perspective, the aim is to provide tools and ontologies to test existing theories and 'explore the vast domain of the yet unknown' with an openness to uncertainty (Nowotny 2015). This method also moves the experimentation of less narrative—if not non-narrative—ways to make history in the digital era. It is not a positivistic revival but a consequence of the belief that 'narrative is not just a set of materials, but it is a quite specific method of organizing those materials' (Altman 2008, 5; who rephrases a definition given at the height of structuralist activity by Stierle 1972, 178, referring to the 'basic structure of all narrative texts (x *is* f *at* t1//g *happens to* x *at* t2//x *is* h *at* t3)' by Danto 1965). Similarly, we can also discuss a famous statement made by the Italian theorist and philosopher Benedetto Croce (1866–1952): 'Where there is no narrative, there is no history' (Croce 1951, 26). In 2008, the American scholar Rick Altman had ironically and futuristically framed the case in the conclusions of his inspiring book on narrative (2008).

> One last foray. If medieval physics clearly grows out of dual-focus assumptions, and its Newtonian successor develops a fundamentally single-focus cause-and-effect model, then we may perhaps recognize in Einstein's famous equation $e = mc^2$ the ultimate multiple-focus hem-naming process, recognizing for the first time that energy and matter can be treated as equals. When energy and matter, action and character, are reduced to the same entity, can the end of narrative be far behind?
>
> (Altman 2008, 339–340)

Altman's theory presented in this book offers powerful potential for describing human activities. In the conclusions, he suggests how his theory might be used to image and explain such varied phenomena as individual texts, literary and film history, social organisation, religion, and political life (Altman 2008, 338). Many other domains might be evoked. Whether the topic is literature, art, or epistemology, we regularly find a historical series that may be usefully described as developing from dual focus through single focus to multiple focus. As the same Altman highlighted in the first pages of his book, among the human endeavours, few are more widely spread or more generally endowed with cultural importance than narrative (Altman 2008, 1–3). Stories are the primary vehicles of personal memory, a mainstay of law, entertainment, and history (Altman 2008, 1). Historically, definitions of narrative have been tightly tied to a particular type of plot. This tendency began with Book VI of Aristotle's *Poetics* (Bywater 1909, 13).

The Greek philosopher informs us that a tragedy is impossible without action, but a tragedy may exist without characters (Altman 2008, 2). Aristotle adopted the notion of the unity of action to build a play around a single unbroken plot thread, eschewing competing storylines, unnecessary characters, and unrelated episodes. Stories must be coherent; they must have a distinct beginning, middle, and end; they must connect their parts through clearly motivated causes; and they must expunge any material unrelated to this unity of action (Altman 2008, 3). At the end of his work, Altman notes that 'we circulate among characters and places, not according to our interests but according to an itinerary fixed by the narrator'. If a 'following' process inaugurates this circulation, the act of reading also involves a tendency towards 'mapping'. This tendency calls on our memory of the text at hand and our prior experience of other texts. Mapping engages the reader in a perpetual return to the past and a constant attempt to define the present in terms of that past, permitting an eventual understanding of the present (Altman 2008, 291–292).

This statement applies wherever humans tell stories or implicitly refer to previously narrated tales. Thus, it must be included in the design of computational models. Stephen Wolfram's effort is to build a full-scale computational language. It is meant to represent the world computationally and provide us with a computational notation (i.e., a series or system of written symbols used to represent numbers, amounts, or elements in music or mathematics) for thinking about the world. The hope is that as mathematical notation helped humanity streamline the use of mathematics and the development of mathematical sciences, similarly, this kind of computational language can increasingly lead to the development of computational x-fields from archaeology to zoology (Wolfram 2022).

From a human sciences perspective, it sounds like a search for the perfect language (Eco 1995) to build a new Tower of Babel (refer to Section 4.2). Otherwise, some critical questions must become machine-understandable. Also, digitally born historians must start thinking algorithmically about human historical experiences (e.g., what is a human action made of, how are they related in space and time, the range of the human condition, and how humans perceive and record external events). Today, we have more questions than answers. What are the theories that must be in this computational-history model? How do we develop efficient compilers? Traditional historians are reasonably concerned because if we want to define a computational rule for the human condition (what does it mean to be in space and time), someone might rightly think that we are essentially reducing the complexity of the humanities to a sophisticated but rather simplifying mathematical equation (Cooper 2014, 124–131). Indeed, in the last 500 years, the history of science has been working on why we humans are not unique. From Copernicus on, humans thought that they were not special at all. We live on a random planet, around a random star, in a random galaxy, and so on (Wootton 2015). Our understanding is based on our perception and imagination of reality, which are the sources and limits of human intellect (Cooper 2014, 87–108). It is a matter of scale and range (Wolfram 2002, 433–434).

References

Altman, Rick (2008). *A Theory of Narrative*. New York: Columbia University Press.

Barton, Nicholas H., Derek E. G. Briggs, Jonathan A. Eisen, David B. Goldstein, & Nipam H. Patel (2007). *Evolution*. Cold Spring Harbor, NY: Cold Spring Harbor Laboratory Press. https://archive.org/details/evolution0000unse_x9v3

Berger, Stefan (2001). "Stefan Berger Responds to Ulrich Muhlack". *Bulletin of the German Historical Institute London*, *23*(1), 21–33. https://www.perspec tivia.net/publikationen/ghi-bulletin/2001-23-1/0021-0033

Bolick, Cheryl Mason (2006). "Digital Archives: Democratizing the Doing of History". *International Journal of Social Education*, *21*(1), 122–134. https://files.eric.ed.gov/fulltext/EJ782136.pdf

Bonner, Anthony (1985). *Selected Works of Ramon Llull (1232-1316)*, translated by Anthony Bonner. Princeton, NJ: Princeton University Press. https://archive.org/details/selectedworksofr00vlllul/mode/2up

Borgman, Christine L. (2015). *Big Data, Little Data, No Data: scholarship in the Networked World*. Cambridge, MA and London: MIT Press. https://doi.org/10.7551/mitpress/9963.003.0001

Bos, Jacques (2010). "Framing a New Mode of Historical Experience. The Renaissance Historiography of Machiavelli and Guicciardini". In *The Making of the Humanities: Volume 1 – Early Modern Europe*, edited by Rens Bod, Jaap Maat, & Thijs Weststeijn, 351–366. Amsterdam: Amsterdam University Press. http://www.jstor.org/stable/j.ctt46n1vz.20

Bowersock, Glen Warren (2007). Lorenzo Valla. *On the Donation of Constantine*. Cambridge, MA: Harvard University Press.

Brandi, Cesare (1950). "La fine dell'Avanguardia". *Immagine*, *2*, 361–433.

Brandi, Cesare (1979). *Scritti sull'arte contemporanea, II*, 57–125. Turin: Einaudi.

Brian Arthur, William (2009). *The Nature of Technology. What It Is and How It Evolves*. New York: Free Press. https://archive.org/details/natureoftechnolo 00arth/mode/2up

Bywater, Ingram (1909). *Aristotle on the Art of Poetry*. Oxford: Clarendon Press. https://archive.org/details/aristotleonarto00aris

Callaway, H. G. (Ed.) (2014). "Arthur Stanley Eddington". In *The Nature of the Physical World. Gifford Lectures of 1927*, An Annotated Edition. Newcastle upon Tyne: Cambridge Scholars Publishing.

Cambria, Erik, & Bebo White (2014). "Jumping NLP Curves: A Review of Natural Language Processing Research". *IEEE Computational Intelligence Magazine*, *9*(2), 48–57. https://doi.org/10.1109/MCI.2014.2307227

Carhart, Michael C. (2019). *Leibniz Discovers Asia. Social Networking in the Republic of Letters*. Baltimore, MD: Johns Hopkins University Press.

Chiang, Yao-Yi, Weiwei Duan, Stefan Leyk, Johannes H. Uhl, & Craig A. Knoblock (2020). *Using Historical Maps in Scientific Studies: Applications, Challenges, and Best Practices*. Cham: Springer Nature Switzerland AG. https://doi.org/10.1007/978-3-319-66908-3

Cohen, Daniel J., & Roy Rosenzweig (2006). *Digital History: A Guide to Gathering, Preserving, and Presenting the Past on the Web*. Philadelphia, PA: University of Pennsylvania Press. https://archive.org/details/digitalhistorygu0000cohe/page/n3/mode/2up

Cooper, Leon N. (2014). *Science and Human Experience. Values, Culture, and the Mind.* Cambridge: Cambridge University Press. http://dx.doi.org/10.1017/CBO9781107337879

Cortada, James W. (1993). *Before the Computer: IBM, NCR, Burroughs, & Remington Rand & the Industry They Created, 1865-1956.* Princeton, NJ: Princeton University Press. https://doi.org/10.1515/9781400872763

Croce, Benedetto (1951). "La storia ridotta sotto il concetto generale dell'arte". In *Primi saggi*, edited by Idem, 3–41. Bari: Laterza.

D'Amour, Alexander, Katherine Heller, Dan Moldovan, Ben Adlam, Babak Alipanahi, Alex Beutel, Christina Chen, Jonathan Deaton, Jacob Eisenstein, Matthew D. Hoffman, Farhad Hormozdiari, Neil Houlsby, Shaobo Hou, Ghassen Jerfel, Alan Karthikesalingam, Mario Lucic, Yi-An Ma, Cory Y. McLean, Diana Mincu, Akinori Mitani, Andrea Montanari, Zachary Nado, Vivek Natarajan, Christopher Nielson, Thomas F. Osborne, Rajiv Raman, Kim Ramasamy, Rory Sayres, Jessica Schrouff, Martin Seneviratne, Shannon Sequeira, Harini Suresh, Victor Veitch, Max Vladymyrov, Xuezhi Wang, Kellie Webster, Steve Yadlowsky, Taedong Yun, Xiaohua Zhai, D. Sculley (2020). "Underspecification Presents Challenges for Credibility in Modern Machine Learning". *arXiv*, Nov 24, 2020. https://arxiv.org/pdf/2011.03395.pdf

Danto, Arthur Coleman (1965). *Analytical Philosophy of History.* Cambridge: Cambridge University Press. https://archive.org/details/analyticalphilos0000dant_k6p5/mode/2up

Denning, Peter J., & Matti Tedre (2019). *Computational Thinking.* Cambridge, MA and London: MIT Press. http://dx.doi.org/10.7551/mitpress/11740.001.0001

Descartes, René (1637). *Discours de la methode pour bien conduire sa raison, & chercher la verité dans les sciences. Plus: La Dioptrique, Les Meteores, et La Geometrie, qui sont des essais de cete Methode.* Leiden: Ian Maire. https://gallica.bnf.fr/ark:/12148/btv1b86069594/f1.item

Domingos, Pedro (2015). *The Master Algorithm: How the Quest for the Ultimate Learning Machine Will Remake Our World.* New York: Basic Books. https://archive.org/details/masteralgorithmh0000domi_q9v1

Dyson, George (2012). *Turing's Cathedral. The Origins of the Digital Universe.* New York: Pantheon Books. https://archive.org/details/turingscathedral0000dyso_n1l6/mode/2up

Eco, Umberto (1995). *The Search for the Perfect Language in the European Culture*, translated [from Italian into English] by James Fentress. Oxford: Wiley-Blackwell (Original work, *La ricerca della lingua perfetta nella cultura europea.* Bari: Editori Laterza, 1993).

Eco, Umberto (2007). *Dall'albero al labirinto.* Milan: Bompiani.

Eco, Umberto (2014). *From the Tree to the Labyrinth: Historical Studies on the Sign and Interpretation*, translated by Anthony Oldcorn. Cambridge, MA: Harvard University Press. https://doi.org/10.4159/9780674728165

Eddington, Arthur Stanley (1929). *The Nature of the Physical World. The Gifford Lectures 1927.* New York and Cambridge: Cambridge University Press. www.cambridge.org/9781107663855

Edmond, Jennifer, Frank Fischer, Laurent Romary, & Toma Tasovac (2020). "Springing the Floor for a Different Kind of Dance: Building DARIAH as a

Twenty-First-Century Research Infrastructure for the Arts and Humanities". In *Digital Technology and the Practices of Humanities Research*, edited by Jennifer Edmond, 207–234. Cambridge: Open Book Publishers. https://doi. org/10.11647/obp.0192.09

Eriksen, Anne (2015). "How to Study History: Nicolas Lenglet Dufresnoy and the Heritage of *ars historica*". *Sjuttonhundratal, 12*. https://doi.org/10.7557/4.3523

Evans, James, & Andrey Rzhetsky (2010a). "Machine Science". *Science, 329*, 399–400. https://doi.org/10.1126/science.1189416

Evans, James, & Andrey Rzhetsky (2010b). "Response". *Science, 330*, 318–319. https://doi.org/10.1126/science.330.6002.318

Galasso, Giuseppe (2000). *Nient'altro che storia*. Bologna: Società Editrice Il Mulino.

Gatti, Hilary (2010). "Giordano Bruno and Metaphor". In Rens Bod, Jaap Maat, & Thijs Weststeijn (Eds.), *The Making of the Humanities: Volume 1 – Early Modern Europe*, 163–176. Amsterdam: Amsterdam University Press. http://www.jstor.org/stable/j.ctt46n1vz.10

Gavin, Michael (2014). "Agent-Based Modeling and Historical Simulation". *Digital Humanities Quarterly, 8*(4). http://www.digitalhumanities.org/dhq/vol/8/4/000195/000195.html

Gerhardt, Immanuel (1875). *Die Philosophischen Schriften von Gottfried Wilhelm Leibniz*, edited by Carl Immanuel Gerhardt. Erste Band, VII, 57–60. Berlin: Weidmannsche Buchhandlung. https://archive.org/details/diephilosophisc05leibgoog/mode/2up

Gianfelici, Francesco (2010). "Machine Science: Truly Machine-Aided". *Science, 330*, 317. https://doi.org/10.1126/science.330.6002.317-b

Gil, Yolanda, Daniel Garijo, Deborah Khider, Craig A Knoblock, Varun Ratnakar, Maximiliano Osorio, Hernán Vargas, Minh Pham, Jay Pujara, Basel Shbita, Binh Vu, Yao-Yi Chiang, Dan Feldman, Yijun Lin, Hayley Song, Vipin Kumar, Ankush Khandelwal, Michael Steinbach, Kshitij Tayal, Shaoming Xu, Suzanne A. Pierce, Lissa Pearson, Daniel Hardesty-Lewis, Ewa Deelman, Rafael Ferreira Da Silva, Rajiv Mayani, Armen R. Kemanian, Yuning Shi, Lorne Leonard, Scott Peckham, Maria Stoica, Kelly Cobourn, Zeya Zhang, Christopher Duffy, & Lele Shu (2021). "Artificial Intelligence for Modeling Complex Systems: Taming the Complexity of Expert Models to Improve Decision Making". *ACM Transactions on Interactive Intelligent Systems, 11*(2), 1–49. https://doi.org/10.1145/3453172

Gilbert, Felix (1990). *History: Politics or Culture? Reflections on Ranke and Burckhardt*. https://doi.org/10.1515/9781400861071

Ginzburg, Carlo (2001). "Conversare con Orion". *Quaderni storici, 23*(3), 905–913. https://www.jstor.org/stable/43779318

Goy-Blanquet, Dominique (2014). *Shakespeare et l'invention de l'histoire guide commenté du théâtre historique*. Paris: Classiques Garnier.

Graham, Shawn, Ian Milligan, & Scott Weingart (Eds.) (2016). *Exploring Big Historical Data. The Historian's Macroscope*. London: Imperial College Press. https://doi.org/10.1142/p981

Gray, Jim (2009). "Jim Gray on eScience: A Transformed Scientific Method". In *The Fourth Paradigm: Data-Intensive Scientific Discovery*, edited by Tony

Hey, Stewart Tansley, & Kristin Tolle, xvii–xxxi. Redmond, WA: Microsoft Research. http://itre.cis.upenn.edu/myl/JimGrayOnE-Science.pdf

Gruber, Thomas Robert (1993). "A Translation Approach to Portable Ontologies". *Knowledge Acquisition, 5*(2), 199–220. https://doi.org/10.1006/knac.1993.1008

Gruber, Thomas Robert (1995). "Toward Principles for the Design of Ontologies Used for Knowledge Sharing". *International Journal of Human-Computer Studies, 43*(4–5), 907–928. https://doi.org/10.1006/ijhc.1995.1081

Guarino, Nicola, Daniel Oberle, & Steffen Staab (2009). "What Is an *Ontology*". In *Handbook on Ontologies*, edited by Steffen Staab, & Rudi Studer, 153–176. Berlin-Heidelberg: Springer Verlag. http://dx.doi.org/10.1007/978-3-540-92673-3_0

Hatzfeld, Helmut (1961). "Three National Deformations of Aristotle: Tesauro, Graciàn, Boileau". *Studi Secenteschi, 2*, 3–21.

Haufe, Chris, Kevin C. Elliott, Richard M. Burian, & Maureen A. O'Malley (2010). "Machine Science: What's Missing". *Science, 330*, 317–318. https://doi.org/10.1126/science.330.6002.317-c

Herlihy, David, & Christiane Klapisch-Zuber (1981). *Census and Property Survey for Florentine Domains and the City of Verona in Fifteenth Century Italy. A User's Guide to the Machine Readable Data File.* Madison, WI: University of Wisconsin, Data and Program Library Service. https://www.disc.wisc.edu/archive/catasto/catasto_data/Catasto.pdf

Hey, Tony, Stewart Tansley, & Kristin Tolle (Eds.) (2009). *The Fourth Paradigm: Data-Intensive Scientific Discovery.* Redmond, WA: Microsoft Research. https://www.microsoft.com/en-us/research/wp-content/uploads/2009/10/Fourth_Paradigm.pdf

Holland, John H. (2018). "Survey of Automata Theory (Ann Arbor MI: The University of Michigan Willow Run Laboratories, 1959)". In *Selected Papers of John H. Holland. A Pioneer in Complexity Science*, edited by Jan W. Vasbinder, & Helena Gao, 1–24. Singapore: World Scientific. https://doi.org/10.1142/10841

Holland, John H., & John H. Miller (1991). "Artificial Adaptive Agents in Economic Theory". *American Economic Review, 81*(2), 365–371. https://www.jstor.org/stable/2006886

King, Ross D., Jem Rowland, Stephen G. Oliver, Michael Young, Wayne Aubrey, Emma Byrne, Maria Liakata, Magdalena Markham, Pinar Pir, Larisa N. Soldatova, Andrew Sparkes, Kenneth E. Whelan, & Amanda Clare (2009). "The Automation of Science". *Science, 324*, 85–98. https://www.science.org/doi/10.1126/science.1165620

Le Roy Ladurie, Emmanuel (1973, 1978). *Le Territoire de L'Historien*, Vol. 1 and Vol 2. Paris: Gallimard. https://archive.org/details/leterritoiredelh0000lero/mode/2up

Lee, Edward T.-Z., & Lotfi Aliasker Zadeh (1969). "Note on Fuzzy Languages". *Information Sciences, 1*, 421–434. https://doi.org/10.1016/0020-0255(69)90025-5

Lenglet du Fresnoy, Nicolas (1713). *Methode pour etudier l'histoire: où aprés avoir établi les principes & l'ordre qu'on doit tenir pour la lire utilement, on fait les remarques necessaires pour ne se pas laisser tromper dans sa lecture: avec un Catalogue des principaux historiens, & des remarques critiques sur la bonté de leurs ouvrages, & sur le choix des meilleures editions.* Paris: Chez Antoine Urbain Coustelier.

Leonelli, Sabina (2010). "Machine Science: The Human Side". *Science, 330*, 317. https://doi.org/10.1126/science.330.6002.317-a

Mabillon, Jean (1681). *De re diplomatica libri VI. In quibus quidquid ad veterum instrumentorum antiquitatem, materiam, scripturam, & stilum; quidquid ad sigilla, monogrammata, subscriptiones, ac notas chronologicas; quidquid inde ad antiquariam, historicam, forensemque disciplinam pertinet, explicatur & illustratur. Accedunt Commentarius de antiquis Regum Francorum Palatiis, Veterum scripturarum varia specimina, tabulis LX comprehensa, Nova ducentorum, et amplius, monumentorum collectio.* Paris: Sumtibus Ludovici Billaine.

Marchesini, Daniela (2004). "L'invenzione del 'primitivo' e l'idea di tempo nell'arte contemporanea". In *Storia della lingua e filologia. Per Alfredo Stussi nel suo sessantacinquesimo compleanno,* edited by Michelangelo Zaccarello, & Lorenzo Tomasin, 321–335. Florence: Edizioni del Galluzzo.

Mitchell, Tom M. (1997). *Machine Learning.* New York: McGraw-Hill. https://archive.org/details/machinelearning0000mitc/mode/2up

Mjolsness, Eric, & Dennis DeCoste (2001). "Machine Learning for Science: State of the Art and Future Prospects". *Science, 293*, 2051–2055. https://doi.org/10.1126/science.293.5537.2051

Montfaucon, Bernard de et al. (1708). *Palæographia Græca, sive, de ortu et progressu literarum Græcarum, et de variis omnium sæculorum scriptionis Græcæ generibus: itemque de abbreviationibus & de notis variarum artium ac disciplinarum. Additis figuris & schematibus ad fidem manuscriptorum codicum.* Paris: Apud Ludovicum Guerin. https://en.calameo.com/read/0001070443b15b4eb3655

Nanetti, Andrea (2010). *Il Codice Morosini. Il mondo visto da Venezia (1094-1433),* 4 vols. Spoleto: Fondazione CISAM. Refer also to Nanetti & Vu 2018.

Nanetti, Andrea (2011). "Atlas of Venetian Messenia. Coron, Modon, Pylos and their islands". In *Archivio di Stato di Venezia & Greek Ministry of Culture.* Imola: Editrice La Mandragora.

Nanetti, Andrea (2014). "Mapping and Visualizing Historical Data". In *Viabilità e insediamenti nell'assetto territoriale di Imola nel Medioevo: sperimentazione esemplare di mappatura e visualizzazione del dato storico [Roads and settlements in the territory of medieval Imola. A case study for historical data mapping and visualisation],* edited by Andrea Nanetti, & Mario Giberti, 253–261. Imola: Editrice La Mandragora.

Nanetti, Andrea (2018). *At the origins of the Venetian Sea State. Coron and Modon, 1204-1209.* Athens: Institute for Historical Research of the National Hellenic Research Foundation.

Nanetti, Andrea (2020). "Thinking History Algorithmically: AI and Machine Learning for a New Science of Heritage." In *Proceedings of the International Conference 'Sacred Geography: Multi-Disciplinary Approaches in Space and Time' ([Kazakhstan, Nazarbayev University] Nur-Sultan, 25-26 September*

2020), edited by Nikolai Tsyrempilov, 80–92. Nur-Sultan: "Foliant" Publishing House. https://eatlas.kz/en/conference/

Nanetti, Andrea (2021a). "Defining Heritage Science. A Consilience Pathway to Treasuring the Complexity of Inheritable Human Experience through Historical Method, AI and ML". *Complexity*, 2021, special issue on *Tales of Two Societies: On the Complexity of the Coevolution between the Physical Space and the Cyber Space*, edited by Shu-Heng Chen (Lead Editor), Simone Alfarano and Dehua Shen (Guest Editors), Article ID 4703820. https://www.hindawi.com/journals/complexity/2021/4703820/

Nanetti, Andrea (2021b). *Venezia e il Peloponneso (992-1718) [Venice and the Peloponnese, 992-1718]*. Venice: Ca' Foscari University Press. http://doi.org/10.30687/978-88-6969-544-5

Nanetti, Andrea, & Mario Giberti (2014). *Viabilità e insediamenti nell'assetto territoriale di Imola nel Medioevo: sperimentazione esemplare di mappatura e visualizzazione del dato storico [Roads and settlements in the territory of medieval Imola. A case study for historical data mapping and visualisation]*. Imola: Editrice La Mandragora.

Nanetti, Andrea, & Siew Ann Cheong (2016). "The World as Seen from Venice (1205-1533) as a Case Study of Scalable Web-Based Automatic Narratives for Interactive Global Histories". *The Asian Review of World Histories*, 4(1), 3–34. https://brill.com/view/journals/arwh/4/1/arwh.4.issue-1.xml

Nanetti, Andrea, & Siew Ann Cheong (2018). "Computational History: From Big Data to Big Simulations". In *Big Data in Computational Social Science and Humanities*, edited by Shu-Heng Chen, 337–363. Cham: Springer International Publishing AG. https://link.springer.com/chapter/10.1007/978-3-319-95465-3_18

Nanetti, Andrea, Siew Ann Cheong, & Mikhail Filippov (2013). "Interactive Global Histories. For a New Information Environment to Increase the Understanding of Historical Processes". In *Proceedings of the International Conference on Culture and Computing 2013" (Ritsumeikan University, Japan, Kyoto, 16-18 September 2013)*, 104–110. Los Alamitos, CA: IEEE Computer Society. https://doi.org/10.1109/CultureComputing.2013.26

Nanetti, Andrea, Angelo Cattaneo, Siew Ann Cheong, & Chin-Yew Lin (2015). "Maps as Knowledge Aggregators: From Renaissance Italy Fra Mauro to Web Search Engines". *The Cartographic Journal*, 52(2), 159–167. https://doi.org/10.1080/00087041.2015.1119472

Nilsson, Nils (2010). *The Quest for Artificial Intelligence*. Cambridge: Cambridge University Press. https://ai.stanford.edu/~nilsson/QAI/qai.pdf

Nowotny, Helga (2015). "The Radical Openness of Science and Innovation: Why Uncertainty is Inherent in the Openness towards the Future". *EMBO Reports*, 16(12), 1601–1604.

Nowotny, Helga (2020). *Life in the Digital Time Machine*. The Second Wittrock Lecture held in Uppsala on 25 February 2020. Uppsala: Swedish Collegium for Advanced Study. http://www.swedishcollegium.se/PDF/general/Life%20in%20the%20Digital%20Time%20Machine_H.%20Nowotny_PDF_web.pdf

Nowotny, Helga (2021). *In AI We Trust: Power, Illusion and Control of Predictive Algorithms*. Cambridge: Polity.

Ottaviani, Alessandro (Ed.) (2006). "Bernardino Telesio". *De rerum natura iuxta propria principia: liber primus et secundus (Romae, apud Antonium Bladum, 1565)*. Turin: Nino Aragno.

Paolucci, Mario, & Stefano Picascia (2011). "Enhancing Collective Filtering with Causal Representation". In *Proceedings of the Second International Conference on Culture and Computing (Japan, Kyoto, 20-22 October 2011)*, 135–135. Los Alamitos, CA: IEEE. https://doi.org/10.1109/Culture-Computing.2011.37

Popper, Karl Raimund (1957). *The Poverty of Historicism*. London: Routledge and Kegan Paul – New York: Harper & Row. https://doi.org/10.4324/9780203538012

Pretz, Kathy (2021). "Stop Calling Everything AI, Machine-Learning Pioneer Says > Michael I. Jordan Explains Why Today's Artificial-Intelligence Systems Aren't Actually Intelligent". *IEEE Spectrum* (blog). The Institute, March 31, 2021. https://spectrum.ieee.org/stop-calling-everything-ai-machinelearning-pioneer-says

Principe, Lawrence M. (2011). *The Scientific Revolution. A Very Short Introduction*. Oxford: Oxford University Press. http://doi.org/10.1093/actrade/9780199567416.001.0001

Raspe, Rudolf Eric (1765). *Oeuvres Philosophiques Latines et Françoises de feu Mr. de Leibnitz*, par Mr. Rudolf Eric Raspe. Amsterdam and Leipzig: Chez Jean Schreuder. https://digital.library.yorku.ca/yul-867141/oeuvres-philosophiques-latines-fran%C3%A7oises-de-feu-mr-de-leibnitz#page/1/mode/2up

Robertson, Douglas S. (1998). *The New Renaissance: Computers and the Next Level of Civilization*. Oxford: Oxford University Press.

Robertson, Douglas S. (2003). *Phase Change: The Computer Revolution in Science and Mathematics*. Oxford: Oxford University Press. https://archive.org/details/phasechange00doug/mode/2up

Seising, Rudolf (2002). *Interview with Prof. Dr. George Lakoff, August 6, 2002*. Berkeley, CA: University of California (Dwinell Hall). Unpublished.

Setz, Wolfram (Ed.) (1976). Lorenzo Valla, *De falso credita et ementita Constantini donatione*. Weimar: Hermann Böhlaus Nachfolger. https://daten.digitale-sammlungen.de/~db/0000/bsb00000635/images/index.html

Spedding, James, Robert Leslie Ellis, & Douglas Denon Heath (Eds.) (1887). "Francis Bacon, *De principiis atque originibus, secundum fabulas Cupidinis et Cæli: sive Parmenidis et Telesii et præcipue Democriti philosophia, tractata in fabula de cupidine*". In *The Works of Francis Bacon*, V, 289–346. Boston, MA: Houghton, Mifflin and Company – Cambridge: The Riverside Press. https://archive.org/details/worksfrancisbaco05bacoiala/mode/2up#information

Stierle, Karlheinz (1972). "L'Histoire comme example, l'example comme histoire". *Poétique*, *10*, 176–198.

Tesauro, Emanuele (1654). *Il cannocchiale aristotelico, o sia, idea delle argutezze heroiche vulgarmente chiamate imprese; et di tutta l'arte simbolica, et lapidaria, contenente ogni genere di figure & inscrittioni espressive di arguti & ingeniosi concetti; esaminata in fonte co' rettorici precetti del divino Aristotele, che comprendono tutta la rettorica, & poetica elocutione.* Turin: Per Giovanni Sinibaldo, Stampator Regio, e Camerale. https://books.google.com.sg/books?id=PzwIo-r5aA0C&pg=PA1&source=gbs_selected_pages&cad=3#v=onepage&q&f=fals

Tesauro, Emanuele (1670). *Il cannocchiale aristotelico o sia idea dell'arguta et ingeniosa elocutione che serve à tutta l'arte oratoria, lapidaria, et simbolica esaminata co' principij del divino Aristotele. Quinta impressine.* Turin: Per Bartolomeo Zavatta.

Tomasin, Lorenzo (2017). *L'impronta digitale. Cultura umanistica e tecnologia.* Rome: Carocci editore.

Trillas, Enric, & Rudolf Seising (2018). "What a Fuzzy Set Is and What It Is not?" In *Frontiers in Computational Intelligence*, edited by Sanaz Mostaghim, Andreas Nürnberger, & Christian Borgelt, 1–20. Cham: Springer International Publishing AG. https://doi.org/10.1007/978-3-319-67789-7_1

Turchin, Peter, Thomas E. Currie, Harvey Whitehouse, Pieter François, Kevin Feeney, Daniel Mullins, Daniel Hoyer, Christina Collins, Stephanie Grohmann, Patrick Savage, Gavin Mendel-Gleason, Edward Turner, Agathe Dupeyron, Enrico Cioni, Jenny Reddish, Jill Levine, Greine Jordan, Eva Brandl, Alice Williams, Rudolf Cesaretti, Marta Krueger, Alessandro Ceccarelli, Joe Figliulo-Rosswurm, Po-Ju Tuan, Peter Peregrine, Arkadiusz Marciniak, Johannes Preiser-Kapeller, Nikolay Kradin, Andrey Korotayev, Alessio Palmisano, David Baker, Julye Bidmead, Peter Bol, David Christian, Connie Cook, Alan Covey, Gary Feinman, Árni Daníel Júlíusson, Axel Kristinsson, John Miksic, Ruth Mostern, Cameron Petrie, Peter Rudiak-Gould, Barend ter Haar, Vesna Wallace, Victor Mair, Liye Xie, John Baines, Elizabeth Bridges, Joseph Manning, Bruce Lockhart, Amy Bogaard, & Charles Spencer (2018). "Quantitative Historical Analysis Uncovers a Single Dimension of Complexity that Structures Global Variation in Human Social Organization". *PNAS*, *115*(2), E144–E151. https://doi.org/10.1073/pnas.1708800115

van Deusen, Neil C. (1932). *Telesio: The First of the Moderns.* New York: Columbia University Press.

Wolfram (2022). "Wolfram Language & System Documentation Center". Accessed May 25, 2022. https://reference.wolfram.com/language

Wolfram, Stephen (2002). *A New Kind of Science.* Champaign, IL: Wolfram Media. https://www.wolframscience.com/nks/

Wootton, David (2015). *The Invention of Science. A New History of the Scientific Revolution.* London: Allen Lane (Penguin Random House, UK). https://archive.org/details/inventionofscien0000woot

Young, Tom, Devamanyu Hazarika, Soujanya Poria, & Erik Cambria (2018). "Recent Trends in Deep Learning Based Natural Language Processing". *IEEE Computational Intelligence Magazine*, *13*(3), 55–75. https://doi.org/10.1109/MCI.2018.2840738

3 History, Films, and Online Video Streaming

3.1 Communicating History with Films

In 2020, Andrea Nanetti and Christoph Hahnheiser started a series of research meetings that acted as a forum to explore how and by what means the production of history-based films could be enhanced by social media platforms. This research is significant for studying and communicating history in our globalised society. It addresses how digitally born world citizens learn about their past that goes beyond regional history (Gruzinski 2015, Epilogue) and create their (hi)stories in the present to build the future they desire (Benzoni 2016, xii–xiii). Thus, in 2021, Cui Yifang was hired as a Research Assistant to work, among others, on a preliminary literature review, the results of which are summarised in Sections 3.1 and 3.3. In addition, part of the content of these two sections has been shared in a paper titled 'Acquiring Knowledge from Online Audiovisual Sources: Opportunities and Challenges for the Audience' (abstract, Nanetti & Cui 2022) at the online conference of the International Association for Media and Communication Research (IAMCR, Beijing, 11–15 July 2022).

According to Jack Duckworth, the use of films (i.e., sets of moving images) for teaching history started as early as the 1930s (Duckworth 1981, 32). This phenomenon gained momentum in the 1960s when educational films for television were intensively produced (Smith 1976, 1–2). In the decade that followed, John E. O'Connor and Martin A. Jackson co-founded the journal *Film & History* and started the Historians' Film Committee, endeavouring to drive investigation and discussions around the subject of filmed history (Toplin & Eudy 2002, 7). Then, towards the end of the twentieth century, an increasing number of people sought and acquired information about the past from moving images rather than from written records or schools (Toplin 1991, 1160). Indeed, the first two decades of the twentieth century saw

DOI: 10.4324/9781003310860-3

an expansion of audiences for history films, documentaries, dramas, and other videos. This trend was accelerated by the booming of the online video streaming industry, or over-the-top (OTT) services. In the digital age, information and communications technology (ICT), from cinema to television, from desktop computers to mobile devices, gave rise to not only a variety of media formats, smart devices, and an opulent amount of content, but also a rich selection of viewing platforms online.

There are several types of moving images that are most often associated with history communication. In Benicia D'sa's perspective, the most common three are documentaries, feature films, and docudramas (D'sa 2005, 9). In the digital age, these formats are generally available for consumption on Subscription Video on Demand (SVOD) sites. Besides these three, period drama and compilation films are also having a close relationship with history. In addition, driven by popularity and accessibility of Advertising-based Video on Demand (AVOD) platforms such as YouTube and TikTok, user-generated content (UGC) has been flourishing, mainly taking the format of short-form videos. UGC will be discussed as the sixth category in this section, but it is to note that some UGC could also be classified as one of the five earlier mentioned categories. Likewise, all the six formats are identified here as theoretical categories; in reality, the borderlines defining each type are often grey or overlapping.

All these types of media need critical tools to allow the users to validate the provenance of historical information and link it to the relevant primary historical sources. Books have footnotes. Media are still waiting for a similar tool in the digital time machine (Nanetti et al. 2016). EHM is currently working on the development of such a tool.

3.1.1 Documentary Films

Documentary films, aka simply documentaries, tend to enjoy a broad definition. John Grierson's definition, 'creative treatment of actuality' was framed in the 1930s and is still regularly referred to upon scholars' attempts to define documentary films today. The purpose of history documentaries, in Betsy McLane's words, is for filmmakers to convey their understanding of historical events, people, and places that they find significant (McLane 2012, 2). The value of history documentaries therefore lies in introducing new viewpoints which may not be prevalent in traditional medias such as history readings and school curricula (Stoddard & Marcus 2010, 281). Moreover, scholars affirmed that documentary films could meet the key objectives of teaching history in 'promoting reasoned judgment, promoting an expanded view of humanity, and deliberating over the common good' (Stoddard & Marcus 2010, 281). As a result, many educators prefer documentaries over other forms of digital media in their history classes.

Yet, issues have been identified in interpreting documentaries. Alan Marcus, Richard Paxton, and Peter Meyerson observed in their research that students see documentaries as trustworthy sources alongside textbooks and primary sources (Marcus et al. 2006, 523). Teachers may also overlook the fact that documentaries are more 'perspective-laden' than objectively true (Hess 2007). Jeremy Stoddard and Robert Toplin argued that documentaries that are not well-researched and more entertainment-oriented would potentially mislead those who have a great trust in such media format (Toplin 1988, Stoddard 2009a, b). Considering the challenge faced by the viewers of the history documentaries mentioned above, it is important to introduce tools to bring critical eyes when accessing documentaries for information about the past. Scholars on multiple occasions also proposed to treat documentaries as supplementary resources for seeking new perspectives, because issues of the past are often controversial and multifaceted (Stoddard 2009a, b, 80, Marcus & Stoddard 2010, 88).

3.1.2 Docudramas

Docudrama or documentary drama, as the term illustrates, comes from 'documentary' and 'drama' and is a hybrid format in between documentary and feature films. Naturally, it bears the characteristics of both documentary and dramatic films. Foluke Ogunleye described docudrama as an audio-visual depiction of real events of the past supported by actual historical footages combined with some artistic performances by actors and actresses (Ogunleye 2005, 480). Although docudramas are more fact-based, D'sa maintained that they are also heavily impacted by the filmmakers' own perspectives and understanding of history (D'sa 2005, 9). The degree of dramatic licence ('creation of materials not established as historical facts or even the violation of known facts') in docudramas is hence affected by subjective opinions and not clearly identifiable (D'sa 2005, 10). Joseph P. McKerns suggested that, based on the amount of information, docudrama may be further categorised into at least three subtypes—'predominantly factual', 'predominantly fictional', and one that 'uses fiction to fill the gaps, large or small, left by the historical record' (McKerns 2019, 24).

Such ambiguity of docudrama between fact and fiction gives rise to its advantages and weaknesses.

Comparing with documentaries which may be more fact-oriented, D'sa suggested that docudramas can engage viewers more effectively driven by its storytelling attribute (D'sa 2005, 10). This is akin to the power of feature films in constructing a vivid and immersive reappearance of the past. Yet, sounder than feature films, docudramas are comparatively more accurate and comprehensive (Ogunleye 2005, 482).

However, the use of docudrama to communicate history is still subject to scrutiny. Janet Staiger, when defining docudrama in the *Encyclopedia of Television*, highlighted three reservations for viewers to pay attention to (Staiger 2013, 738–739). Firstly, docudrama creators apply dramatic license such as created settings and conversations to make sense of the format of a drama (D'sa 2005). This is because completeness and coherence of a play normally entail elements such as 'time', 'location', 'language', 'movement', 'mood', 'symbol', and 'dramatic meaning' as proposed by John O'Toole (1992, 7). Secondly, due to the mixture of fact and fiction, it is challenging for audiences to distinguish the line in between. Such difficulty is mainly caused by docudramas' lack of clarity in indicating the distinction between truth and made-up stories. Finally, although better than feature films, some docudramas still tend to simplify historical narratives. This simplification is possibly due not only to the restriction of duration but also to other factors related to storyboard processes and screenwriters' expertise.

To address the issues discussed, aside from recommending viewers to be more critical in interpreting such media, Alan Rosenthal appealed in the book *Why Docudrama? Fact-fiction on Film and TV* that all docudrama makers should aim to produce more accurate and well-researched works. He quoted David Boulton: 'no invented characters, no invented names, no dramatic devices owing more to the writer's (or director's) creative imagination than to the impeccable record of what happened. For us, docudrama is an exercise in journalism, not dramatic art' (Rosenthal 1999, 9).

3.1.3 Feature Films

Feature films, which may also be referred to as Hollywood films or acted films, are portraying mostly fictional narratives and figures. Although historical feature film may base its stories on a real person and occasion, the representations are mostly dramatic and creative. Robert Brent Toplin and Jason Eudy described such films are an examination of the past in 'innovative, provocative, and unorthodox ways' (Toplin & Eudy 2002, 10) and Scott Metzger highlighted that filmmakers' ambitions must often deal with the rules of commercial market (Metzger 2010, 127).

Most viewers of feature film are aware of its theatrical property and entertaining objective, but historical feature films are still considered to possess educational values towards understanding the past because they influence how the public imagines and visualises the past. However, many studies have shown that historical feature films have positively engaged students in putting further passion and effort in studying history. Feature film's dramatic and entertaining depiction of the past, although not all accurate, stimulates viewers' interest in history and generates a closer connection to historical topics (Toplin & Eudy 2002, 7, Marcus 2005, 62). Scott Alan Metzger and Alan S. Marcus also outlined that the multimedia feature of films builds a past with colour, space, sound, and stories that help audiences to 'visualise' and 'feel' history (Marcus 2005, 65, Metzger 2010, 132). As a result, feature films are a beneficial add-on to complement traditional sources in communicating historical content and increasing the public's awareness of history in general (Jackson 1973).

On the other hand, learning history only through feature films has its own caveat. There is no doubt that these films present more tales than facts (Rosenstone 1988). Robert Rosenstone, while confirming their usefulness, warned that the historical truths exhibited in fictional films are more 'symbolic' and 'metaphorical' than 'literal' (Rosenstone 2004, 33). Unlike peer-reviewed scholarly publications, feature films are mainly dominated by distorted information and illusions because most filmmakers' priority is to tell compelling stories rather than presenting the achievements of scholarly works. To deliver a more convincing account, Scott Alan Metzger asserted that feature films need to take sides and make apparent hero and villain characters, leading to the consequence of oversimplified historical narratives (Metzger 2010, 132). Although some productions engage historians, their contribution varies, and the final call still lies in the hands of scriptwriters, directors, producers, and sponsors (Toplin 1991, 1162, Metzger 2010, 129). Ultimately, the film industry is primarily to produce profitable entertaining works that sell to the widest possible audience.

It was mentioned above that viewers are conscious about the dramatic features of fictional films, yet Alan S. Marcus, Richard J. Paxton, and Peter Meyerson's studies had implied that students, although recognising the limitation of feature films, considered clips shown by teachers in classes were objective and reliable (Marcus et al.

2006, 526). Marcus therefore advocated teachers should proactively develop students' film literacy ('ability to interpret film') and remind them of the dramatic license applied by filmmakers. In addition, Ray E. Scrubber also recommended that historians should be more active in involving in the process of historical film production instead of leaving the creation purely to dramatists (Scrubber 2001).

3.1.4 Historical Dramas

Foluke Ogunleye suggested that historical drama, sometimes referred to as period drama, have laid the foundation for the birth of docudrama (Ogunleye 2005, 482). Sitting under the backdrop of a past period, historical drama consists of less factual representation of history but more fictional imagination than docudrama. On a scale with fiction and fact on the opposing ends, documentary may be placed closest to the factual end out of the four discussed formats so far, followed by docudrama; feature film and historical drama, occasionally used interchangeably, share approximate position towards the fictional pole. Therefore, feature film and historical drama often share similar value and limitations when it comes to history communication.

3.1.5 Compilation Films

Compilation film, also used as a sub-category of documentary from time to time, is defined as productions made mainly by found footages (Beattie 2004, 125, Mulvey 2007, 109). The process of producing compilation films includes the use and juxtaposition of pre-existing clips from sources such as films, drama, newsreel, and television programs. Filmmaker and historian Jay Leyda first coined the term in his book *Films Beget Films* back in 1964, but since then, it appears that there have not been active discussions around the topic. This may be due to the lack of accessible and available shots that are required to complete a coherent project. Keith Beattie stated that without relevant clips, it is challenging for creators to utilise the format of compilation film to put forward comprehensive arguments (Beattie 2004, 126).

3.1.6 User-Generated Content

The so-called AVOD sites, such as YouTube and TikTok, are dominated by UGC. The emergence of UGC therefore took place at the start of social media or Web 2.0 since the beginning of the twenty-first century. The term can be straightforwardly defined as published content online by users, and its forms may be various driven by the liberty of content creators.

The low entrance barrier for making and publishing videos and the accessibility of vast collections online have supported and encouraged the public's participation and interaction in any topics. Claudia Wyrwoll pointed out that users needed no programming or advanced filming skills to produce and upload their works (Wyrwoll 2014, 15). This is reflected in the popularity of short-form videos for which a smart phone and an in-app editing tool are sufficient for any filmmaking layman to be a director and editor on their own. TikTok's launch in 2017, YouTube Shorts in 2020, and the recent Instagram Reels are all tapping on the waves of short videos to appeal to the public. It was estimated that there are over 50 million YouTubers globally and the number is still counting (Koetsier 2020). Not only video-creating became easy, published videos can be easily accessed too. History-wise, it takes no time to search about almost any historical events and figures on social media these days. On YouTube alone, there are numerous channels focusing on history alone. The *History* channel has attracted close to 10 million subscribers with its most-watched clip on Schiavona receiving over 30 million views (HISTORY n.d.).

Richard Azor's research team suggested that with YouTube videos, the process of history learning is more interesting and less abstract (Azor et al. 2020, 318). Browsing history videos uploaded by YouTubers and TikTokers, it is evident that many UGC are presenting bite-sized materials in a fun and creative way. Audiences are not only engaged and inspired to watch more, but they can also choose to do so over their fragmented time. However, one common concern with historical information presented in UGC is that the sources are often unknown. Unlike peer-reviewed and carefully selected written publications, there are generally no references in videos posted on social media for viewers to trace sources (Suciu 2019). Professional editor and writer John Adams-Graf made a critical comment on this by saying that 'a reader could always check a writer's sources to determine whether the printed material was accurate or not. That is lost in YouTube history videos …. Writing and reporting history still requires documenting the trail of reason to the conclusions. Anything less, no matter how attractive or easy to digest; is not history' (Suciu 2019). Additionally, the less restricted freedom in creating and posting videos online leads to decentralised information distribution. Thomas Simonsen argued that there was a lack of intellectual authority and guidance online which resulted in information appearing superficial and disorganised (Simonsen 2011, 73).

Reflecting upon the above limitations, apart from advising viewers to always treat videos from social media sources more critically, organisations like the SVOD provider Boclips has dedicated to video content vetting. Working with content creators, some of whom are also popular YouTube channels such as Crash Course and Weird History, Boclips aims to provide schools and educators with right-cleared videos after realising how information online could be overwhelming and confusing for students ('Boclips: Curated Educational Videos for Student Learning'; refer to Boclips n.d.). InVID is another tool offered to netizens for video verification (Mezaris et al. 2019). First introduced in 2017, InVID has recently been upgraded to InVID WeVerify, a plugin that can be added to Chrome ('Verification Plugin' n.d.). The plugin supports the analysis of a video which includes providing contextual information, extracting, and categorising comments, and fragmenting the video into keyframes to do reverse image search on search engines like Google, Tineye, and Yandex. Yet, InVID WeVerify's key focus is to identify fake or manipulated news reports or footages. For historical content, it seems works in establishing provenance and tracing sources for online UGC are still relatively limited.

Furthermore, it is observed that some historical videos especially on YouTube frequently adopt animation to illustrate historical narratives. Annabelle Honess Roe shared that the animated picture help to resolve the limitations of 'conventional live-action' in film production particularly when telling the past stories (Honess Roe 2016, 48). In the academic side, Kayvan Kousha, Mike Thelwall, and Mahshid Abdoli's investigation also showed that there is a gradual upward trend in citing YouTube videos in research papers because multimedia was better at describing and visualising findings and arguments especially when dealing with performance-based (e.g., music and theatre studies) topics or primary sources such as historical documentaries (Kousha et al. 2012).

3.2 Animated Picture as a Privileged Medium to Screen Historical Narratives in Films

3.2.1 *Using Animation to Adapt Historical Narratives in Films*

In 2018, the research collaboration between Andrea Nanetti and Davide Benvenuti started a research path to explore how and by what means the EHM applications could be empowered by animation (Nanetti & Benvenuti 2019, 2021, Nanetti et al. 2020b). Later, in 2020, they have been assisted by Zaqeer Radzi in a preliminary literature review, the results of which are summarised in this section. As outlined by a renowned animation scholar, Paul Wells, 'history driven animation' can be defined by a 'visual, technical, and subject-oriented consistency ... that ... recognises certain visual and iconography' that serve as 'key signifiers of an implied common language shared by the filmmaker and their audience, which in turn defines the cinematic construction of the historical text'. The historical contexts and facts make up the 'mode of order and integration. They may be recognised as the determining factor that maintains the core historical narrative' (Wells 2002, 43–44). In addition, a film-study scholar, Annabelle Honess Roe, in her influential work on the genre 'Animated Documentary' (2013), stated that 'the use of animation as a representational strategy in documentary ... illustrates the various ways in which one sees and understands their world' (Roe 2013, 2). From Frank Capra's 'Why We Fight' (Capra & Litvak 1942–1945) to Michael Moore's 'Bowling for Columbine' (Moore 2002), the use of animation to contextualise, clarify, and illustrate nonfictional narratives highlights and exemplify high quality use of animation films. Other significant examples of animated documentaries are 'Victory Through Air Power' (Algar et al. 1943), 'Waltz with Bashir' (Folman 2008), 'The Wanted 18' (Shomali & Cowan 2014), 'Walking with Dinosaurs' (Haines & James 1999), etc. (Murray 2017).

According to Roe, an animated documentary allows the audience to see the world in a new light and give alternative perspectives. Still, more importantly, it 'broadens the limits on how reality could be represented' (Roe 2013, 17). For example, in Afarin Eghbal's 'Abuelas' (Eghbal 2011), the animated documentary recounts the story of Argentine mothers during the period of Videla's dictatorship from the 1970s to the 1980s. Moreover, she argues that the centrality of animation within this film is as such that if the animation were to be removed, the meaning of the film would become totally 'incoherent' (Roe 2013, 5). Ultimately, she states that an animated documentary would have to be about the world instead of an imagined world or a fictional one and would be presented to a specific audience, shown in festivals, and reviewed by relevant critics (Roe 2013, 4).

In terms of using animation as a tool to interpret history and adapt to a new digital form, Wells noted that 'animation is, after all, a distinctive film-form, which offers to the adaptation process a unique vocabulary of expression unavailable to the live-action filmmaker' (Wells 1999, 199). In this regard, the added value in filmmaking is that animation is not bound to realism or representation in its execution;

it does not rely on actors in front of the camera or physical locations. Therefore, animation's ability to express stories and states of mind through imaginative visualisation is only limited by the artistic interpretive power of the animator: 'animation accentuates the intended *feeling* of the text through its very abstractness in the use of colour, form, and movement …. Animation simultaneously literalises and abstracts' (Wells 1999, 208).

Moreover, Wells explains that 'the perception of a text unencumbered by the lexicon of a known adaptation must surely be related to the agency of the viewer and the visual codes and conventions that inform that person's perception of the text, as well as the world that surrounds them'. So, Wells determined that animation could bring a historical story into relevance to a modern-day viewer, through the many tools available, including visual style, colour, timing, and sound. Kate Warren added that animation could allow 'sometimes dangerous, stories to be told without the burden of maintaining realism and negotiating *authentic* reconstruction' (Warren 2010, 118). He described how animation is an excellent vehicle to explore the interrelations between memory, fantasy, dream, and experience (Warren 2010).

As a genre, animated documentaries can communicate complex information, historical facts, and events often more effectively than real-life video. As noted by Roe, 'this envisioned information is easier to understand and retain' compared to other oral forms (Roe 2013, 8). It uses visual associations, symbolism, or iconography to relay these facts while pushing the boundaries of animation. As noted by Anna Sowa, in short-form animated documentary films such as 'Nobody's Metaphor' (Sowa 2019), animation became one of the most vibrant aspects of the film in helping to facilitate further discussion (Sowa 2020). In any case, animated documentaries are not meant to be the 'end all be all'. As Hans-Martin Rall noted, 'animated documentaries promise the potential for further research' and open more doors for interdisciplinary work across various schools and fields (Rall et al. 2018, 49). This is the EHM approach to animation to empower the discovery and communicative potential of historical sciences.

3.2.2 Significant Examples of History-Driven Animations

In 2021, Davide Benvenuti, Zaqeer Radzi, and Andrea Nanetti investigated and discussed significant examples of history-driven animation to inform research and development of new approaches to share historical contents (Nanetti et al. 2021). A first innovative example of history-driven animation is 'Loving Vincent' (Kobiela & Welchman 2017). The film focuses on the circumstances of the death of the world-famous Dutch Post-Impressionist painter Vincent Willem van Gogh (1853–1890). The production of this biographical drama experimented a fully painted animated feature film.

'Persepolis' (Paronnaud & Satrapi 2007) is an animated biographical drama film based upon Marjane Satrapi's homonymous autobiographical graphic novel (Satrapi 2004). Persepolis succeeded in giving the viewer an account full of awakening and maturing. The animation skilfully shares with the viewer many emotions of repression, anger, fear, disillusionment, and, finally, maturity and determination. As such, this movie conveys cultural experiences at the individual and community levels. While historical events are depicted, the effect on the protagonist, Marji, and her family places this animation into a unique context. The viewer experiences these events through the eyes and emotions of these lead characters. The visual style used in Persepolis is also significant. With stylistic roots in Japanese Anime and European Art Nouveau, the hard black-and-white style is both comic-like and starkly factual. Persepolis cleverly shows how the visual style can have a powerful effect on how the narrative is received.

A third significant example is 'Waltz with Bashir' (Folman 2008), an animated adult war documentary drama written, produced, and directed by Ari Folman. It depicts Folman searching for the lost memories of his experience as a soldier in the 1982 Lebanon War. The movie is clearly anti-war; the lead protagonist deals with repressed memories created through guilt about his actions in the war. 'Waltz with Bashir' deals less with chronological facts and more with the effects of specific events on an individual. While animated, it uses a relatively accurate, semi-realistic approach, which at times feels more like stylised realism than animation. While the story itself would be just as powerful in an abstract form, the visual style places the movie in the Middle East. This film is a significant example of how location depiction is used to locate the visual and historical context of animation.

These few but significant examples are sufficient to demonstrate how animated representations can have a substantial and profound effect on an audience and perceive personal and historical stories. When the audience is exposed to a story related to their history, the film engages with who they are and the narratives tie to the lives of the individuals becoming personally relevant. However, critical challenges are still unaddressed. For example, among short-form history-driven animation products, we can mention the stop-motion film

'Achilles', directed, written, and animated by Barry Purves in 1995 (Purves 1995). This film explores the complex relationship between Achilles and Patroclus during the Trojan War. According to Homer's Iliad as its primary source, Purves utilised staging and technique to explore the possibilities of introducing eroticism into stop-motion. According to Purves, the idea of 'primal urges' could be explored through the medium of animation. This area was uncharted at the time and could push forward the boundaries of storytelling. The film worked out well by combining Greek iconography, lighting, staging, and 'masked choruses'. Through such techniques, Purves was able to retell the intimate tale of Achilles and Patroclus based on the Iliad itself in a way that had never been done before (Hicks-Jenkins 2013). In addition, this animated film generated a discussion on spiritual or non-platonic love in the relationship between Achilles and Patroclus. However, the audience cannot take a position or argue because the Iliad's passages on which the film is based are not openly shared in relation to the film's scenes.

3.3 Validating Historical Narratives in Films

3.3.1 Acquiring Knowledge from History-Based Films. Opportunities and Challenges for the Audience

The American historians Richard Charles Raack and Robert Brent Toplin argued that when historians and content creators are not the same group of people, which is often the case, quality control becomes difficult for history productions (Raack 1983, 412, Toplin 1988, 1226). However, Raack strongly believed in the power of filmic productions as an 'emphatic reconstruction to convey how historical people witnessed, understood, and lived their lives' (Raack 1983, Weinstein 2001, 27–28). Relatedly, Nicholas Pronay alleged footages on their own can be seen as primary evidence of the period under which they were created, and hence bearing social, cultural, and historical values (Pronay 1983, 366). On the contrary, moving images attracted some shared concerns too. It was demonstrated that history films and videos aim primarily to display filmmakers' perspectives rather than offering a comprehensive assessment of historical issues. These perspectives, although beneficial in introducing original readings of the past, should not be used as sole evidence due to potential prejudice. This is particularly important when it comes to learning history because historical narratives are sometimes instrumentalised to serve as political and social propaganda (Toplin 1988, 1210, Barsch 2020,

67). These challenges are even more relevant today in the online video streaming environment.

Indeed, Robert A. Rosenstone was ultimately sceptical about the possibility of really putting history into films (Rosenstone 1988). However, as outlined by the French historian Serge Gruzinski, full transparency is an illusion not only in the moving image but also in traditional bookish historiography (White 1988, Gruzinski 2015, Chapter 3). The past is gone. Our knowledge of the human experiences in history is based on the traces of these experiences still preserved in our present. The archives and other relics of the past are artificial (i.e., human-made). Yet, in any case, events cannot be confused with their echoes, the documents (Ginzburg 1986). The broad and controversial debate about 'data' in the humanities reflects and addresses this challenge in the digital space (e.g., Owens 2011, Schöch 2013, Kleinman 2016, Rambsy & Kenton 2017, Lavin 2021, Oldman 2021).

The French novelist Marguerite Yourcenar (1903–1987) poetically epitomised this fact in her novel *Souvenirs pieux* ('Pious memories').

> La vie passée est une feuille sèche, craquelée, sans sève ni chlorophylle, criblée de trous, éraillée de déchirures, qui, mise à contre-jour, offre tout au plus le réseau squelettique de ses nervures minces et cassantes. Il faut certains efforts pour lui rendre son aspect charnu et vert de feuille fraiche, pour restituer aux événements ou aux incidents cette plénitude qui comble ceux qui les vivent et les garde d'imaginer autre chose / Past life is a dry, cracked leaf, without sap or chlorophyll, riddled with holes, scratched with tears, which, against the light, offers at most the skeletal network of its thin and brittle veins. It takes some effort to give it back its fleshy, fresh leaf-green appearance, to restore to events or incidents that fullness that fulfills those who experience them and keeps them from imagining something else.
>
> (Yourcenar 1974, 110 / English translation by Andrea Nanetti, based on Yourcenar 1991)

Thus, the central question is whether and how cinematographic creation can make the historical narrative overcome the limits within which it is confined. Can filmmakers retain their creativity and power of witness without sacrificing the critical and philological accuracy transmitted by written history? Does cinema offer a viable alternative to the principle of the single story, of linear rhythm and the relentless concatenation of causes and effects? Serge Gruzinski demonstrated that film directors, like historians, can produce pasts and their works represent more than a gallery of beautiful images (Gruzinski 2015, Chapter 3; referring to Herlihy 1988). In general, moving images can be a practical means to support the understanding of the past. Different audio-visual formats can share similar values, while the proportion of truth in each varies. Additionally, technological advancement has made the existing issues more complicated because of the overwhelming amount of online information via video streaming platforms. The growing of available historical information related to the UGC's burgeoning did not necessarily generate better practices. Realising how online videos can be overwhelming and confusing for students, companies like Boclips have dedicated themselves to video content vetting for the benefit of educators and learners (Boclips n.d.).

InVID WeVerify is another application offered to internet users for video verification (Mezaris et al. 2019) but focuses on identifying fake or manipulated news reports or footage. However, tools to establish provenance and tracing sources for online audio-visuals are still relatively limited for historical content. Even for productions like documentaries that are often perceived as trustworthy sources of historical information, the varying degree of creativity and dramatic license ('creation of materials not established as historical facts or even the violation of known facts') contained in documentary productions can be concerning. From an education studies viewpoint, Diana Hess suggested that documentary films are more 'perspective-laden' than objectively true (Hess 2007). Similarly, Jeremy Stoddard and Robert Brent Toplin also warned that documentaries that are not well-researched and more entertainment-oriented would potentially mislead those who have great trust in such media format (Toplin 1988, Stoddard 2009b). Hence, a review was conducted to assess the tools and metrics OTT sites provide to their audiences for information and provenance checking. The following pages share the outcome of this investigation, for which ten popular OTT platforms have been reviewed and organised in groups according to the approach that they have to information validation.

3.3.1.1 Netflix, Amazon Prime Video, and Disney+

Netflix, Amazon Prime Video, and Disney+ are examples of SVOD players, the content of which is diverse. As a result, these sites provide information for each listed product to assist their subscribers. Apart from basic information such as title, year of release, and duration, streaming sites like Netflix, Amazon, and Disney+ generally offer four main types of information, namely maturity rating, description, credits, and genres.

- Maturity ratings indicate the suitable age group for a particular product so that audiences can make an informed viewing decision. The ratings usually follow the streaming provider's standard and are adjusted according to the laws and policies of each different country.
- Content description is a concise introduction to the film or series that may provoke audiences' interest.
- Credits recognise the crew and cast associated with respective productions and are usually included in the 'details' or 'more' section of the listing or embedded in the open or closing credits within a film or series. In addition, persons' names and titles are commonly credited in the caption for productions that incorporate footage of interviews or speeches of professionals or academicians.
- Genres are categories that each video falls into, such as 'documentary', 'drama', 'romantic', 'comedy', and 'thriller, just to name a few. It is not uncommon to have more than one genre tagged to a particular piece. For example, Amazon Prime Video simultaneously attributed 'Schindler's List' (Spielberg 1993), 'The History of Time Travel' (Kennedy 2014), and 'Lucy and Desi' (Poehler 2022) as a documentary and a drama.

Out of the four elements above, the latter two may be more relevant for anyone who attempts to trace sources or assess the credibility of a production. This relevance relies on the fact that credits generally include names of the writer, screenplay, and history consultants, who give the content a sense of authority. These collaborations improve information traceability to a certain degree but are only limited. Viewers interested in seeking supporting evidence for a particular event or point of view conveyed in the film can choose to go after the writers' or the historians' past and recent works and publications. However, the process is assumed to be tedious because it must be human-curated. Moreover, the works of the historians may not always be easily accessible; even if they are, it can be challenging to locate the relevant proof for the particular statement or incident portrayed in the production by which the viewer was intrigued in the first place. Alternatively, audiences would need to seek other sources to resolve their queries.

Genres assigned by OTT providers can indicate the fabrication level in a film or series. For example, on Netflix, 'docuseries', 'documentaries', 'historical documentaries', 'social and cultural docs', 'period pieces', and 'based on real life' are a few genre examples that are associated with historical subjects. Yet, it does not necessarily suggest that all information contained in productions with these tags is historically correct. One of the critical limitations that documentaries or docudramas have, which similarly apply to the above-listed genres, lies in the blend of fact and fiction within the same production. These limitations make it difficult for audiences to differentiate the truth from the made-up. Sometimes, users can take signs from the genre tags allocated by the OTT sites.

For example, when 'docuseries', 'documentary', 'historical documentary', or 'based on real-life' tags are attributed together with 'drama' to the same film, the picture inevitably contains fictional elements even though it may be history-based. Examples like this are 'The Last Czars' (Netflix 2019), 'Medal of Honor' (Netflix 2018), and 'In the Heart of the Sea' (Howard 2015) on Netflix. However, are the tags sufficient to guide audiences in determining the content's veracity? When Netflix released season four of 'The Crown' (Morgan 2016–2020) in November 2020, UK Culture Secretary Oliver Dowden commented that Netflix should add a fiction warning to alert viewers of 'The Crown' because the young who had no recollection of those past events would mistake the stories as accurate (Bakare 2020). However, Netflix declined the request, given the series has always been classified as drama (BBC 2020). The incident implies that having the genre tags may be practical but is still inadequate for the purpose of content validation.

3.3.1.2 MUBI and Curiosity Stream

MUBI and Curiosity Stream are SVOD suppliers that focus on curating a specific category of films, namely art house films for MUBI and documentaries for Curiosity Stream. Akin to the big streaming players discussed above, MUBI and Curiosity Stream also provide essential information, including title, duration, synopsis, and credits. However, MUBI and Curiosity Stream's maturity ratings are more uncomplicated and straightforward. For instance, MUBI follows four 'Guidance Levels', whereas Curiosity Stream allows the subscriber to turn on the 'Kids Mode' (MUBI n.d.).

Differing from Netflix, Amazon Prime Video, and Disney+, both MUBI and Curiosity Stream provide an outlet for subscribers to review and comment on the works. Although Amazon Prime Video also supports commenting but only via the 'Watch Party' function—a

Figure 3.1 Screenshot of comments for storm over Europe on Curiosity Stream.

Source: Curiosity Stream 2015.

small, closed group of people make an appointment to watch the same content simultaneously online. The comment function that MUBI and Curiosity Stream adopt allows broader audiences to contribute and exchange information, including sharing perspectives regarding the truthfulness of the content. An example observed is 'Storm Over Europe', a documentary about the Germanic tribes and the fall of Rome, offered on Curiosity Stream with Season 1 released in 2015 (Curiosity Stream 2015).

Browsing the comments section (Figure 3.1), one will notice that user Nicholas V. commented, '… why are the Romans wearing Segm[ent] ata armor? Wayyy too early for that'. This dialogue is followed by two replies by Simon U. and Lukas M., suggesting two possible reasons, respectively (i.e., budget constraint and outdated information). Another remark made by Lee B. several months later affirmed the series' value while assuming possible 'overdramatisations' and 'errors'. A similar kind of comment can be seen for other works on Curiosity Stream. These viewers' comments display their critical attitude, which is a competency that many scholars have been advocating when it comes to appreciating and interpreting movies (O'connor 1988, Toplin & Eudy 2002, Marcus & Stoddard 2010, Metzger 2010, Kousha et al. 2012, Barsch 2020). Alan S. Marcus referred to this skill as 'film literacy' (Marcus 2005). However, if the statement about the *lorica segmentata* made by Nicholas V. is accurate, what else may be erroneous in the series? Lukas M.'s comment is also valid because films are produced based on the available knowledge of their times. When new studies reveal more findings, productions of earlier times could contain obsolete information which would be difficult or costly to remedy.

3.3.1.3 YouTube and TikTok

YouTube and TikTok are social media leaders in the AVOD sector, with most site content contributed by the platforms' users. Compared to the SVOD players where content checking and licensing rely solely on the platforms themselves, AVOD sites count on the effort of three parties; creators, viewers, and platforms to govern the appropriateness of the content posted. While both social media players employ machines and human resources to do content checks, they have also publicly outlined community guidelines that list the dos and don'ts for millions of content generators and audiences. The code of conduct includes categories of content that will be banned or removed if a breach occurs. Such policies aim to build a creative and welcoming online environment of 'safety, diversity, inclusion, and authenticity' (TikTok 2022). Not only the creators are reminded to adhere to the rules, but also viewers can report or flag any videos conveniently if they notice any violations such as copyright infringement and deceptive or misinformed practices.

YouTube and TikTok offer content creators an 'information box' (YouTube) or 'caption' (TikTok) to include any additional information such as credits or a list of references. However, it is up to the creators whether to add in and the amount of data to include. TikTok also has a word limit of 300 characters for its caption, which reduces the uploader's flexibility to cover more information (Ahmed 2021), even though TikTokers can still add supplementary information in the comment section. On YouTube, several widely followed channels are offering history-related content, yet only a few provide references besides giving credits. 'Crash Course' (Crash Course n.d.) and 'It's History' (It's History n.d.) are two popular YouTubers that include a reading list for some of their videos on historical subjects. However, it is unclear how much information presented in the videos is from the referred publications and how one may conveniently locate the supporting evidence from the listed materials to a corresponding statement made in these videos. As a result, despite that some YouTubers and TikTokers recognise the need to include sources, unfortunately, neither the 'information box' nor the 'caption' is a convenient instrument for providing references.

Aside from the information box or caption, comments are also supported on YouTube and TikTok. As addressed earlier, allowing comments allows audiences and content creators to exchange perspectives and information. However, YouTubers and TikTokers can disable the comment function for all or selected videos (Google 2022a, TikTok n.d.). For YouTube and TikTok-like AVOD, rather than the sources of information, they seem to be more concerned with copyright issues. This attitude is shown in both companies having relatively comprehensive copyright management programmes, such as YouTube's Content ID and Content Verification Program (Google 2022b) and TikTok's Intellectual Property Policy (TikTok 2021). Their emphasis on copyright may be driven by the nature of their business, as both are requesting content creators to upload original or authorised works.

3.3.1.4 Vimeo

Vimeo's business model is different from the commonly seen SVOD like the ones mentioned earlier. Vimeo charges content creators based on tiered pricing and the viewers watch for free. This choice is because Vimeo offers exclusive benefits for content uploaders, such as higher quality videos, advanced privacy settings, and pay-per-view videos, i.e., transactional video on demand (TVOD). Vimeo's ad-free strategy also helps content creators to engage their audiences more effectively, especially for business purposes. Vimeo shares some standard features with both the SVOD and AVOD sites. For example, the 'community guidelines' and 'comments' sections are akin to that of YouTube and TikTok, whereas 'credits' and 'categories' are like Netflix, Amazon Prime Video, and Disney+'s practices. These features have been discussed in Section 3.3.1.1 on their uses and limitations for information validation.

3.3.1.5 History Channel

'History', often known as the 'History Channel', was originally a television channel curating historical documentaries and docuseries. However, it now supports viewers to stream their content online via SVOD platforms like Hulu and Philo. In 2006, 'History' launched its YouTube channel and, in 2021, a TikTok account. Since then, it regularly posted selected or cropped videos on both platforms. Therefore, the tools and features offered by 'History' for its films and series correspond to those provided by the different OTT providers, as reviewed in the preceding paragraphs. Moreover, it is noted that 'History' describes itself as 'the most trustworthy source of informational entertainment in media' (History n.d.). The choice of words is interesting because producing something both 'trustworthy' and 'entertainment' is not an easy task. Scholars like Stoddard argued that audiences could misread the information conveyed in the works of 'History' as 'objective' and 'neutral', which were, in fact, 'value-laden ideological perspectives'. Stoddard termed such a phenomenon 'the History Channel effect' (Stoddard 2009a, 80).

3.3.1.6 TED

TED has been known for its talks which are viewable online since 2006 (TED n.d.a, b). TED is not technically operating as a pure video streaming provider but a non-profit that aims to spread ideas with its talks, conferences, and community. Their talks can be streamed from their website or TED YouTube channel. Among all the discussed platforms in this chapter, TED is probably the most prudent with information credibility. Their stress on accuracy and transparency is central to TED's content guidelines (TED n.d.a, b). According to the guidelines, TED follows a rigorous process to check presentations' content, including the employment of 'curators', 'fact-checkers', and 'topic-specific advisors' to ensure the information presented is '100% credible' and proper to the knowledge of the time. This approach is analogous to the practice of peer-view for written publications. TED also encourages audiences to raise concerns or flag issues, an exercise like the earlier discussed AVOD platforms.

TED generally provides four sets of information for the videos listed on their official website: introduction, transcript, resource list, and footnotes. Not all four elements are available for every talk published on TED, but the opening and transcript are available in most cases. The introduction section contains an abstract, the speaker's information, and the time and event of the talk. A transcript is provided on the side, in some cases, in multiple language options and can be enabled as subtitles while playing the video. The resource list and footnotes, if available, are more useful for audiences to track provenance. The resource list includes publications relevant to the talk, and the footnotes provide references that correspond to specific statements and timestamps of the talk. 'A History of Indigenous Languages and How to Revitalize Them' (Morcom 2019) and 'The Gender-Fluid History of the Philippines' (Villarta 2020) are two examples where both a resource list and footnotes are provided. Moreover, TED also endeavours to correct any misinformation found in the talks by updating the footnotes (see the correction made for 'How Symbols and Brands Shape Our Humanity' (Millman 2019) or removing the video entirely (TED n.d.a, b). These practices undoubtedly give TED videos more credibility because viewers can go through the references for supporting data, evidence, and the latest updates.

3.3.2 The EHM Approach to Computational Validation of Historical Information in Films

As discussed in Section 1.2, traditionally, historians used citations and notes as standard 'procedures intended to communicate an effect of authenticity' (Ginzburg 2012, 21). Since modern times, historians also normally use the footnote as 'the one form of proof supplied in support of their assertions' (Grafton 1994, 1995, 1997). Yet, these traditional history practices have not entered the audio-visual digital production. Information validation and provenance checking have a long-lasting tradition in historical sciences. Today, history-based films are facing similar challenges without taking advantage of this experience (Baildon & Damico 2009, 265–266, Nanetti et al. 2016). Consequentially, Sam Wineburg and Sarah McGrew's research inferred historians find it problematic when discerning the credibility of information online, not to mention the difficulties for students and the public.

Section 3.3.1 has outlined how online streaming platforms are thriving on the distribution and exchange of information in the audio-visual format. Certainly, as a convenient, accessible, and affordable resource, online videos play an increasingly important role in the people's pursuit of knowledge. However, this vast content often lacks trackable sources, and history-based productions can also be subjective and filled with dramatic licence. Although the video streaming providers have already offered some tools like genre classifications, comments, and selections of references, this information is not always available, satisfying and updated. Even TED—which is the seemingly most meticulous among all the ten platforms reviewed in Section 3.3.1 and follows a thorough process to ensure all information is correct and (hopefully) up to date—does not have annotated references for all its talks online.

To partially address this issue, the industry engages historians to participate more actively in producing history-based films since long (O'connor 1988, 1200–1201, Toplin 1988, 1226). Raack recognised that such a cross-disciplinary effort could generate products that are both 'creative' and 'accurate' and help to improve the public's understanding of the past (Raack 1983, 432). In the meantime, viewers are asked to become more skilled in interpreting moving images starting at a young age. Educators, while using audio-visual media as a supporting device to accompany incumbent methods, bear the responsibility to develop students' film literacy (O'connor 1988, 1208–1209, Baildon & Damico 2009, 280–281, Kelly 2019, 33–34, Barsch 2020, 78). Besides the efforts of history professionals, educators, and audiences, some companies have also endeavoured to resolve the issue of information credibility with examples like Boclips and InVID WeVerify that have been discussed above. Yet, as examined in Section 3.3.1, these attempts seem not sufficient to provide the user with relevant references about the historical information conveyed via online video streaming.

In 2015, following up on a meeting at Microsoft Research in Beijing, Andrea Nanetti, Chin-Yew Lin, and Siew Ann Cheong discussed how EHM could work on the validation of information in the (semi) automatic acquisition of semantic knowledge and machine reading for news indexing/summary taking advantage of the humanities experiences (Nanetti et al. 2016). Since then, inspired by this discussion, EHM is working on a method for video-content validation. In 2021–2022, Andrea Nanetti, assisted by Nur Afiqah Binte Abdul Latiff (Singapore United Traineeship Programme), Peisen Xu (NTU Part-Time Graduate Student Work Scheme), and Yifang Cui (NTU Research Assistant), designed and prototyped an online interactive system for short-form documentary films to serve as a test bed for the for EHM video-content-validation method. As an initial set of video materials, this online interactive system used short-form animated documentaries produced by EHM for Leonardo da Vinci's comments on Francesco di Giorgio Martini's 'Treatise on Architecture' (Nanetti et al. 2020a, Nanetti 2021a–h, Nanetti 2022) and other content-wise-related videos available online (e.g., Royal Collection Trust 2012, The Israel Museum, Jerusalem 2016, The University of Sydney 2018). A parallel set of video materials focused on pre-modern multicultural travel accounts (i.e., Marco Polo, Ibn Battuta, Ma Huan) was selected from online platforms worldwide.

Overall, the EHM online video system involves the communication of five main components: user interaction, front-end, application programming interface (API), back-end, and database management. The request for information moves upstream with each component communicating to the next component after processing the user's request (i.e., the front-end requests the information from the API to obtain the information from the backend). Likewise, information flows from the database to the user through stage-by-stage communications (refer to Figure 3.2). Here, a focus on the back-end system of the NTU video streaming application allows an understanding where the new EHM

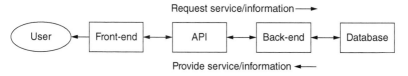

Figure 3.2 High-level flow of information.

Source: Diagram created by Nur Afiqah Binte Abdul Latiff.

video-content-validation method has its foundation. The workflow of the back-end system includes three objectives: database management, mapping objects to fields in the database, and passing instructions to be executed by the back-end system. Figure 3.3 shows the flow of these three objectives through the different objects/classes.

The database, among other information, includes the video URL link retrieved from the cloud storage, Amazon S3 Cloud. So, the database manager can update the SQL database through UpdateSpreadSheetData.php (i.e., a function available in the current EHM dashboard for admin users to update data from a specified Google Sheets file to a SQL database; Figure 3.4). Then, the objects declared in the codes are mapped into the fields of the SQL database (Figure 3.5). This procedure has two steps. First, objects and fields are declared in VidItem and SQL database respectively (Figures 3.6 and 3.7). Afterwards, VideoItemMapper is coded to map the objects in the fields. The items in VidItem can then be used to pass instruction.

The instructions for the back-end system are organised in four main classes: VideoItemDAO, VideoItemSqlDAO, VideoManager, and VideoRS (Figure 3.8). VideoItemDAO and VideoItemSqlDAO were

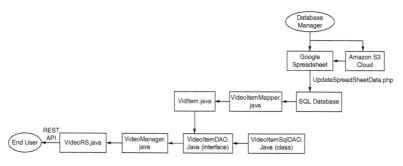

Figure 3.3 Video streaming back-end workflow.

Source: Diagram created by Nur Afiqah Binte Abdul Latiff.

Figure 3.4 Database management.

Source: Diagram created by Nur Afiqah Binte Abdul Latiff.

Figure 3.5 Mapping objects to database fields.

Source: Diagram created by Nur Afiqah Binte Abdul Latiff.

```
11  public class VidItem extends BaseModel {
12      /*
13      VidItem class used to declare objects for the
    model.
14      */
15      private String vidId;
16      private String title;
17      private String projAcronym;
18      private String vidUrl;
19      private String thumbnail;
20      private String description;
21      private String duration;
22      private Integer height;
23      private Integer width;
24  }
25
```

Figure 3.6 Objects in VidItem.java.

Source: Diagram created by Nur Afiqah Binte Abdul Latiff.

used to access data from the SQL database. DAO (Data Access Objects; see Baeldung 2021) is a layer to separate databases from business operations. Using DAO to perform CRUD (Create, Read, Update, Delete) operations, VideoItemDAO and VideoItemSqlDAO can manipulate the database safely. Additionally, DAO allows access to only necessary functions resulting in a cleaner code to pass instructions. A

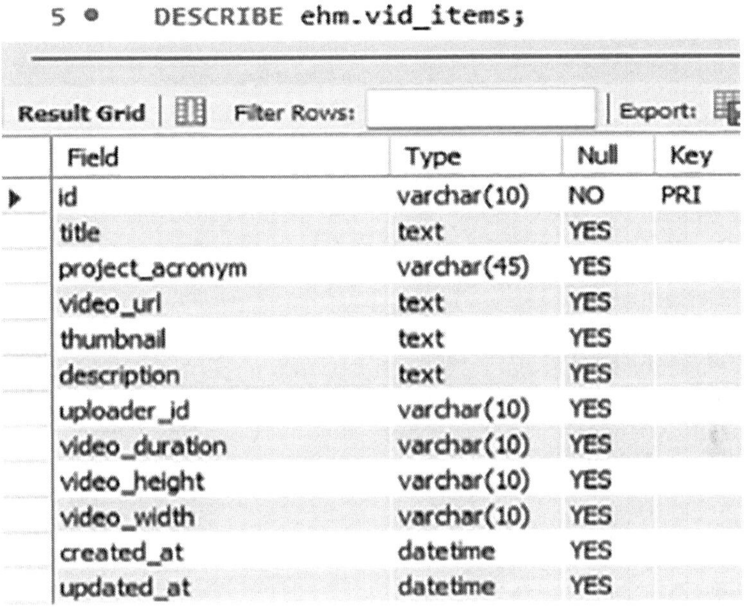

5 ●   DESCRIBE ehm.vid_items;

Field	Type	Null	Key
▶ id	varchar(10)	NO	PRI
title	text	YES	
project_acronym	varchar(45)	YES	
video_url	text	YES	
thumbnail	text	YES	
description	text	YES	
uploader_id	varchar(10)	YES	
video_duration	varchar(10)	YES	
video_height	varchar(10)	YES	
video_width	varchar(10)	YES	
created_at	datetime	YES	
updated_at	datetime	YES	

Result Grid | ▦ Filter Rows: | Export: ▥

Figure 3.7 Field names in SQL database.

Source: Diagram created by Nur Afiqah Binte Abdul Latiff.

VideoManager calls for functions to be executed. These functions include methods to read from the database as declared in the DAO.

Finally, VideoRS allows users to interact (e.g., reading data, executing a function with the website through REST API). VideoRS uses the JAX-RS package that helps developers to create REST API applications (Oracle 2014). The RS class includes *@Path* to perform Hypertext Transfer Protocol (HTTP) methods such as *@GET, @ POST,* and *@DELETE.* The API communicates information between front-end and back-end systems. Testing if the API of the new EHM

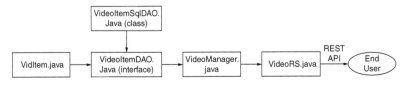

Figure 3.8 Instructions to run the back-end system.

Source: Diagram created by Nur Afiqah Binte Abdul Latiff.

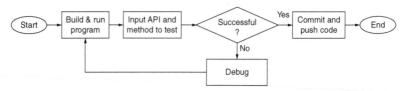

Figure 3.9 Testing the API.

Source: Diagram created by Nur Afiqah Binte Abdul Latiff.

interface performs as desired was done through a platform, Postman. After successfully running the program, a request was sent to test the API in the testing platform as shown in Figure 3.9. Additional query parameters may be required before sending the request.

The EHM suite of tools empowers this simple and robust foundation and brings it towards a FAIRification of historical information, which means high-quality and fast-tracked information (Tóth-Czifra 2020, 236). For example, as a forerunner, the Renaissance engineer Giovanni Fontana (ca 1395–ca 1455) drew an illustration of a magic lantern devised for the projection of devils to frighten the enemy (Birkenmajer 1932, Sparavigna 2013, 3). In Fontana's *Bellicorum insrumentorum liber* (ca 1420), on technology and war machines, he labels the drawing of the magic lantern with a Latin caption, *apparentia nocturna ad terrorem videntium* ('appearing at night to frighten the viewers') (Fontana ca 1420, 70 *recto*). In the mid-seventeenth century, the Flemish Jesuit André Tacquet (1612–1660) used the magic lantern to give an illustrated lecture (Musser 1999, 87). Since then, images have been a constant companion in science lectures, from the magic lantern to computer-powered presentation programmes. This practice moved from slides to films and from illustrated talks to documentaries (Musser 1999, 87–90). The EHM method and tools for video-content validation can be considered a further step in using (moving) images for documentary purposes.

EHM uses human-selected Wikipedia links as multilingual identifiers before automatically investigating the provenance and validation of relevant historical information. Fact-checking uses an automatic and dynamic online federated search for publications, images, and videos. This tool has a uniform design and can share data as described in Section 1.3. Thanks to formal collaborations with academic publishers, including Taylor and Francis, Scopus-Elsevier, and other online resource infrastructures, EHM uses their APIs to provide the service. Finally, the EHM system for videos serves both creators and the audience. On the one hand, EHM provides audio-visual creators of history-based films with a comprehensive set of tools to engage their audiences and generate new historical knowledge as transparently as possible. On the other hand, the audience can verify video content by matching stories with what they can learn from the EHM search tool.

References

Ahmed, Arooj (2021). "TikTok Is Increasing the Caption Character Limit to 300, and Testing A New Tip Feature for Users to Support Their Favorite Creators with". *Digital Information World*, November 2, 2021. https://www. digitalinformationworld.com/2021/11/tiktok-is-increasing-caption-character. html

Algar, James, Clyde Geronimi, & Jack Kinney (Directors) (1943). *Victory through Air Power*. Walt Disney Productions. 1 hr., 10 min.

Azor, Richard Ojinnakaeze, Uche Donatus Asogwa, Edna Nwanyiuzor Ogwu, & Anselm Apex Apeh (2020). "YouTube Audio-Visual Documentaries: Effect on Nigeria Students' Achievement and Interest in History Curriculum". *The Journal of Educational Research 113*(5), 317–326. https://doi.org/10.1080/002 20671.2020.1819182

Baeldung (2021). "The DAO Pattern in Java". Accessed March 23, 2022. https:// www.baeldung.com/java-dao-pattern

Baildon, Mark, & James S. Damico (2009). "How Do We Know? Students Examine Issues of Credibility with a Complicated Multimodal Web-Based Text". *Curriculum Inquiry*, *39*(2), 265–285. https://doi.org/10.1111/J.1467-873X.2009.00443.X

Bakare, Lanre (2020). "UK Culture Secretary to Ask Netflix for 'Health Warning' that the Crown Is Fictional". *The Guardian*, November 29, 2020. https://www.theguardian.com/tv-and-radio/2020/nov/29/the-crown-netflix-health-warning-fictional-oliver-dowden

Barsch, Sebastian (2020). "Does Experience with Digital Storytelling Help Students to Critically Evaluate Educational Videos about History?" *History Education Research Journal*, *17*(1), 67–80. https://doi.org/10.18546/ HERJ.17.1.06

BBC (2020). "The Crown: Netflix Has 'No Plans' for Fiction Warning". December 6, 2020. https://www.bbc.com/news/entertainment-arts-55207871

Beattie, Keith (2004). *Documentary Screens: Non-Fiction Film and Television*. Hampshire and New York: Palgrave Macmillan. https://doi.org/10.1007/ 978-0-230-62803-8

Benzoni, Maria Matilde (2016). "Prefazione all'edizione italiana". In Serge Gruzinski, *Abbiamo ancora bisogno della storia? Il senso del passato nel mondo globalizzato*, xi–xiv. Milan: Raffaello Cortina Editore.

Birkenmajer, Aleksander Ludwik (1932). "Zur Lebensgeschichte und wissen-schaftlichen Tätigkeit von Giovanni Fontana (1395?-1455?)". *Isis*, *17*(1), 34–53. https://www.journals.uchicago.edu/doi/10.1086/346636

Boclips (n.d.). "Curated Educational Videos for Student Learning". https://www.boclips.com/

Capra, Frank, & Anatole Litvak (Directors) (1942–1945). *Why We Fight*. U.S. Army Pictorial Services. 6 hr., 57 min. (7 films).

Crash Course (n.d.). "CrashCourse". *YouTube*. Accessed May 17, 2022. https://www.youtube.com/channel/UCX6b17PVsYBQ0ip5gyeme-Q

Curiosity Stream (2015). "Storm Over Europe | Part 1: Cimbrians and Teutons". Accessed December 8, 2021 (later, removed from the website). https://curiosity stream.com/video/993

D'sa, Benicia (2005). "Social Studies in the Dark: Using Docudramas to Teach History". *The Social Studies* 96(1), 9–13. https://doi.org/10.3200/TSSS.96.1.9-13

Duckworth, Jack (1981). "History on the Screen". *Teaching History* 29(February), 32–35. https://www.jstor.org/stable/43255830

Eghbal, Afarin (Director) (2011). *Abuelas*. National Film and Television School (NFTS). 9 min.

Folman, Ari (Director) (2008). *Waltz with Bashir*. Sony Pictures Classics. 1 hr., 30 min. https://www.amazon.com/Waltz-Bashir-Ron-Ben-Yishai/dp/B0028X38GA

Fontana (ca 1420). *Bellicorum instrumentorum liber, cum figuris et fictitijs literis conscriptus*. MS. Munich: Bayerische Staatsbibliothek, Cod.icon. 242. https://daten.digitale-sammlungen.de/~db/0001/bsb00013084/images/index.html?id=00013084&fip=67.164.64.97&no=4&seite=21

Ginzburg, Carlo (1986). *Il filo e le tracce. Vero falso finto*. Bologna: Feltrinelli (*Threads and Traces. True False Fictive*, translated from Italian to English by Anne C. Tedeschi, & John Tedeschi. Berkeley, Los Angeles, and London: University of California Press, 2012).

Ginzburg, Carlo (2012). "Microhistory, Two or Three Things that I Know About It". In *Threads and Traces. True False Fictive*, translated from Italian to English by Anne C. Tedeschi, & John Tedeschi, 193–214. Berkeley, Los Angeles, and London: University of California Press (Original work: *Il filo e le tracce. Vero falso finto*. Bologna: Feltrinelli, 1986). https://doi.org/10.1086/448699

Google (2022a). "Learn about Comment Settings". Accessed May 12, 2022. https://support.google.com/youtube/answer/9483359#zippy=%2Cdisable-comments

Google (2022b). "Overview of Copyright Management Tools". Accessed May 12, 2022. https://support.google.com/youtube/answer/9245819?hl=en&ref_topic=9282364

Grafton, Anthony (1994). "The Footnote from de Thou to Ranke". *History & Theory*, *33*, 53–76. https://doi.org/10.2307/2505502

Grafton, Anthony (1995). *Die tragischen Ursprünge der deutschen Fußnote*. Berlin: Wagenbach.

Grafton, Anthony (1997). *The Footnote: A Curious History*. Cambridge, MA: Harvard University Press. https://archive.org/details/footnotecurioush0000graf/mode/2up

Gruzinski, Serge (2015). *L'histoire, pour quoi faire?* Paris: Librairie Arthème Fayard.

Haines, Tim, & Jasper James (Directors) (1999). *Walking with Dinosaurs.* BBC Natural History Unit. 3 hr. (6 episodes). https://www.amazon.com/Walking-with-Dinosaurs-Season-1/dp/B000J42WDK

Herlihy, David (1988). "Am I a Camera? Other Reflections on Film and History". *The American Historical Review*, *93*(5), 1186–1192. https://doi.org/10.2307/1873533

Hess, Diana (2007). "From Banished to Brother Outsider, Miss Navajo to An Inconvenient Truth: Documentary Films as Perspective Laden Narratives". *Social Education*, *71*(4), 194–199. https://www.socialstudies.org/system/files/publications/articles/se_710407194.pdf

Hicks-Jenkins, Clive (2013). "Interview with Barry Purves Part 2: In the Realm of the Senses". *Clive Hicks-Jenkins' Artlog*, July 16, 2013. https://clivehicksjenkins.wordpress.com/2013/07/16/interview-with-barry-purves-part-2-in-the-realm-of-the-senses/

History (n.d.). "History". *YouTube*. Accessed May 10, 2022. https://www.youtube.com/c/HISTORY/featured?app=desktop

Honess Roe, Annabelle (2016). "Animated Documentary". In *Contemporary Documentary*, edited by Daniel Marcus, & Selmin Kara, 42–56. London and New York: Routledge. https://doi.org/10.4324/9781315725499

Howard, Ron (Director) (2015). *In the Heart of the Sea.* Warner Bros, Village Roadshow Pictures, and RatPac-Dune Entertainment. 2hr., 1 min. https://www.netflix.com/sg/title/80017529

It's History. (n.d.) "It's History". *YouTube*. Accessed May 17, 2022. https://www.youtube.com/c/ITSHISTORY

Jackson, Martin A. (1973). "Film as a Source Material: Some Preliminary Notes toward a Methodology". *The Journal of Interdisciplinary History*, *4*(1), 73–80. https://doi.org/10.2307/202358

Kelly, Mills T. (2019). *Teaching History in the Digital Age.* Ann Arbor, MI: The University of Michigan.

Kennedy, Ricky (Director) (2014). *The History of Time Travel.* Pineywood Pictures. 1 hr., 11 min. https://www.amazon.com/History-Time-Travel-Daniel-May/dp/B07PB7BK7L/ref=sr_1_91?crid=3T6GZM4JRAQPD&keywords=history&qid=1652773799&refinements=p_n_theme_browse-bin%3A2650367011&rnid=2650362011&s=instant-video&sprefix=history%2Cinstant-video%2C306&sr=1-91

Kleinman, Scott (2016). "Digital Humanities Projects with Small & Unusual Data: Some Experiences from the Trenches". *Scott Kleinman* (blog), March 15, 2016. http://scottkleinman.net/blog/2016/03/15/digital-humanities-projects-with-small-and-unusual-data/

Kobiela, Dorota, & Hugh Welchman (Directors) (2017). *Loving Vincent.* Breakthru Films, Trademark Films. 1 hr., 34 min. https://www.amazon.com/Loving-Vincent-Douglas-Booth/dp/B0792CS9QR

Koetsier, John (2020). "2 Million Creators Make 6-Figure Incomes On YouTube, Instagram, Twitch Globally". *Forbes*, October 5, 2020. https://www.forbes.com/sites/johnkoetsier/2020/10/05/2-million-creators-make-6-figure-incomes-on-youtube-instagram-twitch-globally/?sh=2d95a7fb23be

Kousha, Kayvan, Mike Thelwall, & Mahshid Abdoli (2012). "The Role of Online Videos in Research Communication: A Content Analysis of YouTube Videos Cited in Academic Publications". *Journal of the American Society for Information Science and Technology*, *63*(9), 1710–1727. https://doi.org/10.1002/ASI.22717

Lavin, Matthew (2021). "Why Digital Humanists Should Emphasize Situated Data over Capta". *DHQ: Digital Humanities Quarterly*, *15*(2). http://www.digitalhumanities.org/dhq/vol/15/2/000556/000556.html#:~:text=In%20the%20closing%20section%20of,for%20conversation%20with%20other%20disciplines

Marcus, Alan S., Richard J. Paxton, & Peter Meyerson (2006). "'The Reality of It All': History Students Read the Movies". *Theory & Research in Social Education*, *34*(4), 516–552. https://doi.org/10.1080/00933104.2006.10473320

Marcus, Alan S. (2005). "'It Is as It Was': Feature Film in the History Classroom". *The Social Studies*, *96*(2), 61–67. https://doi.org/10.3200/TSSS.96.2.61-67

Marcus, Alan S., & Jeremy D. Stoddard (2010). "The Inconvenient Truth about Teaching History with Documentary Film: Strategies for Presenting Multiple Perspectives and Teaching Controversial Issues". *The Social Studies*, *100*(6), 279–284. https://doi.org/10.1080/00377990903283957

McKerns, Joseph P. (2019). "Television Docudramas: The Image as History". *Journalism History*, *7*(1), 24–40. https://doi.org/10.1080/00947679.1980.12066937

McLane, Betsy A. (2012). *A New History of Documentary Film*. New York and London: Continuum International Publishing Group. https://doi.org/10.5040/9781501340222

Metzger, Scott Alan (2010). "Maximizing the Educational Power of History Movies in the Classroom". *The Social Studies*, *101*(3), 127–136. https://doi.org/10.1080/00377990903284047

Mezaris, Vasileios, Lyndon Nixon, Symeon Papadopoulos, & Denis Teyssou (Eds.) (2019). *Video Verification in the Fake News Era*. *Video Verification in the Fake News Era*. Cham: Springer International Publishing. https://doi.org/10.1007/978-3-030-26752-0

Millman, Debbie (2019). "How Symbols and Brands Shape Our Humanity". Filmed December 2019 in Palm Springs, US. TED video, 13:37. https://www.ted.com/talks/debbie_millman_how_symbols_and_brands_shape_our_humanity

Moore, Michael (Director) (2002). *Bowling for Columbine*. United Artists. 1 hr., 59 min. https://www.amazon.com/Bowling-Columbine-Jacobo-Arbenz/dp/B0030MGVWQ

Morcom, Lindsay (2019). "A History of Indigenous Languages – and How to Revitalize Them". Filmed February 2019 in Queen's University, Canada. TED video, 13:21. https://www.ted.com/talks/lindsay_morcom_a_history_of_indigenous_languages_and_how_to_revitalize_them?language=en

Morgan, Peter (2016–2020). *The Crown*. Left Bank Pictures, Sony Pictures Television Production UK and Sony Pictures Television. Four seasons. https://www.netflix.com/sg/title/80025678

MUBI (n.d.). "How Can I Check If a Film May Contain Sensitive Content?" Accessed May 13, 2022. https://help.mubi.com/article/266-how-can-i-check-if-a-film-may-contain-sensitive-content

Mulvey, Laura (2007). "Compilation Film as 'Deferred Action': Vincent Monnikendam's Mother Dao, the Turtle-like". In *Projected Shadows: Psychoanalytic Reflections on the Representation of Loss in Europe Cinema*, edited by Andrea Sabbadini, 109–113. London and New York: Routledge. https://doi.org/10.4324/9780203946862-17

Murray, Noel (2017). "10 Great Animated Documentaries". *PBS Independent Lens*, February 14, 2017. https://www.pbs.org/independentlens/blog/great-animated-documentaries/

Musser, Charles (1999). "Documentary". In *The Oxford History of World Cinema. The definitive history of cinema worldwide*, edited by Nowell-Smith, Geoffrey, 86–95. New York: Oxford University Press USA OSA. First published by OUP in 1996. https://ebookcentral.proquest.com/lib/ntusg/detail.action?docID=431159

Nanetti, Andrea (Director) (2021a). On the Width of the Angles. May 14, 2021. Engineering Historical Memory, 1:51. https://ehm-video.s3.ap-southeast-1.amazonaws.com/On+the+width+of+the+angles.mp4

Nanetti, Andrea (Director) (2021b). The Cylinder. May 14, 2021. Engineering Historical Memory, 1:44. https://ehm-video.s3.ap-southeast-1.amazonaws.com/The+Cylinder.mp4

Nanetti, Andrea (Director) (2021c). Heron's Fountain. May 14, 2021. Engineering Historical Memory, 2:57. https://ehm-video.s3.ap-southeast-1.amazonaws.com/On+water+in+the+jar-.mp4

Nanetti, Andrea (Director) (2021d). On the Natural Point. May 14, 2021. Engineering Historical Memory, 1:22. https://ehm-video.s3.ap-southeast-1.amazonaws.com/On+the+natural+point.mp4

Nanetti, Andrea (Director) (2021e). On Centre of Suspended Gravity, viz. How to Raise a Column. May 14, 2021. Engineering Historical Memory, 2:48. https://ehm-video.s3.ap-southeast-1.amazonaws.com/Centre+of+suspended+gravity+(Full+resolution).mp4

Nanetti, Andrea (Director) (2021f). On the Sea Wave. May 14, 2021. Engineering Historical Memory, 1:09. https://ehm-video.s3.ap-southeast-1.amazonaws.com/On+the+wave-.mp4

Nanetti, Andrea (Director) (2021g). On Rope and Weight. Mechanical Devices for Architects. May 14, 2021. Engineering Historical Memory, 1:51. https://ehm-video.s3.ap-southeast-1.amazonaws.com/Rope+and+weight.mp4

Nanetti, Andrea (Director) (2021h). On the Strength of the Rope. May 14, 2021. Engineering Historical Memory, 2:01. https://ehm-video.s3.ap-southeast-1.amazonaws.com/Strength+of+the+rope.mp4

Nanetti, Andrea (Director) (2022). Square and Circle. January 8, 2022. Engineering Historical Memory, 1:17. https://ehm-video.s3.ap-southeast-1.amazonaws.com/Circle+and+Square+MAIN_2.mp4

Nanetti, Andrea, & Davide Benvenuti (2019). "Animation of Two-Dimensional Pictorial Works into Multipurpose Three-Dimensional Objects. The Atlas of the Ships of the Known World depicted in the 1460 Fra Mauro's *Mappa Mundi* as a Showcase". *SCIRES-IT (SCIentific RESearch and Information Technology)*, *9*(2), 29–46. https://doi.org/10.2423%2Fi22394303v9n2p29

Nanetti, Andrea, & Davide Benvenuti (2021). "Engineering Historical Memory and the Interactive Exploration of Archival Documents. The Online Application for Pope Gregory X's Privilege for the Community of Mount Sinai (1274) as a Prototype". *Umanistica Digitale*, *10*, 325–357. https://uman isticadigitale.unibo.it/article/view/12567

Nanetti, Andrea, Zaqeer Radzi, & Davide Benvenuti (2021). "Crafting the Next Generation of Web-Based Learning Tools for Manuscript Artefacts. A Focus on Science, Technology, and Engineering Codices, World Maps, and Archival Documents in Exhibition Settings". *SCIRES-IT (SCIentific RESearch and Information Technology)*, *11*(1), 97–114. http://www.sciresit.it/article/view/13537

Nanetti, Andrea, & Yifang Cui (2022). "Acquiring Knowledge from Online Audiovisual Sources: Opportunities and Challenges for the Audience (Abstract)". In *Online Conference of the International Association for Media and Communication Research (IAMCR)*, Beijing, July 11–15, 2022. https://iamcr.org/beijing2022/abstract-books

Nanetti, Andrea, Chin-Yew Lin, & Siew Ann Cheong (2016). "Provenance and Validation from the Humanities to Automatic Acquisition of Semantic Knowledge and Machine Reading for News and Historical Sources Indexing/Summary". *The Asian Review of World Histories*, *4*(1), 125–132. https://doi.org/10.12773/arwh.2016.4.1.125

Nanetti, Andrea, Davide Benvenuti, Stefano Bertocci, Matteo Bigongiari, & Nguyen Khoi Vu (Eds.) (2020a). Francesco di Giorgio Martini's Treatise I on Civil and Military Architecture (1479-1481 CE). *Engineering Historical Memory*. Accessed May 19, 2022. https://engineeringhistoricalmemory.com/FGM.php

Nanetti, Andrea, Davide Benvenuti, Matteo Bigongiari, Zaqeer Radzi, & Stefano Bertocci (2020b). "Animation for the Study of Renaissance Treatises on Architecture. Francesco di Giorgio Martini's Corinthian Capital as a Showcase". *SCIRES-IT (SCIentific RESearch and Information Technology)*, *10*(2), 19–36. http://www.sciresit.it/article/view/13390/0

Nanetti, Andrea, Zaqeer Radzi, & Davide Benvenuti (2021). "Crafting the Next Generation of Web-Based Learning Tools for Manuscript Artefacts. A Focus on Science, Technology, and Engineering Codices, World Maps, and Archival Documents in Exhibition Settings". *SCIRES-IT (SCIentific RESearch and Information Technology)*, *11*(1), 97–114. http://www.sciresit.it/article/view/13537

Netflix (2018). *Medal of Honor*. Allentown Productions and Compari Entertainment. 7 hr., 18 min. (eight episodes). https://www.netflix.com/sg/title/80169786

Netflix (2019). *The Last Czars*. Nutopia. 4 hr., 31 min. (six episodes). https://www.netflix.com/sg/title/80211648

O'connor, John E. (1988). "History in Images/Images in History: Reflections on the Importance of Film and Television Study for an Understanding of the

Past". *The American Historical Review*, *93*(5), 1200–1209. https://www.jstor.org/stable/1873535

O'Toole, John (1992). *The Process of Drama: Negotiating Art and Meaning*. London and New York: Routledge. https://archive.org/details/processof dramane0000otoo/mode/2up

Ogunleye, Foluke (2005). "Television Docudrama as Alternative Records of History". *History in Africa*, 32, 479–484. https://www.jstor.org/stable/20065757

Oldman, Dominic (2021). "Digital Research, the Legacy of form and Structure and the ResearchSpace System". In *Information and Knowledge Organization in Digital Humanities*, edited by Koraljka Golub, & Ying-Hsang Liu, 131–153. London: Routledge. https://doi.org/10.4324/9781003131816-7

Oracle (2014). "29.2 Creating a RESTful Root Resource Class". Accessed March 25, 2022. https://docs.oracle.com/javaee/7/tutorial/jaxrs002.htm

Owens, Trevor (2011). "Defining Data for Humanists: Text, Artifact, Information or Evidence". *Journal of Digital Humanities*, *1*(1), 6–8. http://journalofdigital humanities.org/1-1/defining-data-for-humanists-by-trevor-owens/

Paronnaud, Vincent, & Marjane Satrapi (Directors) (2007). *Persepolis*. 2.4.7. Films, France 3 Cinéma, The Kennedy/Marshall Company. 1 hr., 36 min. https://www.amazon.com/Persepolis-Simon-Abkarian/dp/B0083GOVLW

Poehler, Amy (Director) (2022). *Lucy and Desi*. Imagine Documentaries and White Horse Pictures. 1 hr., 42 min. https://www.amazon.com/Lucy-Desi-Lucille-Ball/dp/B09QFN8WW9/ref=sr_1_171?crid=3T6GZM4JRAQ PD&keywords=history&qid=1652774158&refinements=p_n_theme_browse-bin%3A2650367011&rnid=2650362011&s=instant-video&sprefix=history%2 Cinstant-video%2C306&sr=1-171

Pronay, Nicholas (1983). "The 'Moving Picture' and Historical Research". *Journal of Contemporary History*, *18*, 365–395. https://www.jstor.org/stable/260543

Purves, Barry (Director) (1995). *Achilles*. Bareboards Productions, Channel Four Television. 11 min. https://mubi.com/films/achilles

Raack, Richard Charles (1983). "Historiography as Cinematography: A Prolegomenon to Film Work for Historians". *Journal of Contemporary History*, *18*(3), 411–438. https://www.jstor.org/stable/260545

Rall, Hans-Martin, Elke Reinhuber, & Wibke Weber (2018). "Little Red Bard: Shakespeare in the Realm of Animated Documentary". In *CONFIA 2018 – 6ᵗʰ International Conference on Illustration & Animation*, 38–50. Barcelos, Portugal: Instituto Politécnico do Cávado e do Ave. https://confia.ipca.pt/files/confia_2018_proceedings.pdf

Rambsy, Kenton (2017). "Cultural Front: Making a Case for "Small Data" Humanities Projects". *Cultural Front* (blog), 13 September. https://www.culturalfront.org/2017/09/making-case-for-small-data-humanities.html?m=1

Roe, Annabelle Honess (2013). *Animated Documentary*. Basingstoke: Palgrave Macmillan. https://link.springer.com/book/10.1057/9781137017468

Rosenstone, Robert A. (1988). "History and Images/History in Words: Reflections on the Possibility of Really Putting History onto Film". *The American Historical Review*, *93*(5), 1173–1185. https://doi.org/10.2307/1873532

Rosenstone, Robert A. (2004). "Inventing Historical Truth on the Silver Screen". *Cinéaste, 29*(2), 29–33. https://www.jstor.org/stable/41689711

Rosenthal, Alan (1999). "Taking the Stage: Developments and Challenges". In *Why Docudrama? Fact-Fiction on Film and TV*, edited by Alan Rosenthal, 1–11. Carbondale and Edwardsville: Southern Illinois University Press. https://archive.org/details/whydocudramafact0000unse/mode/2up

Royal Collection Trust (2012). "Leonardo da Vinci: Anatomist". YouTube video, 3:21. https://youtu.be/SdxEF51kY_4

Satrapi, Marjane (2004). *The Complete Persepolis*. New York: Pantheon Books.

Schöch, Christof (2013). "Big? Smart? Clean? Messy? Data in the Humanities". *Journal of Digital Humanities, 2*(3), 2–13. http://journalofdigitalhumanities.org/2-3/big-smart-clean-messy-data-in-the-humanities/

Scrubber, Ray E. (2001). "Dramatic History or Historical Drama". *Academic Exchange Quarterly, 5*(2), 133–137. http://www.rapidintellect.com/AEQweb/mo133sep.htm

Shomali, Amer, & Paul Cowan (Director) (2014). *The Wanted 18*. National Film Board of Canada. 1 hr., 15 min. https://www.amazon.com/Wanted-18-Alison-Darcy/dp/B073SGGLTY

Simonsen, Thomas Mosebo (2011). "Categorising YouTube". *MedieKultur, 27*(51), 72–93. https://doi.org/10.7146/mediekultur.v27i51.5483

Smith, Paul (1976). "Introduction". In *The Historian and Film*, edited by Paul Smith, 1–14. Cambridge, London, New York, and Melbourne: Cambridge University Press. https://doi.org/10.1017/CBO9780511896910.002

Sowa, Anna (2020). "*Nobody's Metaphor*: A Decolonial Film of Voices, Swords, and Brushstrokes". *Animationstudies 2.0* (blog), September 7, 2020. https://blog.animationstudies.org/?p=3767

Sowa, Remi (Director) (2019). *Nobody's Metaphor*. Chouette Films. 35 min.

Sparavigna, Amelia Carolina (2013). Giovanni de la Fontana, engineer and magician. *arXiv*. https://doi.org/10.48550/arXiv.1304.4588

Spielberg, Steven (Director) (1993). *Schindler's List*. Universal Pictures and Amblin Entertainment. 3 hr., 15 min. https://www.primevideo.com/detail/0OFIS1T1OYW5I7QDNOLWWVI5RZ/ref=atv_dp_share_mv

Staiger, Janet (2013). "Docudrama". In *Encyclopedia of Television*, edited by Horace Newcomb, 738–739. London and New York: Routledge.

Stoddard, Jeremy D. (2009a). "The History Channel Effect". *Phi Delta Kappan, 91*(4), 80. http://dx.doi.org/10.1177/003172171009100420

Stoddard, Jeremy D. (2009b). "The Ideological Implications of Using 'Educational' Film to Teach Controversial Events". *Curriculum Inquiry, 39*(3), 407–433. https://doi.org/10.1111/J.1467-873X.2009.00450.X

Stoddard, Jeremy D., & Alan S. Marcus (2010). "More Than 'Showing What Happened': Exploring the Potential of Teaching History with Film". *The High School Journal, 93*(2), 83–90. http://dx.doi.org/10.1353/hsj.0.0044

Suciu, Peter (2019). "The New History Channel is YouTube, But Can We Trust the Experts?" *Forbes*, October 22, 2019. https://www.forbes.com/sites/petersuciu/2019/10/22/the-new-history-channel-is-youtube-but-can-we-trust-the-experts/?sh=1924a2429213

TED (n.d.a). "History of TED". Accessed December 9, 2021. https://www.ted.com/about/our-organization/history-of-ted

TED (n.d.b). "TED Content Guidelines". Accessed December 9, 2021. https://www.ted.com/about/our-organization/our-policies-terms/ted-content-guidelines

The Israel Museum, Jerusalem (2016). "הדריאנוס: שובו של הקיסר" | Hadrian: An Emperor Cast in Bronze". YouTube video, 4:12. https://www.youtube.com/watch?v=nH2rkmT6tBA&t=252s

The University of Sydney (2018). "Rare Bites: The Renaissance of Euclid's 'Elements'". YouTube video, 31:25. https://www.youtube.com/watch?v=hRhSMCVgJdE

TikTok (2021). "Intellectual Property Policy". Last modified June 7, 2021. https://www.tiktok.com/legal/copyright-policy?lang=en

TikTok (2022). "Community Guidelines". Last modified February 2022. https://www.tiktok.com/community-guidelines

TikTok (n.d.). "Comments". Accessed May 12, 2022. https://support.tiktok.com/en/using-tiktok/messaging-and-notifications/comments

Toplin, Robert Brent (1988). "The Filmmaker as Historian". *The American Historical Review*, *93*(5), 1210–1227. https://www.jstor.org/stable/1873536

Toplin, Robert Brent (1991). "The Historian and Film: A Research Agenda". *The Journal of American History*, *78*(3), 1160–1163. https://doi.org/10.2307/2078957

Toplin, Robert Brent, & Jason Eudy (2002). "The Historian Encounters Film: A Historiography". *OAH Magazine of History*, *16*(4), 7–12. https://www.jstor.org/stable/25163542

Tóth-Czifra, Erzsébet (2020). "The Risk of Losing the Thick Description: Data Management Challenges Faced by the Arts and Humanities in the Evolving FAIR Data Ecosystem". In *Digital Technology and the Practices of Humanities Research*, edited by Jennifer Edmond, 235–266. Cambridge: Open Book Publishers. https://books.openbookpublishers.com/10.11647/obp.0192.pdf

Villarta, France (2020). "The Gender-Fluid History of the Philippines". Filmed February 2020 in Wells Fargo, US. TED video, 10:42. https://www.ted.com/talks/france_villarta_the_gender_fluid_history_of_the_philippines?language=en

Warren, Kate (2010). "Animation, Representation and the Power of the Personal Story: Persepolis". *Screen Education*, *58*, 117–123. https://openresearch-repository.anu.edu.au/bitstream/1885/220341/1/animation%2C%20representation%20and%20the%20power%20of%20the%20personal%20story.pdf

Weinstein, Paul B. (2001). "Movies as the Gateway to History: The History and Film Project". *The History Teacher*, *35*(1), 27–48. https://doi.org/10.2307/3054508

Wells, Paul (1999). "*Thou Art Translated*: Analyzing Animated Adaptations". In *Adaptations: From Text to Screen, Screen to Text*, edited by Deborah Cartmell, & Imelda Whelehan, 199–213. London and New York: Routledge. https://doi.org/10.4324/9781315006192

Wells, Paul (2002). *Animation: Genre and Authorship*. London: Wallflower Press.

WeVerify (n.d.). "Verification Plugin". Accessed May 10, 2022. https://weverify. eu/verification-plugin/

White, Hayden (1988). "Historiography and historiophoty". *The American Historical Review*, *93*(5), 1193–1199. https://doi.org/10.2307/1873534

Wyrwoll, Claudia (2014). *Social Media: Fundamentals, Models, and Ranking of User-Generated Content*. Hamburg: Springer Vieweg. https://doi.org/10.1007/ 978-3-658-06984-1

Yourcenar, Marguerite (1974). *Souvenirs pieux*. Paris: Gallimard.

Yourcenar, Marguerite (1991). *Dear Departed. A Memoir*, translated from French into English by Maria Louise Ascher. Henley-on-Thames: Aidan Ellis Publishing and New York: Farrar, Straus & Giroux.

4 Languages and Cultures at the Computational Turn

4.1 Gazing at the World as Seen from the Others

The French historian Fernand Braudel (1902–1985), in his 1960 essay, *Unité et diversité des sciences de l'homme* (Braudel 1960)/*Unity and Diversity in the Human Sciences* (Braudel 1980, 55–63), took into consideration how to learn from the failure of area studies in the post-World War II United States of America.

> The failure of area studies—in the normative domain, be it understood, for the works which they have inspired or themselves carried out have been by no means inconsiderable—must be a lesson to us. Perhaps our colleagues at Harvard, at Columbia, the members of the bold team in Seattle have not sufficiently widened the circle of their convocations. Hazarding themselves within the narrow confines of the present, in their studies on India or China they have only rarely appealed to historians for help, and never to my knowledge have they turned to geographers.
>
> (Braudel 1980, 62)

With this background, in 1963, Fernand Braudel established the first *Maison des Sciences de l'Homme* in Paris as a research institution to facilitate interdisciplinary research between human sciences and foster international collaboration between scholars. This institution, of which he was the first administrator (1963–1985), allowed him to recruit scholars from all over Europe and afar such as Eric Hobsbawn (1917–2012), who coined the concept of 'invented traditions' for modern national identity and nationalism (Hobsbawm & Ranger 1983, 1), and Immanuel Wallerstein (1930–2019), who pioneered a comprehensive approach to understanding the history and development of the modern world (Wallerstein (2004) provides a general overview of his works

DOI: 10.4324/9781003310860-4

published in the 1970s and 1980s). With this ground-breaking enterprise, Braudel initiated a unique task force to tackle the grand cultural challenge of understanding diversity and postcolonial recomposition or decolonisation in contemporary globalised society, beyond disciplinary boundaries and the Eurocentric modern prejudice (Pomart & Riche 2018).

The above-mentioned comment made by Braudel in 1960 on the failure of the USA area studies programme was similarly confirmed in the 1960s, 1970s, and 1980s (Szanton 2004, 10–11). Indeed in contemporary scholarship, Eurocentrism, which has since been morphing into America-centrism, is still putting the focus on European and North American culture or history to the exclusion of a wider view of the world (including the one of the native Americans) and its related knowledge and wisdom. According to Eugen Weber (1925–2007), Eurocentrism was embedded in the historical profession in the United States of America with the introduction of *Western Civilization* and *Proto-Western Civilisation* courses that can be traced back to 1903–1904 at Harvard University (Weber 1998, 206–207). Carol Gluck explains how America-centrism

> was capable of co-opting large chunks of the world's past, from Ancient Greece to the Renaissance, as part of a telos of History that led to these United States. Europe—as Americans imagined it—became part of America's past. It also constituted, until quite recently, most of what was taught as 'world history' in the schools ... ... Although it is institutionally customary to lump the histories of Asia, Africa, the Middle East, and often even Latin America into one great, undifferentiated "non-West," all 'area studies' were not created equal. Because post-war history drove historiography, U.S. foreign relations made China and Japan loom larger than India, the Middle East more salient than Africa, and the Soviet Union more riveting than the for-decades-disappeared past of Eastern Europe. The regions also created their own differences .... Because these subjects took their place in the universities when America stood at the unprecedently powerful, globally engaged moment in its history, their teleological links to the United States often inverted the European narrative. If Europe was America's past, America was Asia's future ... ... Like a newly energized Hegelian world spirit, American-style modernization appeared as the avatar of universal history, against which the pasts of the non-yet-modern could be measured.
>
> (Gluck 1998, 434)

Among the many innovative fruits inspired by Fernand Braudel and the *Maison des Sciences de l'Homme*, which is still vibrant and at the forefront of human sciences, internationally, the attention goes to three trailblazers, who are of paramount importance for the discourse undertaken by the present essay, because they share transculturalism (Herren et al. 2013, 1–3, 45–46). Transculturalism is crucial to nurture global citizenship with an awareness of the equal cultural value of the *other* (Cuccioletta 2002, König & Rakow 2016). In his famous and influential study on processes of cultural reconfiguration in early modern Cuba first published in 1940 as *Contrapunteo cubano del tabaco y el azúcar/Cuban Counterpoint: Tobacco and Sugar*, the Cuban anthropologist Fernando Ortiz Fernández (1881–1969) introduced the new technical term *transculturación/transculturalism* to describe the impact of cultures on one another as a result of involving the intellectual achievements of more than one people or society (Ortiz 1940, 1973; critical edition edited by Santi 2002). An English translation made from the Spanish by Harriet de Onís was published seven year later (Ortiz 1947) and had two further new editions by different publishers (Ortiz 1995, 2012). The French specialist in Latin American literature and civilisation, Françoise Moulin-Civil, wrote a comprehensive review paper on the impact of this work (Moulin-Civil 2005). According to the British-Polish anthropologist Bronislaw Malinowski (1884–1942), Ortiz aimed 'to replace various expression in use such as cultural exchange, acculturation, diffusion, migration or osmosis of culture, and similar ones that he considered inadequate' (Ortiz 1947, second page of the Introduction).

Since 2010, the journal *Transcultural Studies*, published by the Cluster of Excellence 'Asia and Europe in a Global Context: The Dynamics of Transculturality' of the Ruprecht-Karls-Universität Heidelberg, is 'committed to promoting the knowledge and research of transculturality in all disciplines' (Heidelberg University Publishing n.d.). This concept of transculturalism has also been investigated in different but complementary ways by several authors. Among others, the most prominent have been the seminal book *Orientalism* published by Edward W. Said (1935–2003) in 1978 (refer to Said 1978) and its long-lasting legacy (Curthoys & Ganguly 2007, Gürsoy Sökmen & Ertür 2008a, b), Valentin-Yves Mudimbe's *Invention of Africa* (Mudimbe 1988) that published the results of researches on the forces that shaped African history that the author carried out since 1962, and the unintendidly connected Amartya Sen's insights into the causes of poverty and inequality that, after having married Emma Rothschild in 1991, brought him the Nobel Memorial Prize in Economic Sciences

(1998) and the US National Humanities Medal (BBC 2012). As an indirect fruit of Braudel's *Maison des Sciences de l'Homme* can be also seen *Transcultura* (The International TRANSCULTURA Institute n.d.). *Transcultura* is the institute founded by Alain Le Pichon and Umberto Eco in 1988 on the occasion of the ninth centenary of the University of Bologna to promote reciprocal anthropology ('To renew the conceptual field of the human sciences, limited by the context of Western cultures where it has developed to this day/*pour renouveler le champ conceptuel des sciences humaines, limité par le contexte des cultures occidentales où il s'est développé jusqu'à ce jour*') and connect the international network of researchers and research institutions that Le Pichon was able to initiate with the programme 'Ethnology of France by researchers of the third-world' (*Ethnologie de la France par des chercheurs du tiers-monde*, 1983–1986).

In 1988, Eco, Le Pichon, and a small group of Chinese and African researchers launched a new programme called *Anthropology of the West* to create a transcultural international network able to discuss the *West* from the perspective the *other* according to the criteria proposed by the *other*. They started from the People's Republic of China. The programme organised a first conference *Frontiers of Knowledge* (Guangzhou/Canton, 1991) that developed into a seminar on *Misunderstandings in the Quest for the Universal* (itinerant, from Guangzhou/Canton to Beijing/Peking, 1993), the proceedings of which were published in Chinese as 独角兽与龙 (Le Pichon & Yue 1995a), French as *La Licorne et le Dragon* (Le Pichon & Yue 1995b, 2004, 2005), and English as *The Unicorn and the Dragon* (Le Pichon & Yue 1996). This book was an influential publication for the humanities and the arts in several countries and in different ways. For example, in 2012, the French historian Serge Gruzinski titled *L'aigle et le dragon/ The Eagle and the Dragon* his book on sixteenth-century globalisation (Gruzinski 2012, in French; and 2014, in English). In 2016, the artist Urs Fischer used the subtitle of the book, *Misunderstandings in the Quest for the Universal*, to title his show at the Gagosian Gallery, in New York (Michalarou 2016).

The book *The Unicorn and the Dragon* highlighted 'the role of Chinese culture in the process of invention of the reciprocal knowledge' between East and West. Le Pichon added to his introduction to the 2005 French edition a further significant statement: '*Invention de la connaissance réciproque et recréation, «impératifs catégoriques» que nous impose la mondialisation, si l'on peut encore espérer autre chose que ce magma informe de l'américanisation qui constitue aujourd'hui notre horizon*/Invention of reciprocal knowledge and re-creation, «categorical imperatives» that globalization imposes on us, if we can still hope for something other than the amorphous magma of Americanization which today constitutes our horizon' (Le Pichon & Yue 2005, 16). Later Eco and Le Pichon organised another seminar in Timbuktu (2000) with a follow up in Bologna that, then, promoted a series of conferences in Brussels, Paris, Goa, with a final one in Beijing (2007) focused on 'Order and Disorder', 'New Concepts of War and Peace', 'Human Rights', and 'Social Justice and Harmony'. In 2017, Luca Zan and Kent G. Deng worked on a survey on the East-West debate that is relevant to this discourse (Zan & Deng 2017).

In 1970, the Italian medievalist Gina Fasoli (1905–1992) wrote '*la volontà di conoscere i fatti umani non accetta le separazioni che la politica vorrebbe porre fra gli uomini*/the desire to know about human facts does not accept the separations that politics would like to place among human beings' (Pertusi 1970, 17). In 2001, this statement found an echo in the 'global hypothesis' theorised by Wolf Schäfer as a follow up to the call made by Murray Gell-Mann (1929–2019) to assess the global state of affairs (Gell-Mann 1997):

> Not too long ago the big picture of human history showed a small number of large local civilizations and a large number of small local cultures. The big picture today looks very different. A technoscientific civilization has begun to cover the globe. We are moving toward a global civilization with many local cultures. The local cultures are the flesh and bone of this world and the emerging technoscientific civilization is its nervous system.
>
> (Schäfer 2001, 302)

In 2009, William Brian Arthur published the results of his research on *The Nature of Technology* with the clear statement that 'more than anything else technology creates our world. It creates our wealth, our economy, our very way of being.' However, we still not have a clear understanding of how innovation works. There is no theory of innovation, and the established hegemony of a techno-scientific culture is becoming a major source of social uncertainty and instability that the human sciences need to address (Tomasin 2017, 38–39). Technology does not work alone. Race, religion, and language are more and more sources of uncertainty. India, China, and Africa are playing more and more important roles in the global arena. From the perspective of Thomas Kuhn (1922–1996) and his book on *Structure of Scientific Revolutions*, the global techno-scientific civilisation is the new paradigm shift (Kuhn 1970). In terms of the amelioration of the human condition, it does not offer more certainty for a better life at large than the previous, local, civilisations. However, it appeals to all of us based on promises of a longer and healthier life, a more sustainable economy, a more stable society, a diffused education, etc. The promise is that all this will happen at some point in the future. Academic disciplines, such as the History of Science and Technology (HST) and Science Technology and Society (STS), are studying these topics as key factors for a sustainable future.

Today, one could say that humanity needs all arts and sciences that have been experienced and accumulated over time and across space to guarantee this global techno-scientific civilization a sustainable future. Here, after cultural barriers, comes the issue of linguistic obstacles. From a historical sciences perspective, it is undeniable that the study of the European expansion on the oceans starting in the late fifteenth century must be shared globally (Benzoni 2016, xiii). However, it is also true that for the common good, 'it is only a question of orienting our historical vision, from a vision of conflict to another of shared roots, of adoption and collaboration' (Jacobucci 2015, 184). The treasure of human experiences is indeed a common heritage of humanity.

4.2 A New Tower of Babel?

In 1966, at the fifteenth annual meeting of the National Science Teachers Association, in New York City, Richard Feynman (1918–1988), Nobel Prize winner in Physics (1965), discussing about pseudoscience said that his father already taught him that a certain bird is

> a brown-throated thrush, but in Germany it's called a *Halsenflugel*, and in Chinese they call it a *chung ling* and even if you know all those names for it, you still know nothing about the bird—you only know something about people; what they call that bird. Now that thrush sings, and teaches its young to fly, and flies so many miles away during the summer across the country, and nobody knows how it finds its way', and so forth. There is a difference between the name of the thing and what goes on.
>
> (Feynman 1969, 316)

Gordon Woo saw here an implicit reference to one of Feynman colleagues at Caltech, Murrey Gell-Mann (1929–2019), amateur ornithologist and Nobel Prize in Physics (1969), who knew the names of birds in many languages (Woo 2011, Ch. 3). It may be fully true for the achievements of theoretical physics. Nevertheless, it precludes knowing more about people and their different ways of seeing, which is the treasure of human experiences, and the different languages are part of it.

Indeed, scholars as well did not see language diversities as a privileged opportunity because they based their craft on first-hand (re) reading of primary historiographical sources and all relevant secondary literature in any language. Thus, over centuries, the different languages in which historiographical works were written have been a material obstacle for historians towards a comprehensive study of the history of the world (i.e., of all the people and societies on earth). For a comprehensive survey on the word 'world' (*mundus, universus,* in Latin), refer to the works by Ayesha Ramachandran (2015, 11–12) and Emily Apter (2013, 175–190, *monde*). Today, International English is the lingua franca of both natural and human sciences in research-intensive universities and leading academic communities, worldwide. In the past, human societies have seen similar processes. Knowledge and wisdom have been discussed and transmitted adopting a homogenous language with a canonical writing system. They became common between people whose native languages were different. One can recall Classical Sanskrit, Koine Greek, Classical Latin, Literary Italian, Classical Arabic, Classical Chinese, and so on, depending on the time period and the geographical area that we are focusing on in the Afro-Eurasian *terra continens.*

In 1993, Umberto Eco published a book that was fast translated into English (Eco 1995) about the history of the Western idea that in the Garden of Eden once existed a perfect language, with which humans communicated without any ambiguity the precise identity of all natural things and human thoughts using the so-called *Lingua Adamica* (Schmidt-Biggermann 2008, 97–98). According to the Bible (*Genesis* 11: 1–9), the Tower of Babel was built by the Babylonians in an attempt to reach heaven, 'which God frustrated by confusing the languages of its builders so that they could not understand one another.' Since then, the fall of Babel was felt as a catastrophe for humanity. From Antiquity to at least the Enlightenment, cabbalists, theologians, and philosophers searched for the perfect language, and the idea remained current (Schmidt-Biggermann 2008, 86–99).

> Between 1450 and 1750, Christian cabalists sought above all to develop a unified system of philosophy, drawing on biblical allegory, Neoplatonic, Neopythagorean and partly Hermetic traditions". They aimed to "come closer to the sources of the Adamic

language of paradise, which they believed to be of divine origin. Once mastered, this Adamic language would yield understanding of the nature of all things—and that, in turn, would hasten the end of the world and the return of the Messiah, as had been prophesied in Daniel 12, 4: *plurimi pertransibunt, et multiplex erit scientia.*

(Schmidt-Biggermann 2008, 86)

According to Eco, the 'search for the perfect language' does not seem to have a sustainable solution. He studied, among others, works by Saint Augustine of Hippo (354–430 CE), Dante Alighieri (1265–1321), René Descartes (1596–1650), Jean-Jacques Rousseau (1712–1778), and read treatises on cabbalism, magic, and the history of the study of language and its origins, demonstrating the relationship between language and identity, linguistic and social practices, and emphasising that the search for the perfect language had always ideological motivations (Eco 1993).

Today, International English is in vogue and evidently segregating the English-speaking (and publishing) 'international' academic community from all other scholars who have not yet been made fond of and good at English-centric academic life and the tasks that it involves. In the alternation of hegemonic cultures, spoken and written treasures of human experience have always been put in latency or disappeared. Within the showcase for Afro-Eurasian pre-modern history (ca 1100–1500 CE), linguistic obstacles have been preventing scholars (i.e., true to a thorough knowledge of the multilingual scholarship achieved by humanistic disciplines such as Philology, Palaeography, Diplomatics, and Codicology) to directly access in different vernaculars (e.g., Latin, French, Russian, German, Italian, Swahili, Portuguese, Japanese, Spanish, Dutch, Greek, Korean, Chinese, Malay, Turkic, Indonesian, Arab, Tibetan, Thai, Hindi, Tamil, Bengali):

1 primary historical sources,
2 secondary literature published in print by the different national historiographies in various countries between the sixteenth and the twentieth century, and
3 the contemporary flow of online materials.

Scholars are getting more and more conscious of these linguistic obstacles and become suspicious when they review new books on long-lasting traditional historical topics with a huge bibliography in different languages such as Marco Polo (Watanabe 1986). In 2008,

Longxi Zhang (refer to Zhang 2008) and, in 2018, Gherardo Ortalli (refer to Ortalli 2018), from their different Chinese and Italian perspectives, respectively, raised similar concerns on the (im)possibility for individual scholars to access and evaluate relevant works in all languages. Zhang remarked that even the most reliable Western studies on the *Milione* and on Marco Polo lacked in using Chinese sources. EHM, in collaboration with the research teams led by Eugenio Burgio at the University of Venice Ca' Foscari and Hans-Ulrich Vogel at the University of Tübingen, is publishing a new bibliographical tool as a complement to the publication of the *Codice Diplomatico Poliano*. This tool will be released in 2024 on the occasion of the celebrations for the 700 years from Marco Polo's death (1324–2024).

In confirmation, Ortalli commented that when Zhang mentioned that the best book on Marco Polo was the one published by John Larner in 1999 (refer to Larner 1999), certainly excellent, his selection may have been made only within the publications in English, because of its current linguistic absolute predominance. He then recalled an historiographical article that the Italian medievalist Ovidio Capitani (1930–2012)—with an evident paraphrase of the marginal notes that are found in medieval Latin manuscripts, *Graecum est, non legitur* (it is Greek, it is not readable)—titled *Italicum est, non legitur* (it is Italian, it is not readable) to stigmatise the fact that publications in Italian were neglected by foreign scholars even when they were highly relevant to the historiographical debate (Capitani 1967, Ortalli 2018, 17).

All in all, these linguistic obstacles have prevented historians from unswervingly studying crucial topics, such as trade, conflict, and diplomacy, across national boundaries, and appreciating how, over time and across space, various people, historiographies, and cartographies saw the world and one another in the Afro-Eurasian *terra continens*. On the wealth of how various language see our common world, the lexicographic work published by Barbara Cassin is highly explicative (Cassin 2004). She 'produces wide-span intellectual cartography without a hegemonic global paradigm; that is to say, through interpretive procedures that reveal philosophical world-systems in the making' (Apter 2013, 31). The book covers close to 400 important words that defy easy translation between languages and cultures. It includes terms from more than a dozen languages, with entries written by more than 150 distinguished thinkers. Now, this almost untranslatable book is also available in English (Cassin 2014).

This is an encyclopedic dictionary of close to 400 important philosophical, literary, and political terms and concepts that defy easy—or any—translation from one language and culture to another. Drawn from more than a dozen languages, terms such as *Dasein* (German), *pravda* (Russian), *saudade* (Portuguese), and *stato* (Italian) are thoroughly examined in all their cross-linguistic and cross-cultural complexities. Spanning the classical, medieval, early modern, modern, and contemporary periods, these are terms that influence thinking across the humanities. The entries, written by more than 150 distinguished scholars, describe the origins and meanings of each term, the history and context of its usage, its translations into other languages, and its use in notable texts. The dictionary also includes essays on the special characteristics of particular languages—English, French, German, Greek, Italian, Portuguese, Russian, and Spanish.

(Princeton University Press n.d.)

Each generation is called to (re)read primary sources from the perspective of its own present. In our generation, for the first time ever, primary sources can become machine readable with executable links to Natural Language Processing for secondary literature aggregation in any language. A research question for which the assistance of evolutionary computing systems could be revolutionary would be 'How the global shapes/informs the local and the local informs/shapes the global?' The answer to this question would support national historiographies worldwide to nurture global citizenship as an antidote to intolerance and conflict. Computer connectivity between local and global platforms would be a major opportunity to share systems, applications, and solutions.

In 2016, Jacques Bolo—the author of the book *Philosophy vs AI* published in French in 1996—in a brief comment on the blog of the data scientist Jean Véronis mentioned the French translation of Umberto Eco's *Search for the Perfect Language* (Bolo 2016). Véronis replied to him that 'it was his favourite book and the first recommendation he made to all his students' (Bolo 2016). Indeed, terms and conditions apply with opportunities and limits as the Argentine librarian, writer, and poet Jorge Luis Borges (1899–1986) wrote in his short fiction *La biblioteca de Babel* (The Library of Babel), in which he imagined the universe of knowledge as a gigantic library of all possible books having the same format and printed with the same character set. This short story was part of his collected stories *El Jardín de senderos que se bifurcan* (The Garden of Forking Paths; Borges 1941) that later was included in *Ficciones* (Borges 1944). The English translation was first published in a collection of stories and other writings by Borges titled *Labyrinths* (Yates & Irby 1962, Fresán 2007).

4.3 Computational Approaches as Tools to Overcome Linguistic Obstacles and Cultural Barriers in the Historian's Craft

According to the New Oxford American Dictionary, the Greek word ιστορία/*historia* comes from *histōr*, which means 'the one who saw, the testimony > learned, wise man', and comes from an Indo-European root shared by wit/vit (to know) that gave Sanskrit *veda* 'wisdom' and Latin *videre* 'see', as well as the Old English *witan* of Germanic origin, and is related to Dutch *weten* and German *wissen* (Janda & Joseph 2003, 163). Thus, history is a kind of knowledge acquired by investigation with the intent to generate wisdom and implies the action of 'inquiring/examining', which is a requirement to move from knowledge (knowing how to do something) to wisdom (knowing under which situations to act).

If one agrees with Aristotle (Poetics, 51b), the historians speak of that which exists (of truth), the poets of that which could exist (the possible). In a computational modelling perspective, Michael Gavin (2014) notes that 'on the surface, computational modelling has many of the trappings of science, but their core simulations seem like elaborate fictions: the epistemological opposite of science or history'. He proposes 'that these forms of intellectual inquiry can productively coincide' (Gavin 2014, 1). But it is not as simple as that. Let's give a few significant examples. Ronald Barthes (1915–1980) in his seminal essay on 'The Death of the Author' (Barthes 1967b) followed the structural linguistics of Ferdinand de Saussure (1857–1913) and its anthropological extension made by Claude Lévi-Strauss (1908–2009). In particular, Barthes argued if 'the narrative of past events, subject usually in our culture, from the Greeks onward, to sanction of the historical "science", [...] is really different, for some specific trait and an indisputable relevance, from the imaginary narration, which we can find in epics, novels, drama?' (Barthes 1967a, 5, in French).

On an opposite interpretative angle, we have Carlo Ginzburg (1986, 96–125, and 200–213). 'Under the influence of structuralism, historians oriented themselves towards the identification of structures and of relationships. This identification rejected the perceptions and the intentions of individuals, or turned them into independent experiences, thus separating knowledge from subjective consciousness. In parallel, the number, the series, the quantification, which Carlo Ginzburg (1986) has called Galilei's paradigm, drove history towards a rigorous formulation of structural relationships, the establishment of whose laws became its mission' (Vendrix 1997, 65). The synopsis provided by the publisher for Carlo Ginzburg's essay collection in English translation states that he 'takes a bold stand against naive positivism and allegedly sophisticated neo-scepticism. It looks deeply into questions raised by decades of post-structuralism: What constitutes historical truth? How do we draw a boundary between truth and fiction? What is the relationship between history and memory? How do we grapple with the historical conventions that inform, in different ways, all written documents?' (Ginzburg 2012).

Bernard Williams' famous statement that 'the legacy of Greece to Western philosophy is Western philosophy' (2006, 3) is particularly true in this circumstance, because, as highlighted by Alexander Kerr in the *Introduction* to the *Republic* translated by Benjamin Jowett, Plato made the first attempt to frame a philosophy of history when he defined an order of thought in stating that 'in the brief space of human life, nothing great can be accomplished'; or again, as he afterwards says in the *Laws*, 'Infinite time is the maker of cities' (Jowett 1894). Moreover, Plato's iconic quote from the *Apology of Socrates* (399 BCE) still provides the exact framework: Ὁ δε ἀνεξέταστος βίος οὐ βιωτὸς ἀνθρώπῳ ('The unexamined life is not worth living,' *Apology of Socrates*, 38a). Life is not worth living without ἔλεγχος/*elenchus*, that is examination, argument of disproof or refutation, dialogue; cross-examining, testing, scrutiny especially for purposes of refutation. Such is the Socratic *elenchus*, often referred to also as *exetasis* or scrutiny and as *basanismus* or assay (Vlastos 1983).

Since Herodotus of Halicarnassus (ca 484–ca 425 BCE) in Classical Antiquity, Lorenzo Valla (ca 1407–1457) in the Renaissance, Leopold von Ranke (1795–1886) in Modern Times, and Marc Bloch (1886–1944) in the twentieth century, the critical assessment of the authenticity and reliability of historical sources is the basic and fundamental tool that historians have been using as a *condicio sine qua non* to acquire their data and establish relations such as cause-effect among them (Galasso 2000, 293–353, Ginzburg 2012, 7–24). While the 'procedures used to control and communicate the truth changed over the course of time' (Ginzburg 2012, 231), and the use of the same data can be dramatically different in various accounts bearing on the same past events across time, space, and cultures as well (Grafton & Marchand 1994, Guldi & Armitage 2014, Wang 2016).

Thus, the historians' key problematics have endured for a long period of time. In 1986, Carlo Ginzburg, in his seminal essay on *Clues: Roots of an Evidential Paradigm*, highlighted how history shares with two pseudo sciences, divination and physiognomics, not only roots but also their derivative sciences, law and medicine, that 'conducted their analysis of specific cases, which could be reconstructed only through traces, symptoms, and clues. For the future, there was divination in a strict sense; for the past, the present, and the future, there was medical semiotics in its twofold aspect, diagnostic and prognostic; for the past, there was jurisprudence' (Ginzburg 1989, 104–105, Momigliano 1985).

On 16 May 1969, the 66-year-old French historian Fernand Braudel wrote a three-page *Preface* to a collection of his articles and essays on the nature of history to be reprinted in Paris by Flammarion. The collected works had been written and published in the previous 20 years. The text ended with a statement addressed to the next generation of historians. In the translation made by Sarah Matthews for The Chicago University Press edition published in 1980, it is as follows.

> If I may differ a moment with Emmanuel Le Roy Ladurie, I fear that there is an element of illusion or of alibi in asserting, when speaking of "statistical history," that the historian of the future "will be either a computer programer or nothing at all." What interests me is the programer's program. The historian for the moment should concern himself[/herself] with gathering the human sciences together (could data processing help them to build up a common language?) rather than only with perfecting his own line. The historian of tomorrow will build up this language—or will be nothing at all.
>
> (Braudel 1980, vii–ix)

Michel Foucault (1926–1984), in his seminal book on the determination of truth in the human sciences (Foucault 1966 in French, and 1970 in English), set the stage for this discourse even if he did not mention the impact of computers. Fernand Braudel's persuasion that the historian of tomorrow, to be able to survive as a human scientist, must be able to build up a common language, which can be used by programmers across all the human sciences to write their computer programs, is clear from a historian's perspective. From a computation and machine learning (ML) perspective, one key question needs to be addressed and answered, before taking any action. Why should the historian run such a critical task? Referring to Braudel's 1969 call for unity, it seems that human sciences need to build up a grammar for the computational language that will allow the reloading of the treasure of human experiences through artificial intelligence (AI). Big human sciences data are embedded and embodied in all sorts of artefacts and media that over time and across space have been created by humans to encode their knowledge and values, to make a better use of them in the present and transmit them to future generations as well. In this way, artefacts and media are considered and treated as knowledge aggregators ante litteram. These big data can be named 'THE data', where THE stays for 'Treasure of Human Experiences'. These data is the most valuable component of what is generally called heritage (i.e., what may be inherited) as discussed in Section 1.2.

Historia vero testis temporum, lux veritatis, vita memoriae, magistra vitae, nuntia vetustatis, qua voce alia nisi oratoris immortalitati commendatur? ('By what other voice, too, than that of the orator, is history, the evidence of time, the light of truth, the life of memory, the directress of life, the herald of antiquity, committed to immortality?' Marci Tullii Ciceronis, *De Oratore*, II, 36). If we read this famous quote of Cicero through the lens of the thermodynamic paradigm, which holds that a perfect description of a given moment or set of conditions in history would provide a knowledge of future conditions—and assume that 'the new society comes into being in the womb of the old' (Lechte 2003, 106), our increasingly complex world should cherish as much as possible the treasure of human experiences (the data), to increase resilience and sustainability and to nurture innovation (Cheong et al. 2016, 104–105, Nanetti & Cheong 2018, 358–359). Technology can indeed assist in modelling cultural entities in diverse domains for digital archives (Sugimoto et al. 2021). However, the main call to action is for the humanities (Borgman 2009) and how it can start thinking algorithmically.

On 15 January 2020, Ethan Urie posted a lengthy article on how to start thinking algorithmically in Laurence Bradford's blog 'Learn to Code with Me' (Urie 2020). This overview provides an excellent example of a computer-science perspective on how technology can empower human thinking. This practice breaks problems deterministically down and builds solutions up repeatably. As a research approach, it adverts and opens to the opportunities of AI and ML but does not discuss criticalities and complexities stymied by technological bottlenecks. 'Niche building is an evolutionary activity in which all living organisms engage .... We are in the process of building our next niche for the largest population ever living on earth. It is a digital niche' (Nowotny 2020, 20–21). Yet, overcoming technical limitations needs to be contextualised in specific domains of knowledge to effectively empower related human thinking because algorithmic thinking is a human activity.

This academic performance can effectively benefit from algorithmic data processing only if algorithms facilitate the implementation of individual tasks in the framework of specific disciplines towards augmented human intelligence rather than AI. So, the question is, 'why are we working so hard to make computers that compute better, when we could be using computers to help us think and act better' (Bentley 2022). To EHM, the answer to what's next is to make strong and compelling links to the primary sources of information (the data on which papers or videos are grounded). Otherwise, reviews of reviews risk to shift from facts (i.e., information proved to be true and used as evidence) into the reviewer's opinions (i.e., a view or judgement formed about something, not necessarily based on fact or knowledge). And this has consequences. In history, it is very common to have authors who are unable to directly access primary sources and rely only on translations or secondary literature published in English and available online. These authors are poisoning the advancement of knowledge with easily available and thus highly cited books, papers, and videos. However, history has about 2000 years of experience in this exercise and can provide useful antidots. The challenge is how to balance human digital curation with process automatisation.

Hence, the individuality of the functions is a technological constraint. Identifying the field of knowledge is an epistemological requirement that allows taking into consideration the assumptions of a given discipline before running algorithms based on them. Decisions about what is worth to be inherited require understanding, and, as consistently Umberto Eco argued, problems of interpretation need to be framed in a historical context (Eco 1995). In the case of the historical sciences, this challenge has been discussed as disciplinary assumptions in terms of cultural barriers and linguistic obstacles in this chapter, which summarises, consolidates, and updates the results of two works already published with different perspectives by Andrea Nanetti (2022a, b).

If one agrees with the *World Economic Forum*'s Founder and Executive Chairman, Klaus Schwab, that in the twenty-first century, humanity has entered a Fourth Industrial Revolution (Schwab 2016), some considerations can be made. First, the history of the agricultural revolution was empowered by animal domestication around 8000 BCE. Then, the series of eighteenth-century industrial revolutions followed. Then, 1760–1840 was marked by the advent of mechanical production. Next, the period between the late nineteenth and early twentieth century evolved into mass production. Finally, in the 1960s, semiconductors introduced a new significant disruption. These historical processes teach us that these disruptive events generated unprecedented and unexpected inequalities. Moreover, the communities able to surf their respective early waves caused an unbridgeable gap and built an enormous power over the others (Schwab 2016, 6–13). 'Many see AI through the lens of economic and geopolitical competition,' says Michael P. Sellitto, Deputy Director of the Stanford Institute for Human-Centered AI. '[They] tend to create barriers that preserve their perceived strategic advantages, in access to data or research, for example' (Knight 2019).

Today, one possible scenario is that whoever will be able to empower decision-making with both the treasure of human experiences and big data will lead the planet and reinforce inequality. Otherwise, as Michelangelo Pistoletto would say, humanity can create a Third Paradise, which marks 'the passage to a new level of planetary civilisation, essential to ensure the survival of the human race' (Pistoletto 2003). In Pistoletto's vision, 'the Third Paradise is an evolutionary transition in which human intelligence finds ways to coexist with the intelligence of nature' (Nanetti 2019, Pistoletto 2019, fourth cover page). In this scenario, overcoming linguistic and cultural obstacles in the transcultural (re)reading of primary sources and secondary literature represents a vital tool for showcasing how human sciences can mitigate the tremendous impact of our present techno-scientific paradigm shift on the human condition.

Yet, what is missing in computational history is the macroscopic modelling which grasps big data 'through a process of compression, by selectively reducing complexity until once-obscure patterns and relationships become clear' (Graham et al. 2016, 1). Thus, EHM works on filling this crucial gap following the *Annales* experience (Burguière 2006, 2009), and the evolution of *histoire événementielle* (i.e., event history) into microhistory (Le Goff & Nora 1974; for selected essays in English, Le Goff & Nora 1985). In the EHM system, macroscopic models can be inferred by microhistory. In this perspective, big history emerges from 'all' micro-history interactions. Microhistory studies (theory, Ginzburg 2012, 193–214, exemplified by Ginzburg 1980, Magnússon 2003, 709–716, Trivellato 2011) focus on single historical units/events to ask—as defined by Charles Joyner—'large questions in small places' in contrast with large-scale structural views (Joyner 1999, 1).

References

Apter, Emily (2013). *Against World Literature. On the Politics of Untranslatability*. London and New York: Verso.

Barthes, Roland (1967a). "Le discours de l'histoire". *Social Science Information*, 6(4), 63–75. https://doi.org/10.1177/053901846700600404

Barthes, Roland (1967b). "The Death of the Author, translated by Richard Howard". *Aspen: The Magazine in a Box, 5-6 (The Minimalism Issue)*, Item 3 (*Three Esays*), [First Essay with no page numbers]. https://www.ubu.com/aspen/aspen5and6/threeEssays.html#barthes

BBC (2012). "Indian Nobel Laureate Amartya Sen Honoured in US". 14 February. https://www.bbc.com/news/world-asia-india-17022920

Bentley, Peter (2022). "Augmented Intelligence: What It Is and Why It Will Be Smarter Than AI". *BBC Science Focus Magazine* (blog). February 1, 2022. https://www.sciencefocus.com/future-technology/augmented-intelligence

Benzoni, Maria Matilde (2016). "Prefazione all'edizione italiana". In *Abbiamo ancora bisogno della storia? Il senso del passato nel mondo globalizzato*, edited by Serge Gruzinski, xi–xiv. Milan: Raffaello Cortina Editore.

Bolo, Jacques (1996). *Philosophie contre Intelligence Artificielle*. Paris: Lingua Franca.

Bolo, Jacques (2016). "Umberto Eco and Artificial Intelligence". *Exergue*, March. https://www.exergue.com/h/2016-03/tt/eco-perfect-lang.html

Borges, Jorge Luis (1941). *El Jardín de senderos que se bifurcan*. Buenos Aires: Editorial SUR.

Borges, Jorge Luis (1944). *Ficciones (1935-1944)*. Buenos Aires: Ediciones SUR.

Borgman, Christine L. (2009). "The Digital Future Is Now: A Call to Action for the Humanities". *Digital Humanities Quarterly*, *3*(4). http://www.digitalhumanities.org/dhq/vol/3/4/000077/000077.html

Braudel, Fernand (1960). "Unité et diversité des sciences de l'homme". *Revue de l'enseignement supérieur*, *1*, 17–22.

Braudel, Fernand (1980). *On History*, translated by Sarah Matthews. Chicago, IL: The University of Chicago Press [originally, *Écrits sur l'histoire*. Paris: Flammarion, 1969]. https://archive.org/details/onhistory00brau

Burguière, André (2006). *L'École des Annales: Une histoire intellectuelle*. Paris: Odile Jacob.

Burguière, André (2009). *Annales School: An Intellectual History*. Ithaca, NY: Cornell University Press.

Capitani, Ovidio (1967). "Italicum est, non legitur". *Studi medievali*, *8*, 745–761.

Cassin, Barbara (2004). *Vocabulaire européen des philosophies: Dictionnaire des intraduisibles*. Paris: Le Seuil/Le Robert.

Cassin, Barbara (Ed.) (2014). *Dictionary of Untranslatables: A Philosophical Lexicon*, translated by Emily Apter, Jacques Lezra, & Michael Wood. Princeton, NJ: Princeton University Press. https://archive.org/details/dictionaryofuntr0000unse/mode/2up

Cheong, Siew Ann, Andrea Nanetti, & Mikhail Filippov (2016). "Digital Maps and Automatic Narratives for the Interactive Global Histories". *The Asian Review of World Histories*, *4*(1), 83–123. https://brill.com/view/journals/arwh/4/1/arwh.4.issue-1.xml

Cuccioletta, Donald (2002). "Multiculturalism or Transculturalism: Towards a Cosmopolitan Citizenship". *London Journal of Canadian Studies*, *17* (2001/2002), 1–11. https://is.muni.cz/el/phil/podzim2013/CJVA1M/43514039/reading_3_Transculturality.pdf

Curthoys, Ned, & Debjani Ganguly (Eds.) (2007). *Edward Said: The Legacy of a Public Intellectual*. Melbourne: Melbourne University Press. https://search. informit.org/doi/10.3316/informit.9780522853568

Eco, Umberto (1993). *La ricerca della lingua perfetta nella cultura europea*. Bari: Editori Laterza.

Eco, Umberto (1995). *The Search for the Perfect Language in the European Culture*, translated [from Italian into English] by James Fentress. Oxford: Wiley-Blackwell (Original work, *La ricerca della lingua perfetta nella cultura europea*. Bari: Editori Laterza, 1993).

Feynman, Richard P. (1969). "What Is Science?" *The Physics Teacher*, 7, 313–320. https://doi.org/10.1119/1.2351388

Foucault, Michel (1966). *Les mots et les choses. Une archéologie des sciences humaines*. Paris: Éditions Gallimard. https://monoskop.org/images/4/40/ Foucault_Michel_Les_mots_et_les_choses.pdf

Foucault, Michel (1970). *The Order of Things: An Archaeology of the Human Sciences*, translated from French into English by Alan Sheridan. London: Tavistock Publications and New York: Pantheon Books. https://archive.org/ details/orderofthingsarc00fouc/mode/2up

Fresán, Javier (2007). "De la Biblioteca de Babel a los números normales". *TK*, *19*, 133–139. http://www.asnabi.com/revista/tk19/19fresan.pdf

Galasso, Giuseppe (2000). *Nient'altro che storia*. Bologna: Società Editrice Il Mulino. https://www.darwinbooks.it/doi/10.978.8815/144676/toc

Gavin, Michael (2014). "Agent-Based Modeling and Historical Simulation". *Digital Humanities Quarterly*, *8*(4). http://www.digitalhumanities.org/dhq/ vol/8/4/000195/000195.html

Gell-Mann, Murray (1997). "The Simple and the Complex". In *Complexity, Global Politics, and National Security*, edited by David S. Alberts, & Thomas J. Czerwinski, 3–28. Washington, DC: National Defense University. http:// www.dodccrp.org/files/Alberts_Complexity_Global.pdf

Ginzburg, Carlo (1980). *The Cheese and the Worms: The Cosmos of a 16th-Century Miller*, translated from Italian into English by John Tedeschi, & Anne C. Tedeschi. Baltimore, MD: Johns Hopkins University Press (Original work, *Il formaggio e i vermi. Il cosmo di un mugnaio del '500*. Turin: Einaudi, 1976).

Ginzburg, Carlo (1986). *Il filo e le tracce. Vero falso finto*. Bologna: Feltrinelli.

Ginzburg, Carlo (1989). *Clues, Myths, and the Historical Method*, translated from Italian to English by Anne C. Tedeschi, & John Tedeschi. Baltimore, MD: Johns Hopkins University Press (Original work, *Miti, emblemi, spie*. Turin: Einaudi, 1986). https://archive.org/details/cluesmythshistor0000ginz/ mode/2up

Ginzburg, Carlo (2012). *Threads and Traces. True False Fictive*, translated from Italian to English by Anne C. Tedeschi, & John Tedeschi. Berkeley, Los Angeles, London: University of California Press (Original work, *Il filo e le tracce. Vero falso finto*. Bologna: Feltrinelli, 1986). https://doi.org/10.1086/ 448699

Gluck, Carol (1998). "House of Mirrors. American History-writing on Japan". In *Imagined Histories: American Historians Interpret the Past*, edited by

Anthony Molho, & Gordon S. Wood, 434–454. Princeton, NJ: Princeton University Press. https://doi.org/10.1515/9780691187341-021

Grafton, Antony, & Suzanne L. Marchand (1994). "Proof and Persuasion in History". *History & Theory, 33*(4), 3–4. https://doi.org/10.2307/2505499

Graham, Shawn, Ian Milligan, & Scott Weingart (Eds.) (2016). *Exploring Big Historical Data. The Historian's Macroscope.* London: Imperial College Press. https://doi.org/10.1142/p981

Gruzinski, Serge (2012). *L'aigle et le dragon. Démesure européenne et mondialisation au XVIe siècle.* Paris: Fayard.

Gruzinski, Serge (2014). *The Eagle and the Dragon: Globalization and European Dreams of Conquest in China and America in the Sixteenth Century,* translated [from French into English] by Jean Birrell. Cambridge: Polity Press.

Guldi, Jo, & David Armitage (2014). *The History Manifesto.* Cambridge: Cambridge University Press. https://doi.org/10.1017/9781139923880

Gürsoy Sökmen, Müge, & Başak Ertür (Eds.) (2008a). "Waiting for the Barbarians: A Tribute to Edward W. Said". In *Proceedings of the Homonymous Conference,* organised by the same editors on 25–26 May 2007 at Bogazici University in Istanbul (Turkey). London & New York: Verso.

Gürsoy Sökmen, Müge, & Başak Ertür (Eds.) (2008b). *Barbarları beklerken: Edward W. Said anısına,* translated by Doğan Şahiner. Istanbul: Sona Ertekin. 2010.

Heidelberg University Publishing (n.d.). "The Journal of Transcultural Studies". Accessed May 5, 2022. https://heiup.uni-heidelberg.de/journals/index.php/transcultural/index

Herren, Madeleine, Martin Rüesch, & Christiane Sibille (2013). *Transcultural History: Theories, Methods, Sources.* Heidelberg: Springer Verlag. https://doi.org/10.1007/978-3-642-19196-1

Hobsbawm, Eric, & Terence Ranger (Eds.) (1983). *The Invention of Tradition.* Cambridge: Cambridge University Press. https://doi.org/10.1017/CBO978 1107295636

Jacobucci, Michelangelo (2015). *Le radici di là dal mare. Uno sguardo alle origini della civiltà europea.* Udine: Campanotto Editore.

Janda, Richard D., & Brian D. Joseph (2003). "On Language, Change, and Language Change – Or, Of history, Linguistics, and Historical Linguistics". In *The Handbook of Historical Linguistics,* edited by Brian D. Joseph, & Richard D. Janda, 1–180. Oxford: Blackwell Publishing. https://doi.org/10.1002/9780470756393.ch

Jowett, Benjamin (1894). Plato, *The Republic,* translated by Benjamin Jowett with an Introduction by Alexander Kerr. Oxford: At the Clarendon Press.

Joyner, Charles W. (1999). *Shared Traditions: Southern History and Folk Culture.* Urbana, IL: University of Illinois.

Knight, Will (2019). "The World Economic Forum Wants to Develop Global Rules for AI". *MIT Technology Review* (blog). May 28, 2019. https://www.technologyreview.com/s/613589/the-world-economic-forum-wants-to-develop-global-rules-for-ai

König, Daniel G., & Katja Rakow (2016). "The Transcultural Approach within a Disciplinary Framework: An Introduction". *The Journal of Transcultural Studies*, 7(2), 89–100. https://doi.org/10.17885/heiup.ts.2016.2.23642

Kuhn, Thomas S. (1970). *The Structure of Scientific Revolutions*. Chicago, IL: University of Chicago Press. https://www.lri.fr/~mbl/Stanford/CS477/papers/Kuhn-SSR-2ndEd.pdf

Larner, John (1999). *Marco Polo and the Discovery of the World*. New Haven and London: Yale University Press. https://archive.org/details/marcopolodiscove00john/mode/2up

Le Goff, Jacques, & Pierre Nora (Eds.) (1974). *Faire de l'histoire*, I–III. Paris: Gallimard.

Le Goff, Jacques, & Pierre Nora (Eds.) (1985). *Constructing the Past: Essays in Historical Methodology*. Cambridge: Cambridge University Press.

Le Pichon, Alain, & Dayun Yue/乐黛云 (Eds.) (1995a). 独角兽与龙 - 在寻找中西文化普遍性中的误读 *[Dú jiǎo shòu yǔ lóng - zài xúnzhǎo zhōngxī wénhuà pǔbiàn xìng zhōng de wù dú, The Unicorn and the Dragon – Looking for Misunderstandings in the Quest for the Universal in Chinese and Western Cultures]*. Beijing: Peking University Press. https://sg1lib.org/book/6069123/ae7c18?dsource=recommend

Le Pichon, Alain, & Dayun Yue/乐黛云 (Eds.) (1995b). *La Licorne et le Dragon. Les Malentendus dans la Recherche de l'Universel*. Beijing: Presses Universitaires de Pékin.

Le Pichon, Alain, & Dayun Yue/乐黛云 (Eds.) (1996). *La Licorne et le Dragon/The Unicorn and the Dragon*. Beijing: Presses Universitaires de Pékin/Peking University Press.

Le Pichon, Alain, & Dayun Yue/乐黛云 (Eds.) (2004). *La Licorne et le Dragon. Les Malentendus dans la Recherche de l'Universel*, revised French edition. Beijing: Presses Universitaires de Pékin.

Le Pichon, Alain, & Dayun Yue/乐黛云 (Eds.) (2005). *La Licorne et le Dragon. Les Malentendus dans la Recherche de l'Universel*, revised French edition. Paris: Presses Charles Léopold Meyer.

Lechte, John (2003). *Key Contemporary Concepts. From Abjection to Zeno's Paradox*. New York: SAGE Publications. https://dx.doi.org/10.4135/9781446219638

Magnússon, Sigurdur Gylfi (2003). "'The Singularization of History': Social History and Microhistory within the Postmodern State of Knowledge". *Journal of Social History*, 36(3), 701–735. http://www.jstor.org/stable/3790736

Michalarou, Efi (2016). "ART-PRESENTATION: Urs Fischer's Universe at Gagosian Gallery". *Dreamideamachine ART VIEW*. http://www.dreamideamachine.com/?p=11755

Momigliano, Arnaldo (1985). "History between Medicine and Rhetoric". *Annali della Scuola Normale Superiore di Pisa, Classe di Lettere e Filosofia, Serie III*, 15(3), 767–780. https://www.jstor.org/stable/24307080

Moulin-Civil, Françoise (2005). "El Contrapunteo cubano del tabaco y el azúcar, o el nacimiento de un paradigma". *América. Cahiers du CRICCAL*, 33, 143–150. http://dx.doi.org/10.3406/ameri.2005.1716

Mudimbe, Valentin-Yves (1988). *The Invention of Africa: Gnosis, Philosophy and the Order of Knowledge.* Bloomington, IN: Indiana University Press. https://files.libcom.org/files/zz_v._y._mudimbe_the_invention_of_africa_gnosis_pbook4you_1.pdf

Nanetti, Andrea (2019). "The Third Paradise at NTU Singapore". In *Between Obverse and Reverse*, edited by Michelangelo Pistoletto, 70–75. Roma: Carlo Cambi Editore.

Nanetti, Andrea (2022a). "Overcoming Linguistic Obstacles and Cultural Barriers in the Transcultural (Re)-Reading of Primary Sources and Secondary Literature for Afro-Eurasian Pre-Modern History (1205-1533)". In *Order/Disorder in Asia*, edited by Rila Mukherjee, 485–538. Kolkata: The Asiatic Society.

Nanetti, Andrea (2022b). "Waterways Connecting the Peoples of the World. A Presentation of the EHM Application for Fra Mauro's *Mappa Mundi* as a Virtual Laboratory for Investigating the Maritime Silk Road Discourse in the Digital Time Machine". In *Venezia e il senso del mare. Percezioni e rappresentazioni [Venice and the Sense of the Sea. Perceptions and Portrayals]*, 161–250. Venice: Istituto Veneto di Scienze, Lettere ed Arti.

Nanetti, Andrea, & Siew Ann Cheong (2018). "Computational History: From Big Data to Big Simulations". In *Big Data in Computational Social Science and Humanities*, edited by Shu-Heng Chen, 337–363. Cham: Springer International Publishing AG. https://link.springer.com/chapter/10.1007/978-3-319-95465-3_18

Nowotny, Helga (2020). *Life in the Digital Time Machine.* The Second Wittrock Lecture held in Uppsala on 25 February 2020. Uppsala: Swedish Collegium for Advanced Study.

Ortalli, Gherardo (2018). "Ancora Marco Polo? Vogel per qualcosa di nuovo. Quasi una recensione". *Archivio Veneto*, *149*, 13–23.

Ortiz, Fernando (1940). *Contrapunteo cubano del tabaco y el azúcar.* Havana: Jesus Montero.

Ortiz, Fernando (1947). *Cuban Counterpoint: Tobacco and Sugar*, translated from the Spanish into English by Harriet de Onís. New York: Alfred A. Knopf. https://archive.org/details/cubancounterpoin00orti/mode/2up

Ortiz, Fernando (1973). *Contrapunteo cubano del tabaco y el azúcar.* Barcelona: Ariel.

Ortiz, Fernando (1995). *Cuban Counterpoint: Tobacco and Sugar*, translated from the Spanish into English by Harriet de Onís, new edition with an introductory essay by Fernando Coronil. Durham, NC: Duke University Press.

Ortiz, Fernando (2012). *Cuban Counterpoint: Tobacco and Sugar*, translated from the Spanish into English by Harriet de Onís with an introductory essay by Fernando Coronil, new edition. New York: Knopf Doubleday Publishing Group.

Pertusi, Agostino (Ed.) (1970). *La storiografia veneziana fino al secolo XVI. Aspetti e problemi.* Firenze: Leo S. Olschki Editore.

Pistoletto, Michelangelo (2003). "What is The Third Paradise". Accessed January 15, 2022. http://terzoparadiso.org/en/what-is

Pistoletto, Michelangelo (2019). *Between Obverse and Reverse*. Roma: Carlo Cambi Editore.

Pomart, Julien, & Landry Riche (2018). *Etat général des fonds d'archives conservés par la bibliothèque de la Fondation Maison des sciences de l'homme*, by Julien Pomart, Head of the Archives of the Foundation *Maison des sciences de l'homme*, updated in May 2018 by Landry Riche, Archivist of the Foundation *Maison des sciences de l'homme*. http://nabu.fmsh.fr/archives/search

Princeton University Press (n.d.). "Dictionary of Untranslatables: A Philosophical Lexicon". Accessed May 5, 2022. https://press.princeton.edu/books/hardcover/9780691138701/dictionary-of-untranslatables

Ramachandran, Ayesha (2015). *The Worldmakers: Global Imagining in Early Modern Europe*. Chicago, IL: University of Chicago Press.

Said, Edward W. (1978). *Orientalism*. New York: Pantheon.

Santi, Enrico Mario (Ed.) (2002). Fernando Ortiz, *Contrapunteo cubano del tabaco y el azúcar*. Madrid: Cátedra.

Schäfer, Wolf (2001). "Global Civilisation and Local Cultures: A Crude Look at the Whole". *International Sociology*, *16*(3), 301–319. https://doi.org/10.117 7%2F026858001016003004

Schmidt-Biggermann, Wilhelm (2008). "What is Christian Cabala?" In *Wissensformen*, edited by Werner Oechslin. Stiftung Bibliothek Werner Oechslin (Einsiedeln). Zürich: gta Verlag.

Schwab, Klaus (2016). *The Fourth Industrial Revolution*. New York: Crown Business. https://law.unimelb.edu.au/__data/assets/pdf_file/0005/3385454/Schwab-The_Fourth_Industrial_Revolution_Klaus_S.pdf

Sugimoto, Shigeo, Chiranthi Wijesundara, Tetsuya Mihara, & Kazufumi Fukuda (2021). "Modeling Cultural Entities in Diverse Domains for Digital Archives". In *Information and Knowledge Organization in Digital Humanities*, edited by Koraljka Golub, & Ying-Hsang Liu, 25–42. London: Routledge. https://doi.org/10.4324/9781003131816-2

Szanton, David L. (2004). "The Origin, Nature and Challenges of Area Studies in the United States". In *The Politics of Knowledge: Area Studies and the Disciplines*, edited by David L. Szanton, 1–33. Berkeley, CA: University of California Press. https://escholarship.org/uc/item/59n2d2n1

The International TRANSCULTURA Institute (n.d.). "Institut International TRANSCULTURA". Accessed May 4, 2022. http://transcultura.org/?page_id=569&lang=en

Tomasin, Lorenzo (2017). *L'impronta digitale. Cultura umanistica e tecnologia*. Roma: Carocci editore.

Trivellato, Francesca (2011). "Is There a Future for Italian Microhistory in the Age of Global History?" *California Italian Studies*, *2*(1). https://doi.org/10.5070/C321009025

Urie, Ethan (2020). "How to Start Thinking Algorithmically. A Beginner's Guide to Algorithmic Thinking". *Learn to Code with Me* (blog). *Laurence Bradford*. January 15, 2020. https://learntocodewith.me/posts/algorithmic-thinking/ (accessed July 19, 2020).

Vendrix, Philippe (1997). "Cognitive Sciences and Historical Sciences in Music: Ways Towards Conciliation". In *Perception and Cognition of Music*, edited by Irene Deliège, & John Sloboda, 64–74. Hove: Psychology Press. https://halshs.archives-ouvertes.fr/halshs-00265891

Vlastos, Gregory (1983). "The Socratic Elenchus". *Oxford Studies in Ancient Philosophy*, *1*, 27–58.

Wallerstein, Immanuel (2004). *World Systems Analysis: An Introduction*. Durham, NC: Duke University Press. https://www.jstor.org/stable/j.ctv11smzx1

Wang, Gungwu (2016). "Heritage and History". In *Videorecording of the 3rd Singapore Heritage Science Conference*, Nanyang Technological University Singapore, 25–26 January 2016. https://www.paralimes.org/events/past-events-video-recordings-and-slides/conference-3rd-singapore-heritage-science/

Watanabe, Hiroshi (Compiler) (1986). *Marco Polo Bibliography, 1477–1983*. Tokyo: Toyo Bunko.

Weber, Eugen (1998). "Western Civilization". In *Imagined Histories: American Historians Interpret the Past*, edited by Anthony Molho, & Gordon S. Wood, 206–221. Princeton, NJ: Princeton University Press. https://doi.org/10.1515/9780691187341-012

Williams, Bernard (2006). *The Sense of the Past*. Princeton, NJ: Princeton University Press. https://doi.org/10.1515/9781400827107

Woo, Gordon (2011). *Calculating Catastrophe*. London: Imperial College Press.

Yates, Donald A., & James E. Irby (Eds.) (1962). Jorge Luis Borges, *Labyrinths. Selected Stories and Other Writings*, preface by André Maurois. New York: New Directions. https://archive.org/details/labyrinths0000unse_y9b3/mode/2up

Zan, Luca, & Kent G. Deng (2017). "Micro Foundations in the Great Divergence Debate: Opening up the Perspective". *Accounting History*, *22*(4), 530–553. https://doi.org/10.1177/1032373217729865

Zhang, Longxi (2008). "Marco Polo, Chinese Cultural Identity, and an Alternative Model of East-West Encounter". In *Marco Polo and the Encounter of East and West*, edited by Suzanne Conklin Akbari, & Amilcare Iannucci, 280–296. Toronto: University of Toronto Press. https://doi.org/10.3138/9781442688582-013

5 EHM Showcase on Afro-Eurasia (ca 1100–1500 CE)

5.1 EHM Computational Engineering of Afro-Eurasian Communication Networks with a Focus on Waterways

The interested historiographical fields are global history (Olstein 2015), world history (Toynbee 1934–1961, Wallerstein 1974, Mazlish 1998, Weinstein 2005), and agent-based modelling and simulations (ABMSs) of big historical data (Holland & Miller 1991, Graham et al. 2016). The showcase is the Afro-Eurasian *terra continens*, its people, and their interactions. The historiographical context is the intercontinental communication networks by sea and overland. The German geographer Ferdinand Freiherr von Richthofen (1833–1905) first identified these networks in two papers given at the Berlin Geographic Society (Richthofen 1876, 1877) and, later, in his magnum opus, *China* (1877–1912). Later, as highlighted by Richard Foltz in 1999, 'historians such as Fernand Braudel [1902–1985], Immanuel Wallerstein [1930-2019], André Gunder Frank [1929–2005], Jerry Bentley [1949-2012], and others had consistently confirmed that the Eurocentric view is excessively narrow because Afro-Eurasian networks have been already in use for at least three millennia' before the world-systems supposedly first emerged with the European discoveries in the fifteenth century (Foltz 2010, 137, Abulafia 2019, xvii, 6–8, 920).

In this historiographical context, the infrastructure of ports of trade and sea lanes is a significant focus to showcase the EHM computational approach to the (re)reading of primary historical sources (Nanetti 2022). This infrastructure can be considered one intercontinental communication and trade network. Though, before Modernity, it was highly segmented and did not evenly gather pace across all the seas (Lippman Abu-Lughod 1989, Gilroy 1993, 17, Rediker 2004, Abulafia 2019, xxi–xxiii). Historiographically, it did not become a system before the 'historicisation of the ocean' viz. the overcoming of the nation-state perspective in the approach to the study of maritime

DOI: 10.4324/9781003310860-5

communications (Klein & Mackenthun 2004). The assumption is that ports of trade and sea routes determined each other and worked as a system of systems built from the ground up (North 2016, 2019, 21). The outcomes of the 50th Datini Conference on 'Maritime Networks as a Factor of European Integration (Prato, Italy, 13-17 May 2018)' (Nigro 2019) are relevant. Although the conference dealt with the history of European trade ports between late medieval times and the early modern period, the research results go beyond the geographical limits of the Mediterranean Sea and the North-East Atlantic Ocean. Besides the last section on 'Intercontinental exchanges', all research questions that identify the other parts of the book are globally relevant: 'how did shipping routes serve as a connecting force?', 'how did nodal points bring together different commercial spheres?', 'to what extent did free trade and protection facilitate the integration of maritime networks?', 'which features of cultural exchange served to integrate maritime networks or were their particular products?'. As highlighted by Michael North in the closure of his keynote titled 'Connected Seas', 'putting regional maritime histories into a comparative international perspective is one of the main tasks of our future research' (North 2019, 25).

However, it is vague how this interdependency and connectivity functioned. And it is unclear how to understand it historically using all available information provided in different languages by various historiographies. Hence, EHM introduced the ABMS approach to studying sea-based interactions between East and West Afro-Eurasian trade systems. ABMS uses computational modelling for simulating the tentative interaction of autonomous agents, viz. real-world entities, within an environment called the system (Macal & North 2007, Mayr 2011). Here, the system is the sea routes network, the identifying knots of which are the ports of trade reached by private vessels and public convoys. Each port can be construed as an autonomous agent. Human and natural factors determine the agents' attributes, resources, life cycle, and interactions. The working hypothesis is that the web of the sea lanes regularly used by shipping could be simulated, putting the historical network of trade ports in the natural context of the virtual sea routes determined by prevailing sea currents and winds. If climate did not change in the last ca 3,000 years, climatological winds and currents can contribute to virtually reconstructing potential sea lanes (Nanetti 2022, subchapter 3). On the pattern of such a virtual network, communications and trade that happened by sea, as witnessed by archaeological findings and written records about vessels and voyages, can be plotted to validate the picture in a computational history approach (Nanetti & Cheong 2018).

The heterogeneous information needed to feed an ABMS Data Template is available in scholarly literature and databases, but it has not been aggregated in a single searchable space yet. EHM proposes a method to reconstruct the sea routes on which goods and people moved since the Neolithic. This method has three phases. Firstly, we map the interaction between climate and geological parameters. Secondly, we relate them to the geographical distribution of archaeological data, such as terrestrial and submarine sites, artefacts, shipwrecks, epigraphs of mariners and representations of ships. And thirdly, we connect them to other written records. The information can be identified in prevailing sea currents and winds, earthquakes and other cataclysms, voyages and itineraries of merchants and other travellers, evidence of goods coming from identifiable places, and shipwrecks. Andrea Nanetti and Siew Ann Cheong have introduced the theoretical framework of requirements and prescriptions to build data-driven simulations (Nanetti & Cheong 2018, 353–354). The starting point is the database of the primary historical sources engineered and accessible as applications on EHM (Nanetti et al. 2022a) and their representation in four-dimensional space-time (Niccolucci & Hermon 2016).

Firstly, EHM identifies the following items with different modalities in the ontology of the entities used in database engineering.

- Necessarily: agents. They are the entities, considered individuals and collective wholes (i.e., governments, families), capable of setting goals, interacting with other agents, and reacting to the environment and its changes.
- Necessarily: events. From which can be extracted the actions needed to achieve goals.
- Possibly: environmental conditions (and other agents). They are the most important external factors influencing the agents' decision-making process.
- Possibly: preferences (built-in conditions). They are the arbitrary choices the agents make to pursue their goals.

Secondly, the database needs to facilitate or at least allow for retrieving agent-action-condition (who did what and why) triplets so that historians can visualise the frequencies of actions taken under specific conditions by agents and how they depend on time and space. We then codify the most frequent or most critical agent-action-condition triplets as our rules for the ABM. If preferences can be inferred, these will also be included. Otherwise, by consulting human experts, EHM may endow agents with heterogeneous preferences consistent with peoples' behaviours of that time and space as input parameters for our ABM. At this point, EHM is ready to write the computer program to simulate the ABM (Nanetti & Cheong 2018, 355).

The virtual routes, traced by the study of prehistoric civilisation, especially that of the Aegean in the Mediterranean Sea, seem not to have varied, according to the testimony of successive historical periods. If valid, these routes can be identified as the greatest, if not *the* continuity, factor in the history of communications by sea (for the Mediterranean Sea, Murray 1987, Pryor 1989, Nanetti 2011, 46–47; for the Atlantic Ocean, Goldsmith & Richardson 1987; for the Indian Ocean, Fernández-Armesto 2000, 14–16; Beaujard 2012, 32–40). Along the shores and in the open sea, underwater archaeologists are discovering more and more sites and shipwrecks. A direct citation is helpful for underwater findings, for which a database of shipwreck information is still lacking (a rare example, limited to the Mediterranean Sea, is Parker 1992).

> Coastal waters represent the greatest danger to ships and seafarers, as ships are most commonly lost at the intersection of water and shore. Ships sinking in deep water undergo a gradual transition. Deep-submergence archaeology refers to the archaeological study of cultural resources beyond the limits of traditional diving. At great depths in the sea, the totality of archaeological exploration—discovering, recording, excavating, and recovering—requires function-specific tools. Deep Submergence Archaeological Excavations (DSAE) uses a remarkable existent toolkit designed for various oceanographic purposes besides studying ancient shipwrecks. What is lacking at present is a comprehensive methodology for deep-water excavation. The ultimate goal of DSAE is to develop the technologies and the skills that permit expeditions to excavate and safely raise the contents and hull of an entire ship for conservation, study, and display.
>
> (Wachsmann 2012)

However, underwater archaeology provides evidence only with goods that did not perish underwater (e.g., ceramic, glass). As an example, highlighted by David Abulafia (2019, illustration 13, between pp. 184–185, 162–165, 929), 'the Belitung wreck contained 70,000 pots, the largest collection of late Tang pottery ever found, including many pieces from Changsha in central China. It probably carried silk, but that has disintegrated (Krahl et al. 2010)'. In addition, in Singapore, Fuxi Gan and his research team edited a collection of suitable methods to study glass that could also be applied to the sea trade (Gan et al.

2009). As for other goods more likely to decay underwater, scholarship mainly relies on written records to know whether, when and where specific commodities travelled by sea.

The record of individuals or people groups moving by sea from one place to another and the goods they carried is an enormous and highly diversified treasure of human experiences. This information is dispersed in various primary historical sources (e.g., archival documents, travel accounts, maps, chronicles). For example, the American historian Michael McCormick published a register of 828 records of maritime travels dated between 700 and 900 CE (McCormick 2001, 852–972). This register is an excellent but rare specimen of historical information collected in a way that can become a machine-understandable database with little effort. On the contrary, most highly relevant publications do not share the basic information collected by the authors to substantiate their theories and narratives (e.g., Pryor 1988, 87–101, Casson 1994, Tagliacozzo & Chang 2011, Gerritsen & Riello 2015). Encyclopaedic works such as *Trade, Travel, and Exploration in the Middle Ages. An Encyclopedia* (Block Friedman et al. 2000) give a glimpse of the vastness of the work which needs to be done to process this treasure trove of human experiences in a machine-understandable system.

The tracing of therapeutic commodities across cultures and languages as practices by Michal Stanley-Baker is an excellent showcase for studying goods across Afro-Eurasia. Stanley-Baker's 'Drugs Across Asia' project (Stanley-Baker n.d.) combines various digital tools to identify and track the migration of materia medica across digitised manuscripts in multiple languages and map their geographic spread, ancient and modern. Additionally, this project links materia medica to science databases describing biochemical contents and metabolic targets in the human body. In this way, the project speaks across multiple disciplines forging new pathways for collaborative research across history, traditional medicine, ethnopharmacology and botany, and modern drug research. Since 2018, Stanley Baker's early pilots have taken three primary forms and engaged several interdisciplinary collaborations with other scholars: large text corpora of searchable digital transcriptions of citable manuscripts, semi-automated text tagging, and comparative digital mapping of multiple text editions via historical-GIS databases such as those hosted in the Fairbank Center for Chinese Studies at Harvard University and in the Center for Historical Geographical Studies at Fudan University (2016) and in the Dharma Drum Institute of Liberal Arts (DILA) (2008).

The core database is a large textual corpus of Buddhist, Daoist, and materia medica sources (Stanley-Baker et al. 2018) that allows automated discovery of massive term clusters (including, but not limited to, indigenous Chinese drug names). It reveals each term's distribution across titles, genres, and time (Stanley-Baker & Chong 2019). Selected texts are individually tagged using semi-automated methods that allow context discovery of complex internal patterns and constitute a new type of annotated critical edition at the primary source (Stanley-Baker et al. 2020a, Tu et al. 2020). Texts tagged with locations using historical GIS databases such as those hosted at Harvard, and Dharma Drum can be used to digitally map the contents, revealing hitherto unseen geographic distributions and the contours of early trade networks (Stanley-Baker et al. 2020b).

These three pilot studies serve as a proof-of-concept for the project 'Polyglot Asian Medicine' (2019) that addresses the problem of how to identify ancient drugs across different languages. At Nanyang Technological University Singapore, the project is currently the subject of a three-way interdisciplinary collaboration between researchers of the School of Humanities, the Chinese Medical Clinic and the Centre for Biomedical Informatics at the Lee Kong Chian School of Medicine. In addition to full-text medical manuscript databases, some with high-resolution images, this project identifies Malay, Chinese, and Abui ethnobotanical terms. It also links them to the corresponding scientific names via the Kew Gardens' 'Medicinal Plant Name Services' (Royal Botanic Gardens Kew Science 2021), biodiversity maps (Global Biodiversity Information Facility n.d.), the 'Biodiversity Heritage Library' (n.d.), and numerous other web-based projects compiling plant chemistry and their metabolic targets in the human body (e.g., SuperTCM 2020, SymMap 2021).

In collaboration with Michael Stanley-Baker and his research team, EHM aims to leverage this machine-understandable information on therapeutic commodities to work on a cloud-based application for goods on EHM. This new EHM application aggregates information about things that can (or are believed to) be medicinal for humans and animals. Still, it traces also the culturally diverse use of other commodities made across space and over time (Gerritsen & Riello 2015, 1–28). Because, in the same place and simultaneously, the same item can be traditionally used for different purposes (e.g., drugs, perfumes, food) and be taxed differently, accordingly, as happened, for example, between Constantinople and Venice in the Middle Age (Tucci 2004, Lauritzen 2017, 22–43).

The law issued in 533 by Constantinople and applied to Italy from 554 mentions various categories of luxury goods (*Digest* 24.1.7;

34.2), and that of medicines (*Digest* 41.1.27) stand out. These two categories demonstrate an overlapping of the different trades of the maker or seller of perfumes and spices. The confusion is because the same ingredients could be used to create perfumes or medicines.
(Lauritzen 2017, footnote 12 at p. 30)

The confusion is apparent in the *Lexikon* of Hesychius, where the term 'pimentarius' is explained as pharmacist and perfumer: 'πιμ εντάριος: φαρμακός και μυρεψός'.
(*ibidem*, referring to Hesychius, *Lexicon*, pi.2296, in Schmidt 1861–1862)

However, the preservation of relevant documents dated before the eleventh century is a rare case. Realities such as Cairo's genizah and, more in general, the European historical archives can only suggest how much we have lost from the past in other times and regions of Afro-Eurasia that used writing to keep track of tax records and other ordinary transactions. Thanks to the edition of the letters of Jewish traders that Shelomo Dov Goiten (1900–1985) published in 1974 (refer to Goiten 1974) and his later masterful work that used this source to study the Mediterranean society (Goiten 1967–1993); the documentation of Cairo's genizah widely contributed to the reconstruction of the movements of Jewish merchants in the Mediterranean Sea and the Indian Ocean in the eleventh century (Goldberg 2012). The documentation preserved in European historical archives provides scholars with a tremendous contribution to studying the history of medieval and early modern trade and communications by land and sea. Yet, surprisingly, there is no comprehensive study offering a synthesis of the impact of these archives on international historiographies. The International Council on Archives (2022) is a first and unique reference point.

Besides, the more famous and popular some travel accounts and chronicles became, the more they put other texts in latency, made societies forget previous accounts, and, ultimately, caused their loss. In terms of literary texts, archetypes are organised aggregations of selected knowledge and wisdom from a past that usually does not provide any more trace of its human experiences. The reasons are practical and straightforward. Firstly, these works lowered the need to access earlier repositories of human experiences, and, finally, when their reputation grew, they put a gravestone on what was before them. This loss is the price that cultures pay for codifying and formalising existing knowledge and practices into comprehensive, organised systems. For example, from Western classical antiquity, only about one per cent of Ancient Greek and Latin works are still available today.

The transmission of texts written in these two languages was very successful compared to other ancient languages, without mentioning what has been intentionally dispersed or destroyed. Two examples are significant and famous. According to Pliny the Elder, in 146 BCE, in Carthage (North Africa), the Roman senate 'bestowed the libraries of that city upon the petty kings of Africa' and only Mago's *Treatise on Agriculture* was preserved to be translated into Latin (*Naturalis Historia*, Book 18, 5.22). Evidence of a fire that destroyed about 40,000 scrolls is related to Julius Caesar's siege of the city of Alexandria (Egypt) in 48 BCE (MacLeod 2004, 7, quoting Seneca the Younger, who cited Titus Livius, *Ab Urbe Condita*). Afterwards, the Library of Alexandria was restored and finally destroyed when Amr ibn al-As conquered the city in 642 CE (Delia 1992).

Thus, while history must rely on the earliest known proof of something, the testimony of archaeological and archival records, annals, chronicles, travel accounts, maps, etc., cannot be construed as evidence that anything did not exist before what that testimony itself records. On the contrary, as an example, when we read that something is 'of Mesopotamian origin', it must instead be understood that the most ancient testimony of that human experience dates to Sumer and Akkadian pieces of literature. Indeed, most if not all knowledge and wisdom that the civilisation of Sumer recorded using pictographs starting in the fourth millennium BCE must eventually have already been part of that culture. Since when? We do not know (Geller 1997, Dalley 1998). The same could be argued about later developments of writing in Egypt, India, Crete, Syria, Palestine, and China (Ong 1982, Godart 2001). Similarly, we do not know if and how often long-distance sea travels happened before their first evidence. Therefore, we can assume that the existing historical and archaeological evidence of sea lanes illustrates a situation consolidated much earlier. Alike, accessible evidence of exchange between East and West suggests that human societies traded goods that came from very far away by sea much earlier than what mainstream archaeology usually acknowledges.

EHM aims to link all this information to a specific time and space coordinates, run ABMS, and offer the opportunity to plot it in navigation charts (e.g., Zheng He's, edited by Nanetti et al. 2022b) and other maps of Afro-Eurasia (e.g., Fra Mauro's, edited by Nanetti et al. 2019). An EHM research team (Siew Ann Cheong, Nguyen Khoi Vu, and Andrea Nanetti) started to work on ABMS in 2019. However, there

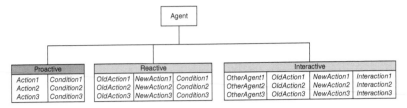

Figure 5.1 Identification of the ABM Data Template characteristics of a computational agent to be mapped from a primary source. An agent must be 'proactive', viz. able to set goals and, under the right conditions, execute them; 'reactive', viz. able to respond to features or changes in the environment; 'interactive', viz. able to change its course of action because another agent's course of action prevents the agent from executing its preferred action.

are many challenges when we consider the task of running ABMS starting from primary sources. Firstly, records in any primary source have structures peculiar to the typology or even the individual primary source itself. Hence, they are considered unstructured from a computational perspective because they are not written down in a relational database. Thus, many human curations are needed to build up historical databases from primary historical sources. Nevertheless, these databases are not enough for building an ABMS, even when they are searchable since they were not specifically created to facilitate the creation of computer simulations. Therefore, existing databases require further human curation for their purposeful reorganisation in the form of an ABM Data Template to get started with agent-based modelling. For example, refer to Figure 5.1.

Secondly, once relevant primary historical sources have been processed and aggregated on EHM to gain information on environmental features and changes, the ABM Data Template is still challenging for its constant updating and being logically disconnected. As a result, the ABMS built using the ABM Data Template at a given time will differ from the next one that uses an updated ABM Data Template. A solution to this updating problem is to organise the ABMS efforts into a source-compiler-executable framework, as shown in Figure 5.2.

This software engineering framework does not solve the updating problem alone but allows us to think of a solution from a very different perspective. Indeed, the ABM Data Template must behave like a source code when we refer to the ABM Data Template as a source. The agents described in the ABM Data Template must be declared as software 'objects' and their defining codes as well. It also means that agent actions, reactions, and interactions must be definable as software

Figure 5.2 Source-compiler-executable framework commonly used in the software engineering industry, whereby the source can be frequently updated (with the help of a versioning system) to cater to evolving demands and can be transformed by a compiler into an executable. The number of executable versions can be as large as the number of source versions. The idea is that a historian wanting to run a historical ABMS would download the most recent version of the ABM Data Template, make some modifications, compile it, and then run the executable. The compiler needs to be seldomly updated because it does not need to know what changes have been made to the ABM Data Template.

functions. We want the compiler to read the ABM Data Template, copy out the object and function definitions, instantiate agents, and initialise their list of actions/reactions/interactions based on the list provided by the user. In a sense, the ABM Data Template must be a hybrid document. Presented to historians, it will be a list of agent actions/reactions/interactions they can add to, with proper references to the primary sources. Presented to a computational scientist, it must be a list of object and function definitions to be assembled by the compiler into an executable script. Presumably, historians would not be able to provide these object/function definitions, so the ABM Data Template must be updated by two groups of people: the historians and the computational scientists. We must also build the compiler to issue warnings to the computational scientists to tell them which definitions are missing and need to be added. Often, there are missing object/function definitions because historians have done a recent update, but computational scientists have not.

Notwithstanding the continuous updating process, the ABM Data Template remains logically disconnected because the evidence available in existing primary historical sources does not cover the totality of the agent's behaviour. Therefore, inferences are needed before compiling the ABM Data Template into an executable that can be simulated. However, such inferences cannot be included in the ABM Data Template, as it can only contain records traceable back to recognised primary sources. Inferences represent hypotheses of which we do not have direct but only indirect evidence. The EHM solution to this logical disconnection problem, within the source-compiler-executable framework, is to list the inferences in a separate (updateable) library called ABM Inferences Library. It can

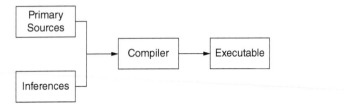

Figure 5.3 The compiler reads in primary sources (ABM Data Template) and inferences (ABM Inferences Library) and combines their object/function definitions to run the ABMS.

be organised as the ABM Data Template. Then, the inferences can be compiled within the source-compiler-executable framework, as shown in Figure 5.3.

At this point, secondary literature interpretations can also be added to the simulation to surrogate a lake of necessary inference. For example, by reading the seminal book of the American sociologist Janet Lippman Abu-Lughod (1928–2013), *Before European Hegemony: The World System A.D. 1250–1350,* published by Oxford University Press in 1989, EHM builds up agent/function definitions and assembles them into an ABM Historiography Library that the compiler can read in, on its own, to integrate necessary inferences and run simulations using the framework shown below in Figure 5.4. Yet, one should refrain from the temptation to create many different ABM Historiography Libraries for each secondary-literature item. They represent interpretations, and their validation cannot be tested by pitting them against each other but by running them in parallel with the information available in existing primary sources.

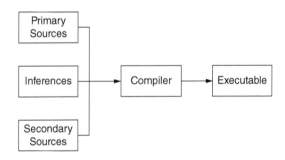

Figure 5.4 The compiler can read primary sources, inferences, and secondary sources and combine them into an executable simulation as a scalable approach to data-driven ABMS.

5.2 Venetian State-Run Galley Convoys as a Testbed to Design ABMs and Run Simulations

In studying ports of trade, sea lanes, environmental events, and their relationships, a critical discussion is about how to move from current practices into a computational discipline. An option is to adopt ABMS as a method, focus on essential questions of history and relevant data sets, and, thus, empower relevant knowledge discovery. Joshua M. Epstein, in his 2008 Bastille Day keynote address given to the Second World Congress on Social Simulation, George Mason University, and earlier speeches at the Institute of Medicine, the University of Michigan, and the Santa Fe Institute, clarified the difference between explanation and prediction as modelling goals and offered sixteen reasons other than prediction to build a model. Epstein's research 'also challenges the common assumption that scientific theories arise from and summarise data, when often, theories precede and guide data collection; without theory, in other words, it is not clear what data to collect' (Epstein 2008).

In 2017, EHM started to work on its first example of how to develop an exploratory ABMS was designed and implemented. Two members of the EHM research team (Siew Ann Cheong and Andrea Nanetti) proposed to Nguyen Khoi Vu (Talented Program, Faculty of Physics, Vietnam National University of Science, Hanoi) to focus his internship at Nanyang Technological University Singapore on historical trading and commodity data from Venice between 1200 and 1700. A series of correlated reasons informed this initial choice. First, Venice is the earliest global power that carefully and continuously preserved documentation of its history for over 1,000 years. Today, we have more than 70 kilometres of shelves of archival documents, which witnessed the activities carried out by the government offices in the day-to-day administration of their duties (Tiepolo 1994). In addition, a complementary collection of about 2,000 handwritten chronicles narrates and comments on selected events related to both the Republic of Venice and the world as seen from its perspective (Vespignani 2018, vii–xii). These corpora can indeed be used as a privileged laboratory (i.e., a space isolated in time as a closed physical system) to run ABMS and experiment with how this exercise can contribute to the advancement of learning in historical sciences. This laboratory can work towards a better understanding of the complex relationship among trade, conflict, and diplomacy at the intercontinental level (Nanetti 2010, xiii–xix, Nanetti & Vu 2018, Nanetti 2021, 24–25). The internship outcome was Vu's final year thesis at the Vietnam National University of Science (Vu 2018).

Afterwards, Vu was hired as Research Assistant at Nanyang Technological University Singapore to contribute to the implementation of the EHM algorithms under the supervision of Andrea Nanetti and Siew Ann Cheong from 2019 to 2020. Later, in 2020, another scholar, Alan M. Stahl (Princeton University), joined the EHM team. The team collegially decided to work on the Venetian state-run galley convoys from 1400 to 1433 as a relatively 'small data paradigm' (Posner 2015, Hekler et al. 2019) because of several benefits. First, the Venetian state-run galley convoys are a well-studied international economic actor (Stöckly 1995).

Le système de l'Incanto des galées du marché à Venise offers the first complete analysis of the medieval Venetian system of auctioning (*Incanto*) the state-owned galleys for commercial use. The *Incanti* (auction records) reveal a pattern of progressive intervention by the state in sea trading and the evolution of a corpus of statutes governing private navigation. The work traces the growth and interdependency of the eight state shipping lines. By establishing the infrastructure necessary for international commerce, the state (or rather the patriciate) enabled the involvement in trade—in roles ranging from sponsor to captain to arquebusier—of a large number of nobles with only modest capitals. This study also examines the structures of such participation (patrician family associations) and shows how these defined the career patterns of nobles and guided the emergence of a noble merchant oligarchy in medieval Venice.

(Stöckly 1995, abstract)

Notwithstanding that these early eight convoys lasted for centuries, 'as to the number of active ships, the peak was reached in the fifteenth century, with 180 galleys in circulation in the 1430s and 1440s' (Pezzolo 2013, 263). Moreover, in 2018, Andrea Nanetti designed an EHM application (Nanetti & Vu 2018) for the Morosini Codex (1400–1433), a financial and economic diary of the world as seen by the Venetian patrician Antonio, son of Marco Morosini (Nanetti 2010). This diary recorded detailed information about the state-run galley convoys from 1400 to 1433. Likewise, Alan M. Stahl contributed to the critical edition and study of Michael of Rhodes' manuscript (dated 1434). This work aggregates the experience and knowledge of his author, who sailed on more than 40 voyages and took part in five major sea battles, rising through the galley ranks from oarsman to commander (Long et al. 2019). Concurrently, Stahl shared a reach database that he had populated over the years. The database contains the record of about 1,500 voyages and 24,000 holdings extracted from about 9,000 archival documents dated between 1365 and 1443, including Deliberations of the Venetian Senate, the main deliberative body of the Republic of Venice.

Furthermore, the focus on the early fifteenth century is significant because of the historical relevance of this period for the study of world history and the dawn of modern globalisation in the pre-modern Afro-Eurasian communication networks. The recorded information on the Venetian state-run galley convoys—despite its unrivalled richness of documentation to study the economic history of the early fifteenth-century Euro-Mediterranean trade—does not cover all events. As recent and meaningful examples, there are Stefania Montemezzo's use of the late fifteenth-century Foscari ledgers to catch a glimpse of the system of public navigation in Renaissance Venice (Montemezzo 2019) and Gerassimon Pagratis and Renard Gluzman's GIS-based maps of voyages for the years 1497 and 1514 with a focus on Candia (Gluzman & Pagratis 2019).

So, even the rich records of the Venetian Republic somehow lack the historical-information granularity desired to fulfil the requirements of an ABMS. Furthermore, this limited data resolution is evident when research moves from the Mediterranean into the Indian Ocean. However, existing historical records are fascinating, as demonstrated by Alan M. Stahl in his study on and Venetian and Muslim merchants in Tana in the Late Middle Ages (Stahl 2019) and as encouraged by the same author when he gave a talk on the Venetian ducat in India encouraging the audience to track Venetian coins in the Indian subcontinent (Stahl 2004). In all ports of trade where the so-called Silk Road, by sea and overland, met the Euro-Mediterranean trade systems, we can start a meaningful investigation. Thus, the EHM experimental goal is to simulate relevant events not mentioned in the available historical documentation. EHM designed and built an ABM to simulate some critical scenarios for shipping between Venice and the ports of call and trade of the Venetian state-run galley convoys. The ABM works to estimate how galleys sailed between ports (calibrating the total recorded voyage time along with physical factors such as velocity) and cargo space value in the state convoys (concerning the fact that piracy affected private merchant ships with no protection).

In creating the ABM, EHM started with two historical sources: archival documents (Deliberations of the Senate of Venice) and a narrative source (the Morosini codex; Nanetti 2010, 2018). The two primary quantitative data sets are the state-auction prices for the convoys and the loading capacity of the ships (galleys, light galleys, and cogs). The database was populated by combining information from the Morosini codex and the Senate deliberations. The ships have also been studied with 3D visualisation models (Nanetti & Benvenuti 2019). This ABM can simulate both recorded and unrecorded historical events through specific rules of action, including proactivity (i.e., an action to achieve the agent's goal), reactivity (i.e., a change in the action because of changes in the environment), and interactivity (i.e., a change in the action as a result of interactions with other agents). The EHM team mentioned above has identified several challenges and matched them with potential solutions for this first ABM.

Identified challenges	*Potential solutions*
Unlike secondary literature, this database aims to be continuously updatable online. When the database is updated, the simulation needs to be updated in a scalable way (automatically or semi-automatically).	Source compiler executable framework. An Excel spreadsheet is generated automatically by the database. It contains the latest updates and serves as the source code of simulations. Then, a Python programe works as a compiler and reads in the Excel spreadsheet to generate a Python simulation programe. This Python simulation programe plays the role of an executable. So, whenever the user wants to run a simulation, EHM generates an Excel spreadsheet with the latest updated data set and an executable file.
Proliferation of agent types, action types, and condition types. If this challenge is not addressed, there are far too many agents, actions, and conditions to deal with in a scalable manner. For example, in the records of the Senate Deliberations, some galleys and cogs are mentioned explicitly in some documents but only implicitly identifiable as ships in other documents (without information about the type of ship). On an Afro-Eurasian scale, unspecified types can only increase when other primary historical sources are compiled (e.g., Arabic, Swahili, Chinese, Malay, Thai).	Eventually, EHM could simulate each ship type, action type, and condition type extracted from primary sources in the long run. But initially, it is better to run more direct simulations without discriminating between different subtypes of agents. Within given Excel spreadsheets, EHM can define various levels of mapping between the recorded agent type and the simulated agent type. For example, suppose cogs and galleys are not treated differently. In that case, only a single ship agent type is simulated, viz. the cog agent type and galley agent type are mapped in the simulation as a ship agent type.

(Continued)

Identified challenges	*Potential solutions*
Identification of primary agency (i.e., the agent that initiates the action according to a primary source). Example: On 27 July 1405, the captain of the State convoy of Flanders sent a land dispatch asking to stay longer than planned, and the Senate approved the request). In this case, the question is whether the agency is the State convoy, the Senate, or an interaction between the two.	EHM proposes using a chronological disambiguation system (i.e., the agent acting first is the initiator and the agent reacting is the interaction).
Dynamic Agency. Example: The State convoy to Bruges consisted of 4–6 galleys. They first sailed from Venice to the Isle of Sandwich. There, the convoy broke up: 2–3 galleys headed for Sluys (Bruges), and 2–3 galleys headed for London. After trading there, the two galley groups met up again at the Isle of Sandwich to reform the convoy and sail back to Venice. Therefore, it is necessary to accord agency to both groups and treat the two groups as distinct agents.	A straightforward potential solution is to treat each galley as an agent because they can exercise agency in making decisions. However, when galleys form groups, they surrender their decision-making agency to a representative (the captain) and let him be the one making decisions for all of them. Thus, a second and better option is to create two new agents when a convoy splits into two and, similarly, creates a new single agent when the two convoys merge into one. This second framework allows agents to have preferred actions or interactions to develop new agents and obliterate themselves.
Gaps in the primary sources. Example: The Senate approved the request by captain Fantin Michiel, but there is no record of the initial commission given to the captain by the Senate before departure. A complete picture can only be obtained by combining various primary sources (e.g., Morosini Codex and Senate Deliberations). However, in several cases, not all information is available.	Two ways can be experimented with to deal with gaps in primary sources. The first way consists of preparing additional source codes that offer interpretations only linking different records to keep the database as accessible as possible from arbitrary interpretations (i.e., professional assessments made by historians to connect events). This framework also allows for simulated scenarios consisting of fictitious chronologies. Another way to solve this challenge is to incorporate secondary source interpretations in loadable modules for the simulations. However, this incurs the below challenge.

(Continued)

Identified challenges	Potential solutions
Secondary literature does not refer to primary sources or considers only an arbitrary (i.e., not entirely justifiable) selection. For example, the State convoys are well described in the Michael of Rhodes website (2005) without links to the primary sources that informed the work. Again, Stöckly (1995) considers only a selection and not all available primary sources about the *Incanti*.	This challenge requires computational engineering of secondary literature that links each historian's statement to all potentially related primary sources and not only to the ones used and mentioned by the author of the interpretation. In this direction, the EHM search engine (publications, images, videos, news) is an innovative and scalable solution (see Section 1.3).

Finally, to visualise the simulation results generated by the ABM, the first scenario was the Francesco de Cesanis marine chart dated 1421 (Nanetti 2010). In the Afro-Eurasian context, the research team chose the Fra Mauro map (Nanetti et al. 2019). For this visualisation, the research team created a Source-Compiler-Executable Simulation of Random Walk in one or two dimensions for the ships (Figure 5.5). It is the initial and most simple ABMS developed within EHM. It is the preliminary testbed to build up a whole source-compiler-executable framework for historical ABMS. This random walk is easy to program, with different boundary conditions. If the random walker cannot pass through a wall, the walls represent 'fixed' or 'reflecting boundary' conditions.

If we do not use complicated data structures, this simulation can be achieved using a simple Python code such as the following one written by Nguyen Khoi Vu.

```
import numpy as np
# random walk within 8 x 8 grid
N = 8
# the walls are at x = 0, y = 0, and x = 9, y = 9
# probabilities p = [pN, pE, pS, pW, q]
p = np.array([0.2, 0.2, 0.2, 0.2, 0.2])
# r = position of random walker
r = np.random.randint(1, 8, (1, 2))
# number of time steps to simulate
T = 100
# start simulation
for t in range(T):
    # choose a random direction
    d = np.random.randint(0, 4)
    # update position of random walker
```

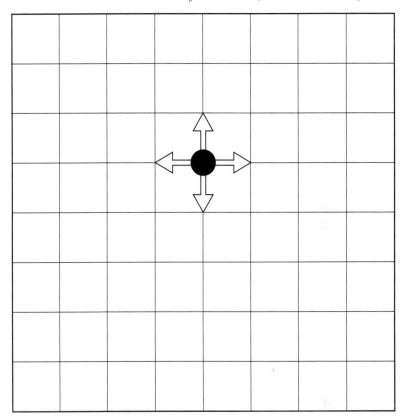

Figure 5.5 Random walk in two dimensions by Nguyen Khoi Vu. The solid
black circle represents the random walker, which can only occupy
sites at the intersection of the thin grid lines. At any point in time,
the random walker can take a step north, with probability p_N, or
a step east, with probability p_E, or a step south, with probability
p_S, or a step west, with probability p_W, or stay put, with probability
$q = 1 - p_N - p_E - p_S - p_W$, except when the random walker is next to
a wall. The random walker is not allowed to pass through a wall.
Therefore, it takes only the allowed steps away from the wall or
stays put, with different probabilities.

```
if d == 0:
    r = r + np.array([0, 1])
if d == 1:
    r = r + np.array([1, 0])
if d == 2:
    r = r + np.array([0, -1])
if d == 3:
```

```
        r = r + np.array([-1, 0])
        # no need to do anything if d == 4
        # check if random walker has gone into the
walls
        if r[0] == 0:
            r[0] = 1
        if r[0] == 9:
            r[0] = 8
        if r[1] == 0:
            r[1] = 1
        if r[1] == 9:
            r[1] = 8
```

In the above Python code, the probability of the forbidden move is added to *q*. Still, a more complicated Python code is needed if we want to redistribute this any other way. As mentioned earlier, EHM wants to simulate this random walk within the source-compiler-executable framework. Therefore, in the design of the 'Random Walker Source', it was taken into consideration that the steps north, south, east, west, or staying put are agent preferred actions, whereas staying clear of the walls represents a reaction to the environment. Since this simulation visualises a single random walker, there is no need to specify any inter-actions. Ultimately, this simple initial step showcases the scalability of the EHM computational approach.

5.3 Framing EHM in the Silk Road Discourse

The German geographer Ferdinand Freiherr von Richthofen (1833–1905) was a pioneer in the scholarly investigation of Eurasian intercontinental networks by sea and land (Waugh 2007, Whitfield 2007, Chin 2013, Hansen 2017, Jacobs 2020, Liu 2020, Wahlquist 2020, Hansen 2021; and an animation based on Waugh's paper, Nanetti & Luo 2016). However, the term 'silk road(s)', *Seidenstraße(n)*, which he used a few times, was not coined by him. So far, the earliest evidence of the use of this term is related to the German geographer Carl Ritter (1779–1859) and dates to 1838. However, a closer study of the works used by Ritter (e.g., Abel Rémasut, Julius Klaproth, Jean Baptiste Bourguignon d'Anville) could even bring the term further back in time (Mertens 2019).

Indeed, Richthofen's most significant contribution lay in having recognised the significance of the intercontinental networks by sea and land. In 1876, he first used the term silk road in a lecture on 'Communication by Sea' given at the Berlin Geographic Society

(Richthofen 1876). He referred to a specific overland route, which ran from the Mediterranean to the western side of the Pamir mountains in what is today Tajikistan. Here began *Serica*, the Land of Silk, as it was known in Greek and Roman Antiquity. Richthofen refers to Ptolemy and Plinius the Elder as he retrieved the information from another German geographer, Carl Ritter (1779–1859), in a book published in 1838 (Mertens 2019, Figure 3 at p. 4, reproducing Ritter 1838, 692).

> Außer diesem südlichen maritimen Wege über Ceilon, Indien und das persisch-arabische Meer, von welchem aus mit der Waare die Griechen und Römer den ächtchinesischen Namen der Seide, *Sericum*, (σήρ, *Sir*, bei Chinesen) kennen lernen konnten, wenn er ihnen nicht auf nördlicherm Wege über Persien durch Ctesias zugekommen, öffnet sich aber fast gleichzeitig der nördliche continentale Weg der Seidenstraße, von China gegen den Westen zum kaspischen See hin. Dies ergiebt sich aus Plinius (VI. 20) und Ptolemäus Berichten von der Seidencultur, dem Seidenhandel und der Serenstraße zu den Sinen, nach *Marinus Tyrius* Aussagen von dem macedonischen Handelsmanne und Reisenden Maës (genannt *Titianus*, s. *Ptolem.* I.
>
> (Ritter 1838, 692)

In 1877, Richthofen, lecturing in the same venue, emphasised that the concept of transcontinental silk roads (*transcontinentaler Seidenstraßen*) lost its meaning after 120 CE when the Han dynasty had retreated from Central Asia (Richthofen 1877). In 1877, he resumed the topic incidentally in his magnum opus *China* (Richthofen 1877–1912, I, 459–462). After that, however, he did not use 'silk road' anymore in his works.

For Richthofen, in the development of complex societies, the interaction across space and time was equally important as the response they gave to the challenges of the surrounding environment (Waugh 2007, 2–3). Furthermore, he emphasised the significance of Eurasian maritime trade routes over land transport networks because intercontinental communication networks over sea demonstrated more resilience and continuity. This fact deserved further attention. It was this belief that, from 1900 until his death, in 1905, led him to establish and serve as founding director of 'The Institute and Museum for the Study of the Sea' (*Das Institut und das Museum für Meereskunde*) as independent research and educational institution of the University of Berlin (Schuster 2007, Museum für Meerkunde, n.d.).

But how a German word incidentally used by a few German geographers was adopted internationally and became the keyword to name all Afro-Eurasian communication and trade networks by land and sea? The attractiveness of the term silk road rose over the years as Richthofen's students—Albert Hermann (1886–1945), Sven Anders Hedin (1865–1952), and Marc Aurel Stein (1862–1943)—gave lectures and published books about their travels by land over these trade routes. These books gained recognition from Europeans who craved adventurous expeditions to exotic countries. But the real boom in the popularity of the term silk road came about with a Sino-Japanese television show broadcast in the 1980s. The multimillion-dollar 30-part television spectacular *The Silk Road* sparked the imagination of millions of people around Asia (Waugh 2007, 5–7). As a result, the term silk road was used as a double synecdoche (i.e., a part representing the whole) for the entire Eurasian commercial and cultural exchanges network. Silk represented all traded goods; one road meant all intercontinental communication networks by land and sea. Since then, the 'Silk Road' has titled the most disparate media products: from historical narratives (e.g., Frankopan 2015, discussing the roads of faiths, revolutions, concord, furs, heave, gold, silver, catastrophe, with a conclusion on 'The New Silk Road', to which the same author dedicated a further book in 2018 with considerations on a new potential world order; Cardini & Vanoli 2017) to exhibition projects (e.g., with reliable historical narratives, Nara National Museum & Nara Prefectural Museum 1988; D'Arelli & Callieri 2011), through museum settings (Davies 2012).

Later, the term silk road was also used as a metaphor (i.e., applied to an object or action to which it is not applicable) to brand disparate successful initiatives that span almost all subjects. On the one hand, the Silk Road website was created by Ross William Ulbricht as a marketplace to buy and sell illicit drugs, contraband goods, and services, such as computer hacking.

> The FBI shut it down in October 2013, resulting in a seizure of $3.6 millions of funds in escrow. The shutdown also led to the arrest of Ross Ulbricht, the alleged founder and chief operator of the site, known by users as the Dread Pirate Roberts.
>
> (Lacson & Jones 2016)

On 29 May 2015, in the Federal District Court in Manhattan, Ulbricht, 31, was sentenced to life in prison by the judge, Katherine B. Forrest, for his role as what prosecutors described as 'the kingpin of a world-wide digital drug-trafficking enterprise' (Weiser 2015).

On the other hand, the Silk Road Universities Network is supported by UNESCO. 'The project aims to revive the spirit of peace, coexistence and co-prosperity, which is represented by the Silk Road, a symbol of the East-West civilisational exchange. Also, it aspires to uphold the spirit on a global scale' (UNESCO 2018). The 2002 annual Smithsonian Folklife Festival on the National Mall in Washington, D.C., was dedicated to 'The Silk Road: Connecting Cultures, Creating Trust'. It was the Smithsonian's answer to the 11-September-2001 attacks (Slobin 2003, Andrea 2014, 114–115). In terms of trade and communication networks, the Iraqi journalist, Iqbal al-Qazwini, outlined the controversial American physical economist and international statesman Lyndon H. LaRouche Jr. (1922–2019). LaRouche Jr was the spiritual father of the revival of a land-based 'New Silk Road' or Eurasian Land-Bridge, which aims to link the continents through a network of ground transportation (al-Qazwini 2003, Simpfendorfer 2009, Ch. 1). Laurence M. Hecht praised LaRouche's idea to develop economic development corridors across Eurasia. The plan was to create a rail linkage from Eurasia to the Americas via the Strait of Bering. It was seen as a disruptive agenda to foster modernisation, improve living standards for about two-thirds of the world's population, and 'finally, shift the international economic balance from maritime to land-based power' (Hecht 2003).

Today, the most well-known use of the 'New Silk Road' belongs to the Chinese government, which refers to more excellent connectivity between Afro-Eurasian regions and uniting them under one umbrella to promote economic development. From a historical perspective, refer to the works by Peter Frankopan (2015, 2018). From a political sciences perspective, refer to *Research Handbook on the Belt and Road Initiative*, edited by Liow, Joseph Chinyong, Hong Liu, and Gong Xue (2021). This collected-study book investigates the transformative impact of the Belt and Road Initiative (BRI), addressing key questions regarding its economic, political, and strategic consequences from different angles: What does the Chinese government hope to achieve with the BRI? How have recipient states responded? And what are its potential opportunities and risks?

In September 2013, the CCP secretary-general, Xi Jinping, announced a land-based economic programme called 'Silk Road Economic Belt' during an official visit to Kazakhstan (Ministry of Foreign Affairs of the People's Republic of China 2013). In October

2013, in a speech to the Indonesian Parliament, he launched its sea-based counterpart called '21ˢᵗ Century Maritime Silk Road.'

> Observers said the proposal, made by Xi during a speech to the Indonesian Parliament, aimed at enhancing maritime partnership against the backdrop that China's geopolitical ties with its Southeast Asian neighbours brings both opportunities for cooperation and challenges from territorial disputes.
>
> (Wu & Zhang 2013)

As early as October 2013, China linked this initiative to the creation of the Asian Infrastructure Investment Bank to lend money for projects (AIIB n.d., Lichtenstein 2018, Ch. 1), and later, in 2014, to the Silk Road Fund for complemental business investments (SRF n.d.; Page 2014). In 2015, these initiatives were unified and together renamed in English as 'Belt and Road' (in Chinese, 一带一路, 'One Belt One Road') with an equity of about one trillion yuan (US$160 billion; refer to National Development and Reform Commission of the PRC 2015). However, even if, in the new label, this economic initiative has a unified aegis, the land networks ('One Belt') and the sea routes ('One Road') are discernible as a duality in the way in which they are phrased. For a thorough study of OBOR narratives from a Southeast Asian perspective and with particular attention paid to the balance between overland and maritime trade routes, the *Proceedings of the seminar jointly organised by the Confucius Institute of Nanyang Technological University Singapore and the International Zheng He Society (Singapore, 19 December 2015)* are punctual (Lim et al. 2016). According to one of the finest Southeast Asian intellectuals, the historian Gungwu Wang, a reason can be that modern Chinese history is all about land (Ooi 2015).

> The Chinese records are obsessed with the north and the west for security and political reasons. From the south, there was no danger. So, there was no reason to talk about it. But, today, China has started to think about danger coming from the sea and the south. That's why there is a balance starting to look at the maritime branch as equally important.
>
> (Wang 2020)

Since 2013, on the internet, many reports, policy documents, news articles, etc. are available about this initiative that, with more than 100 countries on board (Figure 5.6), could impact the lives of 4.4 billion

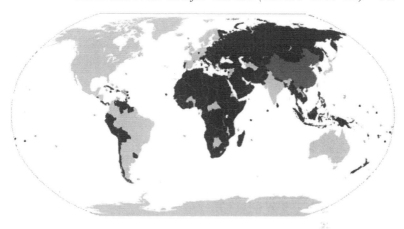

Figure 5.6 Map of the countries (in black) which signed cooperation documents related to the Belt and Road Initiative with China (in dark grey) by 5 February 2021. This map continues to be updated on Wikimedia Commons https://commons.wikimedia.org/wiki/File:Belt_and_Road_Initiative_participant_map.svg (accessed on 2022-05-10).

people, more than half of the global population, with far-reaching social and economic effects. But there is no place where this valuable information can be brought all together in a single open-access searchable system. In 2018, according to the United Nations Conference on Trade and Development, maritime transport was the backbone of international trade and the global economy. Around 80 per cent of global trade by volume and over 70 per cent of global trade by value are carried by sea and are handled by ports worldwide (United Nations Conference on Trade and Development 2018). In 2020, the trend increased (United Nations Conference on Trade and Development 2020). As presented in previous sections of this essay, historically, intercontinental communication and trade networks by sea demonstrated a greater continuity and resilience than land-based networks and acted as a web to connect river-based regional networks to the world. However, the antinomies of land vs sea communication systems and the consequential dichotomy between land and sea powers originated economic conflicts at the domestic and foreign policy levels (Hecht 2003, 2). Therefore, EHM is working on creating a knowledge aggregator powered by sentiment analysis algorithms (Cambria et al. 2020) to understand *The Silk Road: Histories, Initiatives, People* (Nanetti & Vu 2021). Past and present are working together to design a better future. The study of the long and deep roots of the Silk Road discourse can benefit from understanding the modalities of the European interaction with Southeast Asia (Reid 2000).

5.4 Epilogue without Conclusion

This chapter closes this book. It showcased why, how, and by what means EHM is unfolding the knowledge embodied in primary historical sources and lays it out online in the digital space. EHM empowers the historian's craft with human digital curation and automatic multilingual and multimodal database processing. The vision is that, by these means, scholars could faster and more comprehensively penetrate the foundations of previously accumulated knowledge and, ultimately, discover the hitherto unattainable depth and breadth of historical insight. The immediate results can be listed in this epilogue as the beginning of a research pathway in which EHM is a visual gateway to digital historical knowledge.

This outcome is made possible by the open-access aggregation of the results of multiple research projects based in different regions of the world to overcome today's limits in research funding, namely short-term investments (i.e., one-to-three year-long projects) and localism (preference for one's area or region). This effort in aggregating research results has two significant outcomes. Firstly, it provides scholars with an increasing number of interconnected databases of high-quality human-curated digital information that can be construed as a connectivity set of research infrastructure sharable with machine learning algorithms. Secondly, it becomes easier to explore history beyond national historiographies, the short-sighted parochial strategies of which act like a Shirt of Nessus for the historical understanding of the world as seen from the others.

As an epilogue, therefore, but without a conclusion, we can cite the final lines of the last poem, *Il termine* ('The end,' 2004–2005), by the Italian poet Mario Luzi (1914–2005). The poet, thinking if his enterprise had ended there, poses the alternative that 'a new impossible climb was born/this he feared, this he desired' (Ramat 2005, 3). As Silvio Ramat writes, commenting on it, in Luzi's last poems, environments and occasions may change, 'but there is a spring urgency, the germ of transformation, the breath of renewal' (Ramat 2005, 4). The final wishes this book makes to EHM are imbued with this spirit of constant rebirth.

References

Abulafia, David (2019). *The Boundless Sea. A Human History of the Oceans.* London: Penguin Books.

AIIB (n.d.). "Asian Infrastructure Investment Bank". Accessed May 9, 2022. https://www.aiib.org/en/index.html

al-Qazwini, Iqbal (2003). "Major International Crisis Need Giant Project to Overcome Them". *Asharq Al-Awsat*, January 23, 2003.

Andrea, Alfred J. (2014). "The Silk Road in World History: A Review Essay". *Asian Review of World Histories*, *2*(1), 105–127. http://dx.doi.org/10.12773/arwh.2014.2.1.105

Beaujard, Philippe (2012). *Les mondes de l'océan Indien, Tome I. De la formation de l'État au premier système-monde afro-eurasien (4ᵉ millénaire av. J.-C.-6ᵉ siècle apr. J.-C.)*. Paris: Armand Colin.

Biodiversity Heritage Library (n.d.). "Biodiversity Heritage Library". Accessed May 25, 2022. https://www.biodiversitylibrary.org/

Block Friedman, John, Kristen Mossler Figg, Scott D. Westrem, & Gregory G. Guzman (Eds.) (2000). *Trade, Travel, and Exploration in the Middle Ages. An Encyclopedia*. London: Routledge. https://doi.org/10.4324/9781315160047

Cambria, Erik, Jonathan K. Chandra, Andrea Nanetti (2020). "One Belt, One Road, One Sentiment? A Hybrid Approach to Mining Opinions about the New Silk Road Initiative". *2020 International Conference on Data Mining Workshops (ICDMW)*, 2020, 7–14. https://doi.org/10.1109/ICDMW51313.2020.00011

Cardini, Franco, & Alessandro Vanoli (2017). *La Via della Seta. Una storia millenaria tra Oriente e Occidente*. Bologna: Il Mulino.

Casson, Lionel (1994). *Travel in the Ancient World*. Baltimore, MD: Johns Hopkins University Press. https://archive.org/details/travelinancientw0000cass/mode/2up

Chin, Tamara (2013). "The Invention of the Silk Road, 1877". *Critical Inquiry*, *40*(1), 194–219. https://doi.org/10.1086/673232

D'Arelli, Francesco, & Pierfrancesco Callieri (Eds.) (2011). *A Oriente: città, uomini e dei sulle vie della seta [Catalogue of the exhibition]*. Milan: Electa.

Dalley, Stephanie (1998). *The Legacy of Mesopotamia*. Oxford: Oxford University Press. https://archive.org/details/legacyofmesopota0000dall/mode/2up

Davies, Stephen (2012). "Maritime Museums: Who Needs Them?" *Nalanda-Sriwijaya Centre Working Paper*, *11*(May), 1–46. https://www.iseas.edu.sg/images/pdf/nsc_working_paper_series_11.pdf

Delia, Diana (1992). "From Romance to Rhetoric: The Alexandrian Library in Classical and Islamic Traditions". *The American Historical Review*, *97*(5), 1449–1467. https://doi.org/10.2307/2165947

Dharma Drum Institute of Liberal Arts (DILA) (2008). "Buddhist Studies Authority Database Project". Accessed May 25, 2022. https://authority.dila.edu.tw

Epstein, Joshua M. (2008). "Why Model?" *Journal of Artificial Societies and Social Simulation*, *11*(4), 12. https://www.jasss.org/11/4/12.html

Fairbank Center for Chinese Studies (Harvard University) and Center for Historical Geographical Studies (Fudan University) (2016). "CHGIS V6 [China Historical Geographic Information System]". December 2016. https://sites.fas.harvard.edu/~chgis/data/chgis/v6

Fernández-Armesto, Felipe (2000). "The Indian Ocean in World History". In *Vasco da Gama and the Linking of Europe and Asia*, edited by Anthony Disney and Emily Booth, 11–30. New York and New Delhi: Oxford University Press.

Foltz, Richard (2010). *Religions of the Silk Road. Premodern Patterns of Globalization*, second edition. New York and Houndmills, UK: Palgrave Macmillan (1999). https://doi.org/10.1057/9780230109100

Frankopan, Peter (2015). *The Silk Roads. A New History of the World.* London: Bloomsbury Publishing. https://archive.org/details/silkroadsnewhist 0000fran_c9j0/mode/2up

Frankopan, Peter (2018). *The New Silk Road. The Present and Future of the World.* London: Bloomsbury Publishing.

Gan, Fuxi, Robert H. Brill, & Shouyun Tian (Eds.) (2009). *Ancient glass research along the Silk Road.* Singapore: World Scientific. https://doi.org/10.1142/6964

Geller, Markham J. (1997). "The Last Wedge". *Zeitschrift für Assyriologie und Vorderasiatische Archäologie, 87*, 43–95. https://doi.org/10.1515/zava. 1997.87.1.43

Gerritsen, Anne, & Giorgio Riello (Eds.) (2015). *The Global Lives of Things: The Material Culture of Connections in the Early Modern World.* London: Routledge. https://doi.org/10.4324/9781315672908

Gilroy, Paul (1993). *The Black Atlantic: Modernity and Double-Consciousness.* Cambridge: Harvard University Press.

Global Biodiversity Information Facility (n.d.). "GBIF | Global Biodiversity Information Facility". Accessed May 25, 2022. https://www.gbif.org/

Gluzman, Renard, & Gerassimon Pagratis (2019). "Tracking Venice's Maritime Traffic in the First Age of Globalization: A Geospatial Analysis". *Nigro, 2019*, 135–153. http://dx.doi.org/10.36253/978-88-6453-857-0.08

Godart, Louis (2001). *L'invenzione della scrittura. Dal Nilo alla Grecia, with a new Introduction.* Turin: Einaudi (1992).

Goiten, Shelomo Dov (1967–1993). *A Mediterranean society: the Jewish communities of the Arab world as portrayed in the documents of the Cairo* Geniza, 6 vols. (I. *Economic Foundations*, 1967; II. *The Community*, 1967; III. *The Family*, 1978; IV. *Daily Life*, 1983; V. *The Individual. Portrait of a Mediterranean personality of the High Middle Ages as reflected in the Cairo Geniza*, 1978; VI. *Cumulative Indexes*, prepared by Paula Sanders, 1993). Berkeley & Los Angeles: University of California Press, & London: Cambridge University Press.

Goiten, Shelomo Dov (1974). *Letters of Jewish Traders.* Princeton, NJ: Princeton University Press. https://www.jstor.org/stable/j.ctt13x1c4d

Goldberg, Jessica L. (2012). *Trade and Institutions in the Medieval Mediterranean. The Geniza Merchants and their Business World.* Cambridge: Cambridge University Press. https://doi.org/10.1017/CBO9780511794209

Goldsmith, Roger A., & Philip L. Richardson (1987). *Reconstructing Columbus's First Transatlantic Track and Landfall Using Climatological Winds and Currents.* Woods Hole, MA: Woods Hole Oceanographic Institution. https://www.doi.org/10.1575/1912/4341

Graham, Shawn, Ian Milligan, & Scott Weingart (Eds.) (2016). *Exploring Big Historical Data. The Historian's Macroscope.* London: Imperial College Press. https://doi.org/10.1142/p981

Hansen, Valerie (2017). *The Silk Road: A New History with Documents.* New York: Oxford University Press.

Hansen, Valerie (2021). "The Classical Silk Road: Trade and Connectivity across Central Asia, 100 BCE–1200 CE". In *Oxford Research Encyclopedia of Asian History*, online. https://doi.org/10.1093/acrefore/9780190277727.013.576

Hecht, Laurence (2003). "Editorial: Science and the new Silk Road". *21st Century Science & Technology Magazine, 15*(4), 3–4. https://21sci-tech.com/articles/wint02-03/new_silk_road.html

Hekler, Eric B., Predrag Klasnja, Guillaume Chevance, Natalie M. Golaszewski, Dana Lewis, & Ida Sim (2019). "Why We Need a Small Data Paradigm". *BMC Medicine 17*(133), 1–9. https://doi.org/10.1186/s12916-019-1366-x

Holland, John H., & John H. Miller (1991). "Artificial Adaptive Agents in Economic Theory". *American Economic Review, 81*(2), 365–371. https://www.jstor.org/stable/2006886

International Council on Archives (2022). "International Council on Archives". Accessed May 8, 2022. ica.org/en

Jacobs, Justin M. (2020). "The Concept of the Silk Road in the 19th and 20th Centuries". In *Oxford Research Encyclopedia of Asian History*, online. https://doi.org/10.1093/acrefore/9780190277727.013.164

Klein, Bernhard, & Gesa Mackenthun (Eds.) (2004). *Sea Changes. Historicizing the Ocean.* London & New York: Routledge. https://doi.org/10.4324/9780203498538

Krahl, Regina, John Guy, J. Keith Wilson, & Julian Raby (Eds.) (2010). *Shipwrecked: Tang Treasures and Monsoon Winds.* Singapore & Washington, DC: Arthur M. Sackler Gallery, Smithsonian Institution, the National Heritage Board of Singapore, and the Singapore Tourism Board.

Lacson, Wesley, & Beata Jones (2016). "The 21st Century DarkNet Market: Lessons from the Fall of Silk Road". *International Journal of Cyber Criminology, 10*(1), 40–61. http://dx.doi.org/10.5281/zenodo.58521

Lauritzen, Frederick (2017). "Byzantine Perfumery". In *The History of Perfume in Venice*, edited by Messinis, Anna, 22–43. Venice: Lineadacqua.

Lichtenstein, Natalie. G. (2018). *A Comparative Guide to the Asian Infrastructure Investment Bank.* Oxford: Oxford University Press. https://doi.org/10.1093/law/9780198821960.001.0001

Lim, Tai Wei, Henry Hing Lee Chan, Katherine Hui-Yi Tseng, Wen Xin Lim (Eds.) (2016). *China's One Belt One Road initiative [Proceedings of the seminar jointly organised by the Confucius Institute of Nanyang Technological University Singapore and the International Zheng He Society, Singapore, 19 December 2015].* London: Imperial College Press.

Liow, Joseph Chinyong, Hong Liu, & Gong Xue (Eds.) (2021). *Research Handbook on the Belt and Road Initiative.* Cheltenham, UK & Northampton, MA: Edward Elgar Publishing. https://doi.org/10.4337/9781789908718

Lippman Abu-Lughod, Janet (1989). *Before European Hegemony: The World System A.D. 1250–1350.* New York: Oxford University Press.

Long, Pamela O., David McGee, & Alan M. Stahl (Eds.) (2019). *The Book of Michael of Rhodes.* 3 vols. Cambridge, MA: MIT Press.

Macal, Charles M., & Michael J. North (2007). "Agent-Based Modeling and Simulation: Desktop ABMS". In *Proceedings of the 2007 Winter*

Simulation Conference, edited by Shane G. Henderson, Bahar Biller, Ming-Hua Hsieh, John Shortle, Jeffrey D. Tew, and Russel R. Barton, 95–106. Los Alamitos: IEEE. https://citeseerx.ist.psu.edu/viewdoc/download?doi=10.1.1.467.6515&rep=rep1&type=pdf.

MacLeod, Roy (Ed.) (2004). *The Library of Alexandria: Centre of Learning in the Ancient World*. London: I.B. Tauris & Co. Ltd. http://dx.doi.org/10.5040/9780755625949.

Mayr, Erasmus (2011). *Understanding Human Agency*. Oxford: Oxford University Press. https://doi.org/10.1093/acprof:oso/9780199606214.001.0001.

Mazlish, Bruce (1998). "Comparing Global History to World History". *The Journal of Interdisciplinary History*, *28*(3), 385–395. https://www.jstor.org/stable/205420.

McCormick, Michael (2001). *Origins of the European Economy. Communications and Commerce AD 300–900*. Cambridge & New York: Cambridge University Press. https://doi.org/10.1017/CBO9781107050693.

Mertens, Matthias (2019). "Did Richthofen Really Coin 'The Silk Road'?" *The Silk Road*, *17*, 1–9. https://edspace.american.edu/silkroadjournal/wp-content/uploads/sites/984/2020/02/2-Mertens-Did-Richthofen-Really-Coin-the-Silk-Road.pdf.

Michael of Rhodes (2005). "A Medieval Mariner and His Manuscript". Institute and Museum of the History of Science. Accessed May 10, 2022. https://brunelleschi.imss.fi.it/michaelofrhodes/.

Ministry of Foreign Affairs of the People's Republic of China (2013). "Promote Friendship Between Our People and Work Together to Build a Bright Future". [Speech by H.E. Xi Jinping at Nazarbayev University, Kazakhstan], September 8, 2013. https://www.fmprc.gov.cn/ce/cebel/eng/zxxx/t1078088.htm.

Montemezzo, Stefania (2019). "Ships and Trade: The Role of Public Navigation in Renaissance Venice". *Nigro*, *2019*, 473–484. http://dx.doi.org/10.36253/978-88-6453-857-0.24

Murray, William M. (1987). "Do Modern Winds Equal Ancient Winds?" *Mediterranean Historical Review*, *2*(2), 139–167. https://doi.org/10.1080/09518968708569525

Museum für Meerkunde (n.d.). "Wissenshaftliche Sammlungen der Humboldt-Universität zu Berlin". Accessed May 9, 2022. https://www.sammlungen.hu-berlin.de/sammlungen/museum-fuer-meereskunde

Nanetti, Andrea (2010). *Il Codice Morosini. Il mondo visto da Venezia (1094–1433)*. 4 vols. Spoleto: Fondazione CISAM. Refer also to Nanetti & Vu 2018.

Nanetti, Andrea (2011). *Atlas of Venetian Messenia. Coron, Modon, Pylos and their islands*. Archivio di Stato di Venezia & Greek Ministry of Culture. Imola, Italy: Editrice La Mandragora.

Nanetti, Andrea (2021). *Venezia e il Peloponneso (992–1718) [Venice and the Peloponnese, 992–1718]*. Venice: Ca' Foscari University Press. http://doi.org/10.30687/978-88-6969-544-5

Nanetti, Andrea (2022). "Waterways Connecting the Peoples of the World. A presentation of the EHM application for Fra Mauro's *mappa mundi* as a virtual laboratory for investigating the Maritime Silk Road discourse in the digital time machine". In *Venezia e il senso del mare. Percezioni e rappresentazioni [Venice and the sense of the sea. Perceptions and portrayals]*, 161–250. Venice: Istituto Veneto di Scienze, Lettere ed Arti.

Nanetti, Andrea, & Shen Shen Luo (2016). "The Silk Road". Engineering Historical Memory. Last modified June 16, 2016. https://engineeringhistoricalmemory.com/Images/silk_road/silk-road-opening.mp4

Nanetti, Andrea, & Siew Ann Cheong (2018). "Computational History: From Big Data to Big Simulations". In Chen, Shu-Heng Chen (Ed.), *Big Data in Computational Social Science and Humanities*, 337–363. Cham (Switzerland): Springer International Publishing AG. https://link.springer.com/chapter/10.1007/978-3-319-95465-3_18

Nanetti, Andrea, & Nguyen Khoi Vu (Eds.) (2018 onwards). *The Morosini Codex (1095-1433)*. Vernacular Venetian text with translation into English by J. Melville Jones et al. https://engineeringhistoricalmemory.com/Morosini Codex.php

Nanetti, Andrea, & Davide Benvenuti (2019). "Animation of Two-Dimensional Pictorial Works into Multipurpose Three-Dimensional Objects. The Atlas of the Ships of the Known World Depicted in the 1460 Fra Mauro's *mappa mundi* as a Showcase". *SCIRES-IT (SCIentific RESearch and Information Technology)*, 9(2), 29–46. https://doi.org/10.2423%2Fi22394303v9n2p29

Nanetti, Andrea, & Nguyen Khoi Vu (Eds.) (2021 onwards). "The Silk Road. Histories, Initiatives, People. A Multiapplication for Heritage Science". Engineering Historical Memory. Last modified June 26, 2021. https://engineeringhistoricalmemory.com/SilkRoad.php

Nanetti, Andrea, Piero Falchetta, & Nguyen Khoi Vu (Eds.) (2019). "Fra Mauro's Mappa Mundi (1460)". Vernacular Venetian text with translations into English and Chinese supervised by Piero Falchetta and Daniele Beltrame, respectively. Engineering Historical Memory. Last modified November 29, 2019. https://engineeringhistoricalmemory.com/FraMauro.php

Nanetti, Andrea, et al. (2022a). "Homepage". Engineering Historical Memory. Accessed May 9, 2022. https://engineeringhistoricalmemory.com

Nanetti, Andrea, Chuchen Ping, & Nguyen Khoi Vu (Eds.) (2022b). "Zheng He's Navigation Chart (ca 1421–1430 CE) aka The Máo Kūn's Map/Wǔbèi Zhì Chart (offered to the throne in 1628)". Engineering Historical Memory. Last modified July 26, 2022. https://engineeringhistoricalmemory.com/MaoKunMap.php

Nara National Museum, & Nara Prefectural Museum (1988). シルクロード 大文明展. シルクロード *(The Grand Exhibition of Silk Road civilizations)* [4-volume Catalogue: *The Oasis and Steppe Routes, The Sea Route, The Route of Buddhist Art*, Nara-shi, Japan]. Nara: Nara National Museum, Nara Prefectural Museum.

National Development and Reform Commission of the PRC (2015). "我委等 有关部门规范'一带一路'倡议英文译法 [The Commission and other relevant departments standardise the English translation of "the Belt and Road" initiative]". September 21, 2015. https://web.archive.org/web/20190511191431/http://www.ndrc.gov.cn/gzdt/201509/t20150921_751695.html

Niccolucci, Franco, & Sorin Hermon (2016). "Representing Gazetteers and Period Thesauri in Four-Dimensional Space-Time". *International Journal on Digital Libraries*, *17*, 63–69. https://doi.org/10.1007/s00799-015-0159-x

Nigro, Giampiero (Ed.) (2019). *Reti marittime come fattori dell'integrazione europea/Maritime Networks as a Factor in European Integration [Proceedings of the 50ᵗʰ Week of Studies, (Prato, 13–17 May 2018)]*. Florence: Florence University Press.

North, Michael (2016). *Zwischen Hafen und Horizont. Weltgeshichte der Meere*. Munich: C.H. Beck.

North, Michael (2019). "Mari connessi". *Nigro, 2019*, 5–25. https://doi.org/10.36253/978-88-6453-857-0.02

Olstein, Diego (2015). *Thinking History Globally*. Houndmills & New York: Palgrave Macmillan. https://link.springer.com/book/10.1057/9781137318145

Ong, Walter J. (1982). *Orality and Literacy. The Technologies of the Word*. London & New York: Methuen. https://monoskop.org/images/d/db/Ong_Walter_J_Orality_and_Literacy_2nd_ed.pdf

Ooi, Kee Beng (2015). *The Eurasian Core and its Edges: Dialogues with Wang Gungwu on the History of the World*. Singapore: ISEAS–Yusof Ishak Institute. https://doi.org/10.1355/9789814519861

Page, Jeremy (2014). "China to Contribute $40 Billion to Silk Road Fund". *The Wall Street Journal*, November 8, 2014. https://www.wsj.com/articles/china-to-contribute-40-billion-to-silk-road-fund-1415454995

Parker, Anthony John (1992). *Ancient Shipwrecks of the Mediterranean and the Roman Provinces*. Oxford: Tempus Reparatum. https://doi.org/10.30861/9780860547365

Pezzolo, Luciano (2013). "The Venetian Economy". In Dursteler, Eric R. (Ed.), *A Companion to Venetian History, 1400–1797*, 255–289. Leiden & New York: E. J. Brill. https://doi.org/10.1163/9789004252523_007

Polyglot Asian Medicine (2019). "Polyglot Medical Traditions in Maritime Southeast Asia". Accessed May 25, 2022. https://www.polyglotasianmedicine.com/

Posner, Mariam (2015). "Humanities Data: A Necessary Contradiction". *Miriam Posner* (blog). 25 June. https://miriamposner.com/blog/humanities-data-a-necessary-contradiction

Pryor, John H. (1988). *Geography, Technology, and War. Studies in the Maritime History of the Mediterranean, 649–1571*. Cambridge: Cambridge University Press. https://doi.org/10.1017/CBO9780511562501

Pryor, John H. (1989). "Winds, Waves, and Rocks: The Routes and the Perils Along Them". In *Maritime Aspects of Migration*, edited by Friedland, Klaus, 71–85. Cologne: Böhlau.

Ramat, Silvio (2005). *Mario Luzi. La fine del viaggio terrestre*. Accessed May 29, 2022. https://www.yumpu.com/it/document/view/15619603/mario-luzi-la-fine-del-viaggio-terrestre-poesia

Rediker, Marcus (2004). "The Red Atlantic; or, 'a terrible blast swept over the heaving sea'". In *Sea Changes: Historicizing the Ocean*, edited by Klein,

Bernhard, & Gesa Mackenthun, 111–130. New York: Routledge. https://doi. org/10.4324/9780203498538

Reid, Anthony (2000). "Five Centuries, Five Modalities: European Interaction with Southeast Asia, 1497–1997". In *Vasco da Gama and the linking of Europe and Asia*, edited by Anthony Disney and Emily Booth, 167–177. New Delhi and New York: Oxford University Press.

Richthofen, Ferdinand von (1876). "Über den Seeverkehr nach und von China im Altertum und Mittelalter". *Verhandlungen der Gesellschaft für Erdkunde zu Berlin, 1876*, 86–97.

Richthofen, Ferdinand von (1877). "Über die zentralasiatischen Seidenstraßen bis zum 2. Jh. n. Chr". *Verhandlungen der Gesellschaft für Erdkunde zu Berlin, 1877*, 96–122.

Richthofen, Ferdinand von (1877–1912). *China. Ergebnisse eigener Reisen und darauf gegründeter Studien*. 5 vols. Berlin: Reimer.

Ritter, Carl (1838). *Die Erdkunde von Asien. 3. Buch: West-Asien*, Band VI: *Iranische Welt*, in *Die Erdkunde im Verhältniß zur Natur und zur Geschichte des Menschen, oder allgemeine vergleichende Geographie, als sichere Grundlage des Studiums und Unterrichts in physicalischen und historischen Wissenschaften*, zweite Ausgabe, achter Theil. Berlin: Reimer.

Royal Botanic Gardens Kew Science (2021). "Medicinal Plant Names Services". Last modified December 2021. https://mpns.science.kew.org/

Schmidt, Mauricius (Ed.) (1861–1862). *Hesychii Alexandrini lexicon*. Jenae: Sumptibus Hermanni Dufftii.

Schuster, Claudia (2007). "Das Institut und Museum für Meereskunde in Berlin – Forschung, Volksbildung und Flottenpropaganda". In *Kolonialismus hierzulande – Eine Spurensuche in Deutschland*, edited by van der Heyden, Ulrich, & Joachim Zeller, 150–152. Erfurt: Sutton. https://www.degruyter. com/database/HBOL/entry/hb.20808901/html

Simpfendorfer, Ben (2009). *The New Silk Road: How a Rising Arab World is Turning Away from the West and Rediscovering China*. London: Palgrave Macmillan. https://doi.org/10.1057/9780230233652

Slobin, Mark (2003). "The Silk Road Wends its Way to Washington". *Middle Eastern Studies Association Bulletin, 36*, 194–199. https://www.jstor.org/ stable/23062749

SRF (n.d.). "丝路基金 [Silk Road Fund]". Accessed May 10, 2022. http://www. silkroadfund.com.cn

Stahl, Alan M. (2004). "The Venetian Ducat in India". In *Foreign Coins found in the Indian Sub-Continent. Proceedings of the 4th International Colloquium of the Indian Institute of Research in Numismatic Studies (Mumbai, 8-10 January 1995)*, edited by MacDowall, David William, & Amiteshwar Jha, 97–98. Maharashtra, India: IIRNS Publications.

Stahl, Alan M. (2019). "Where the Silk Road Met the Wool Trade: Venetian and Muslim Merchants in Tana in the Late Middle Ages". In *Crusading and Trading between West and East: Studies in Honour of David Jacoby*, edited by Menache, Sophia, Benjamin Z. Kedar, & Michel Balard (Eds.),

351–364. London & New York: Routledge. https://doi.org/10.4324/9781315142753

Stanley-Baker, Michael (n.d.). "Drugs Across Asia". Accessed May 25, 2022. https://michaelstanley-baker.com/drugs-across-asia/

Stanley-Baker, Michael, & William Chong Eng Keat (2019). "Materia Medica in Chinese Religious Sources: Towards A Critical Digital Philology for modelling Knowledge Distribution in Early Chinese Texts". In *Proceedings of the 2019 Pacific Neighborhood Consortium Annual Conference and Joint Meetings (PNC)*, edited by 项洁 [Hsiang Jieh], & Michael Stanley-Baker (Eds.), 1–8. IEEE Xplore. https://ieeexplore.ieee.org/document/8939627

Stanley-Baker, Michael, 陈诗沛 [Chen Shih-Pei], 杜协昌 [Tu Hsieh-Chang], & 洪一梅[Hung I-Mei] (2018). "DAOBUDMED6D: Daoist Buddhist and Medical Corpus from the Six Dynasties". *Research Center for Digital Humanities, National Taiwan University*, August 1, 2018. http://doi.airiti.com/Landing Page/NTURCDH/10.6681/NTURCDH.DB_DocuSkyDaoBudMed6D/Text

Stanley-Baker, Michael, 许多多 [Xu Duoduo], & William Chong Eng Keat (2020a). *Bencaojing jizhu 本草经集注 in Three Layers*. DR-NTU (Data), V4. https://doi.org/10.21979/N9/K4WS29

Stanley-Baker, Michael, 许多多 [Xu Duoduo], 陈诗沛 [Chen Shih-Pei], 张端 [Zhang Duan], & 杜协昌 [Tu Hsieh-Chang] (2020b). In 洪振洲 [Hung Joey], & 洪一梅 [Hung I-Mei] (Eds.), *Collected Annotations of the Materia Medica (Bencaojing jizhu 本草经集注)*, Vol. 2. Taipei: National Taiwan University Press. http://doi.org/10.6681/NTURCDH.DB_DocuSkyBencaojing/Text

Stöckly, Doris (1995). *Le système de l'Incanto des galées du marché à Venise, fin XIIIᵉ-milieu XVᵉ siécle*. Leiden, New York & Cologne: E. J. Brill. https://doi.org/10.1163/9789004474178

SuperTCM (2020). "SuperTCM V2.0". Accessed May 25, 2022. https://bioinf-applied.charite.de/supertcm/

SymMap (2021). "SymMap v2". Accessed May 25, 2022. http://www.symmap.org/

Tagliacozzo, Eric, & Wen-Chin Chang (Eds.) (2011). *Chinese Circulations: Capital, Commodities, and Networks in Southeast Asia*. Durham: Duke University Press. https://doi.org/10.1215/9780822393573

Tiepolo, Maria Francesca (1994). "Archivio di Stato di Venezia". In *Guida Generale degli Archivi di Stato Italiani*, edited by Carucci, Paola, Piero D'Angiolini, & Claudio Pavone, 857–1148. Rome: Ministero per i beni culturali e ambientali; Ufficio centrale per i beni archivistici. http://www.maas.ccr.it/PDF/Venezia.pdf

Toynbee, Arnold J. (1934–1961). *A Study of History*. 12 vols. London: Oxford University Press.

Tu, Hsieh-Chang, Hsiang Jieh, Hung I-Mei, & Hu Chijui (2020). "DocuSky, A Personal Digital Humanities Platform for Scholars". *Journal of Chinese History 中国历史学刊*, 4(2), 564–580. http://doi.org/10.1017/jch.2020.28

Tucci, Ugo (2004). "Farmaci e aromi nel commercio veneziano delle spezie". In *Rotte mediterranee e baluardi di sanità*, edited by Vanzan Marchini, Nelli-Elena (Ed.), 95–100. Milan: Skira.

United Nations Conference on Trade and Development (2018). *Review of Maritime Transport 2018*. New York: United Nations Publications. https://unctad.org/system/files/official-document/rmt2018_en.pdf

United Nations Conference on Trade and Development (2020). *Review of Maritime Transport 2020*. New York: United Nations Publications. https://unctad.org/system/files/official-document/rmt2020_en.pdf

United Nations Educational, Scientific and Cultural Organization (2018). "The General Assembly of Silk-road Universities Network". Accessed May 10, 2022. https://en.unesco.org/creativity/policy-monitoring-platform/general-assembly-silk-road

Vespignani, Giorgio (2018). *La cronachistica veneziana fonte per lo studio delle relazioni tra Bisanzio e Venezia*. Spoleto: Fondazione CISAM.

Vu, Nguyen Khoi (2018). *Historical Agent-Based Model and Simulation*. Submitted in partial fulfilment of the requirements for the degree of Bachelor of Sciences in Physics (Talented Program). Supervisors: Siew Ann Cheong, Andrea Nanetti, Nguyen Tien Cuong. Hanoi: Vietnam National University of Science, Faculty of Physics.

Wachsmann, Shelly (2012). "Deep-Submergence Archaeology". In *The Oxford Handbook of Maritime Archaeology*, edited by Ford, Ben, Donny L. Hamilton, & Alexis Catsambis (Eds.), online publication. https://doi.org/10.1093/oxfordhb/9780199336005.013.0009

Wahlquist, Håkan (2020). "Albert Herrmann: A Missing Link in Establishing the Silk Road as a Concept for Trans-Eurasian Networks of Trade". *Environment and Planning C: Politics and Space*, 38(5), 803–808. https://doi.org/10.1177%2F2399654420911410a

Wallerstein, Immanuel (1974). "The Rise and Future Demise of the World Capitalist System: Concepts for Comparative Analysis". *Comparative Studies in Society and History*, 16(4), 387–415. https://www.jstor.org/stable/178015

Wang, Gungwu (2020). "Comment to the lecture". In Eric Tagliacozzo, *A Transnational Horizon: Sino-Southeast Asia's Historical "Adolescence"*, lecture given for the National University of Singapore, Belt and Road Initiative (BRI) Cluster, December 3, 2020. https://fass.nus.edu.sg/belt-and-road-initiative-bri-cluster

Waugh, Daniel C. (2007). "Richthofen's 'Silk Roads': Toward the Archaeology of a Concept". *The Silk Road*, 5(1), 1–10. https://faculty.washington.edu/dwaugh/publications/waughrichthofen2010.pdf

Weinstein, Barbara (2005). "History Without a Cause? Grand Narratives, World History, and the Postcolonial Dilemma". *International Review of Social History*, 50(1), 71–93. https://doi.org/10.1017/S0020859004001865

Weiser, Benjamin (2015). "Ross Ulbricht, Creator of Silk Road Website Is Sentenced to Life in Prison". *The New York Times*, May 29, 2015. https://www.nytimes.com/2015/05/30/nyregion/ross-ulbricht-creator-of-silk-road-website-is-sentenced-to-life-in-prison.html

Whitfield, Susan (2007). "Was there a Silk Road?" *Asian Medicine*, 3(2), 201–213. https://doi.org/10.1163/157342008X307839

Wu, Jiao, & Yunbi Zhang (2013). "XI IN CALL FOR BUILDING OF A NEW 'MARITIME SILK ROAD'". *China Daily USA*, October 4, 2013. http://usa.chinadaily.com.cn/china/2013-10/04/content_17008940.htm

刘进宝 [Liu, Jinbao] (2020). "关于李希霍芬'丝绸之路'命名的辨析 [Discussion on the Naming of Richthofen's 'Silk Road']". 中华文史论丛 *[Journal of Chinese Literature and History]*, *2*, 43–53.

Index

Printed and bound by CPI Group (UK) Ltd, Croydon, CR0 4YY

17/10/2024

01775680-0009